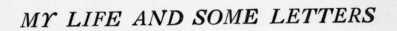

MY LIFE AND SOME LETTERS

MRS. PATRICK CAMPBELL

MY LIFE AND SOME LETTERS

BY

MRS. PATRICK CAMPBELL

(BEATRICE STELLA CORNWALLIS-WEST)

WITH ILLUSTRATIONS

NEW YORK
DODD, MEAD AND COMPANY
1922

DEDICATION

I CAME out by the stagedoor of the Duke of York's Theatre at a quarter-past twelve on the first night of the production of *Madame Sand,* by Phillip Moeller. A girl of about fifteen, bare-headed, was standing against the wall, evidently waiting for some one. I said:

"What are you waiting for?"

"To see you."

"Where do you live?"

"At Richmond."

"How are you going to get back?"

"Walk. I walked here early this morning. I wanted to get a good place to see the play, and I did: and now I have been waiting to see *you.*"

Then, with a wild young look of ecstasy, she vanished into the night.

To her I dedicate this book.

ILLUSTRATIONS

ILLUSTRATIONS

MY LIFE AND SOME LETTERS

MY LIFE AND SOME LETTERS

CHAPTER I.

WITH some little difficulty I have gathered together the following romantic and rather remarkable facts of my family history:—

My grandfather, John Tanner, was a descendant of Thomas Tanner, Bishop of St. Asaph; born 1693, died 1735. He had a son, Thomas Tanner, who was Rector of "St. Edmund The King and Martyr," and Rector of Merstham, Surrey; also Prebendary of Canterbury.

*   *   *   *   *

My grandfather went out to India as a very young man, and eventually became Army Contractor to the British East India Company. He made a large fortune—married Mary Ann Davis in 1823. They lived at Byculla Park, Bombay; seven children were born to them, the eldest—my father—John Tanner; William, Oscar, Fred, Emily, Emma, and my dear "Uncle Harry" (Henry Ward Tanner).

My father and my mother, Maria Luigia Giovanna Romanini, fell helplessly in love at their first meeting: my mother could not speak a word of English, and my father not a word of Italian. He was twenty-one, she was seventeen.

The marriage caused great excitement in Bombay at the time, my father being the heir of one of the richest Anglo-Indians, my mother the daughter of an Italian political exile. They had six children, three born in India, my two brothers and myself in London.

*   *   *   *   *

My father, it seems, managed to get through two large fortunes; he was careless with money, exceptionally generous, delighting in business enterprise and speculation. I had a letter from him in June, 1893, which gives an account of his early financial difficulties. After mentioning some trouble connected with a Consular post, he writes:—

"I can scarcely imagine how nearly half a million pounds sterling which I possessed in 1864 could have been dissipated, but the fact is that I was overtaken in my vast expectations by two severe crises in London. To this day our Government is owing me £50,000 or more, compensation for valuable services, and losses I sustained, during the Indian Mutiny. All the Executive Offices of our Government in the Ordnance and Commissariat gave their unqualified endorsement to my claim, but it eventually fell through. I was badly treated, indeed, and upon appealing to Lord Derby, recently dead, he offered a suggestion to the Local Government as a

'pis aller' out of the difficulty. There it ended. My
good friend, Isaac Butt, M. P., offered to agitate the matter in Parliament, but being very rich on my return from
India in 1872, I had destroyed my documents. It was on
record and will be found in the Archives of the War
Office that 'but for the celerity and magnitude of Mr.
Tanner's Ordnance Supplies the guns could not have been
brought into position or the capture of Delhi ef-
fected.' . . ."

People who knew my father well, spoke with much
love of his extraordinary kindliness and buoyant
spirits.

*   *   *   *   *

My Italian grandfather, Count Angelo Romanini,
born in Brescia, was at one time a man of considerable position. We have a tradition that he owned
large estates of chestnut groves.

During the Austro-Italian War he joined the
Democratic Society known as the Carbonari and fell
into serious political trouble. Aided by a firman
from the Sultan of Turkey, Abdul Medjid, he
travelled unmolested over Eastern Europe.

My grandmother, Rosa Polinelli, came from Mi-
lan. They had eight beautiful daughters, six of
whom under the age of eighteen married Englishmen.

My grandfather had a passionate love for horses.
We were told when we were children of his going
into a stable, where there was a wild, unmanageable

creature that no one would approach, and of his coming out in twenty minutes leading the animal, feeding from his hand.

Owing, no doubt, chiefly to this power and affection he became for a time the proprietor of an equestrian company.

Unfortunately, whenever I asked questions about this "Circus," which interested.me profoundly, I was hushed. Only my mother smiled, and I thought that some day she would tell me about it, but she never did.

*   *   *   *   *

People say that if they read the old letters of their mothers and grandmothers, it is difficult to realise that they were creatures of flesh and blood; and if the chronicle be enriched with some high adventure or escapade, it only makes an impression as though a brightly coloured foreign bird flew through a quiet garden.

My own experience is different. My Italian mother and her beautiful sisters were invested for me with great romantic glamour that has remained with me. And the few stories I was told about their youthful adventures delight me now as they did when I was a child, and felt proud they were my people.

My life appeared to me to have sprung from a magical past, in which Italy, Persia, India—white houses with flat roofs, white-robed Arabs, and lovely Arab horses—and my beautiful aunts—were all seen through a mist of childish imaginings; built upon stories I was told, photographs and letters I had seen, my mother's sweet singing voice, her delicious Italian accent, her guitar, and the many languages she spoke, among them Greek and Arabic.

It is because of the effect these things made upon my childish mind that I record them briefly.

These were the names of my aunts:—Regina, Stella, Carolina, Angela, Theresa, and Theodora, and another who died very young. The story of the death of this beloved youngest child shows my grandfather as a man of passionate feeling—he turned her sick room almost into a chapel, with candles and crucifixes: prayers were said continuously. The child died—my grandfather blew out the candles, broke the crucifixes, and was never known to pray again.

*　　*　　*　　*　　*

A caravan, with my grandfather and grandmother, their children mounted ahead on Arab horses! This picture was probably fixed in my childish mind by the following anecdote. My aunts, whilst riding, found a poor woman who had just given birth to a child by the roadside; not knowing what to do, they slipped off their petticoats and left them with her, to the dismay of their mother when they returned to the caravan.

Eventually my grandfather travelled to India and,

I believe, settled for some time in Bombay. His eldest daughter, Aunt Regina, married Richard Stevens, British Consul at Tabriz, Persia.

My Uncle Richard's official work took him away from Aunt Regina a great deal, and the following story I treasured. One evening, tired of waiting for him, she dressed herself in his uniform, with his sword at her side. When he returned late at night and opened the door of his wife's bedroom, he saw in the dim light a young officer standing with his back to him. His horror and dismay can be imagined! The "young man" turned round, and he met his wife's laughing eyes.

They had a son, Hadji Baba Stevens, to whom the then Shah of Persia stood godfather. He worked as a young man on the *Indian Pioneer* with Mr. Rudyard Kipling. His sister married an Englishman, Henry Soutar. She with her husband and children were handsomely ransomed by the English Government from, I believe, Bulgarian brigands, when Mr. Gladstone was Prime Minister. There was a touching story connected with this: 'one of the brigands walked back for many miles to find a doll the youngest child had dropped. . . .

*   *   *   *   *

Aunt Stella eloped when she was sixteen with a well-known Bavarian artist, Alexander Svoboda. My grandfather would not tolerate this love affair, and he must, I think, have locked her into a room, for we were told she escaped by climbing up the wide chimney of a Moorish house, her sisters helping her to drag up a box by a rope. I take it she was successfully helped down into the street, where Svoboda was waiting for her. . . .

Svoboda was always painting my Aunt Stella; especially her feet, which were very lovely. The marriage was not happy; Svoboda was intensely jealous. Aunt Stella had a bird, which she used to feed from her lips. One day this infuriated Svoboda, who, in a fit of jealousy, wrung the bird's neck before her eyes. . . .

My Aunt Stella died at twenty-nine, leaving behind her just this little sequence: her beauty, her young love, her escape up the chimney, her bird killed to spite her, and her early death.

I was named after her; and I wish I could give the mysterious impression this little history made upon my childish thoughts.

*   *   *   *   *

My Aunt Theresa, a light-hearted, merry girl, married an English lawyer, who piously on his wedding night knelt on the bed to pray. The gay Theresa, irritated by prayers said in such a way at such a time, pushed him off the bed onto the floor. Her wedding night was spent in tears. . . .

A year or two afterwards my uncle took his adored young wife and child home to England. She caught a chill on the voyage, and within a few days she and her baby died at the Buckingham Palace Hotel.

Of Aunt Angela, I know only that she married a certain Mr. Henry Lacey, the son of an English clergyman. Aunt Carolina married a Scotchman, Captain Gunn Fraser.

Aunt Dora, my youngest aunt, married a Mr. James Vere Cumins. When I met this uncle in America for the first time a few years ago, I saw an unusually handsome man, with a pointed beard and blue eyes. As a youth he had great expectations: this he could never forget. He worked hard to support my Aunt Dora, a hearty, handsome woman, who sang well and adored her five children. My uncle and aunt are both dead, but their children are still living in Texas.

Which of my aunts it was who had a tame crow that used to fly into the woods and when she clapped her hands return to her, I do not know: or which aunt sold her monkey for a basketful of pistachio nuts. I was told she pulled the monkey by its tail into her window, thinking he was falling, and he never forgave her the indignity. This she could not bear, so she sold him for a large basket of her favourite nuts. Her sisters refused to share them with her; and the story that she ate them all herself in defiance and became ill, I could always understand.

My father's eldest sister, Aunt Emily, married

Baron von Jasmund—closely related to the Imperial House of Hapsburg. The story that has come down to us about this gentleman is rather mysterious. I give it for what it is worth:—

Aunt Emily eloped from a school in England where Baron von Jasmund was a professor. In time my grandfather forgave this marriage. They lived in London and entertained largely. I heard that for a season they took Dorchester House, and my eldest brother and sister remember playing with their German cousins on the great staircase. Von Jasmund and his wife and family eventually went to America.

Many years afterwards, when I was acting in America, two young men called to see me, and claimed cousinship—Mortimer and Wasa von Jasmund. Later I met their charming and pretty sister, Hildegarde, and their youngest brother, Seymour.

I cannot resist quoting from letters written by Hildegarde, after our meeting, to my Uncle Harry. They show she inherited a fine sensibility from her mother:

> " 'Brainerd,'
> "Minn.
> "January 25th, 1902.

"My dear Uncle,

"You will experience surprise, I am sure, at a communication from me, but as I am your very own niece I feel that I can take the liberty. My delight at hearing from a real live uncle was unbounded. To think that after a lapse of so many years, years of hoping, longing, waiting, we should at last find, in a most unexpected and unforeseen way, some of my dear mother's people. . . .

"How many times during these long years we have wondered about you all. We have written many letters, but it was impossible to find any of you. All that we knew was that mother had two brothers, John and Fred, and this information we obtained from some old pictures. You who have had your friends and family about you cannot conceive what it means for four helpless, mother-less children, with an irresponsible father, to be dropped in a strange land with absolutely no one to look after them. Thanks to a most merciful Providence, we fell in good hands, and received the best care and kindest treat-ment, and all the advantages it was possible for our new friends to give us. . . .

"Write to me of my dearest mother. Do not hesitate for fear of hurting my feelings. I feel that her only re-gret at dying must have been parting with her chil-dren. , . .

"Most affectionately,

"HILDEGARDE VON J. COURTNEY

"(nèe von Jasmund)."

"February 11th, 1903.

"My dear Uncle Harry,

"My meeting with Beatrice* was a most pleasant oc-casion for me. I reached Chicago on Saturday, and went alone to the matinée. The first vision I had of Beatrice was as she entered the stage as 'Magda.' It was one of loveliness. I was charmed, delighted! . . . Her chief charm lies, to me, in her sweet unaffectedness and that air of exquisite refinement. . . . Seeing her, brought back strange and sad memories. Memories of that dear mother, whose love I have always missed so sorely, and I wept through the entire performance. I

* My family always called me Beatrice.

was unfit to go out in the evening, so did not see her in
The Joys of Living, very much to my regret. I saw
her in all her other plays. . . . I am doubly anxious
to see you all after hearing Beatrice talk of you. She
spoke most lovingly and tenderly of you, dear uncle, and
I know you must be the nicest and noblest of men. . . .
I am glad you could see a little resemblance to mother
in my picture. I have always thought the lower part of
my face was like her. I am 5 ft. 5 in. in height. Was
mother as tall? . . ."

Extract from letter written by my Uncle Harry to
Seymour von Jasmund.

"23, Glebe Place,
"Chelsea.
"26th October, 1902.

"My dear Seymour,
    "Immediately on receipt of your letter of 6th instant,
I wrote to a cousin of ours, Mrs. Hogarth; who is
about 77 years old, and she, when we were children, took
care of us after our mother's death. She lives at some
distance out of London. . . . I thought she might be
able to give me some information in answer to the questions contained in your letter. She replied:
    " 'I have been looking over some papers I have not
seen for years, and am pleased to say I came upon a copy
of poor Emily's marriage certificate, with other papers
relating to the Baron, which I should like you to see.'
    "These documents she has now handed to me. They
consist of:
    "1. Copy of Marriage Certificate, 1851.
    "2.   Do.   Document (written in German).
    "3.   Do.   Do.   Do.   1851.

"4.   Do.   Do.   Do.   1851.

"5. Letter written by your father to his father-in-law. . . . 11th January, 1852, St. Goarshausen.

" 'I wish to forward the above to one of you, and, as I don't know Wasa's whereabouts, I will send them to your brother Mortimer, who, I suppose, has the first right to them next to Wasa.' "

The following is a copy of the christening certificate of Seymour von Jasmund, the youngest child, who was born in Canada:

"Seymour Theodore Algernon Wasa von Jasmund, born at Mooretown, Ontario, September 3rd, 1864.

"Son of Charles Albert Theodore and Emily Mathilda Rebecca von Jasmund.

"Baptised at the City Hotel, St. Clair, Michigan, on December 24th, 1864, by Rev. B. J. Prichard.

"Sponsors (by Proxy) :
"Henry Stuart Wortley.
"Lady Jane Muncaster.
"Capt. Alfred Drummond.
"England."

*   *   *   *   *

I remember my beloved mother first when I was about three years old—tall, pale, dressed in black, with long, white, delicate hands. I fancy she was mourning my eldest brother, who had died suddenly at school, and two loved sisters she had lost. My father was away in India.

My earliest recollection is of her walking up and down a long room, and I walking close behind her, feeling very proud to be following her up and down that long room.

When my mother sang to me I listened under an enchantment.

She gave me her great love of beauty. She could not pass beauty by unnoticed. . . .

I never heard her laugh or saw her gay. I remember no bitterness or harsh speaking, but I know now what as a child I could not guess; sorrow had silenced the song of life in her.

Italian women differ from Englishwomen in their reserve: in the Southern heart there is no *chill*, however great the suffering.

My father in these early days I do not recall. I neither remember being caressed by him nor having any sense of his love for me; my whole adoration was for my mother.

I remember, when I was a very young girl, talking to her about some new acquaintances with whom she did not wish me to be intimate—people who were odd, noisy, vulgar, rich, full of gaiety and high spirits. They fascinated me, though in some strange way they offended my taste. I remember my mother listening gravely for some time to my questions, and then saying gently: "We have an Italian proverb—'Only the sweep knows what is up the chimney.'"

From my mother I learnt my love of music. Schubert was my first love. She sang his songs in French with a touching unsentimental simplicity.

Dante and Tasso, and Ariosto, together with her Bible, were always by her bed.

After her death I found these few lines translated from Dante in her handwriting:—

"When the leaves are falling and thou are come
"To seek my cross in Camposanto. . . .
"In a ·humble corner thou wilt find it,
"And many flowers near it born. . . .
"Gather thou, then, for thy fair tresses
"The flowers born of my heart . . . they are
"The songs I thought, but did not write. . . .
"The words of love I did not tell thee."

My mother spoke to me with enthusiasm of the Italian actors, Salvini, Rossi, and Madame Ristori; also of the singers, Mario and Grisi and Adelina Patti. I do not think she ever saw any of our English players; if she did, I never heard her speak of them.

She loved her children and her grandchildren. Not a flower or a colour, not a sound, line or movement that had loveliness escaped her. She loved animals, especially horses, birds, and dogs; so life must have given her joy: but the impression she has left upon me is one of abiding melancholy and beauty. Her religion was simple, "simple as truth's simplicity." She was a Roman Catholic.

My father was a cheerful believer in the Darwinian theory.

I remember a story my mother told me about an Arab horse she used to ride in the Row: hearing the music of a regimental band passing, the horse began to lie down and try to roll over. My mother kept her seat, and the people who were standing by, watching, said under their breath: "Circus rider." She smiled as she told me this story, and thrilled me with the idea that the horse must have been a performing horse that had learnt to bow or dance to music, and perhaps roll over "dead" at some given cue.

*   *   *   *   *

I remember clearly my first grief. There was a children's party given by my father—a Christmas tree with a lovely fairy doll holding a golden sceptre in her hand, and with, what appeared to me, a diamond crown upon her head, standing on the tips of her toes, with stars all about her and lights— lights everywhere—and toys of all descriptions and colours hanging everywhere beneath her feet.

At the foot of the tree were large crackers—bigger than I—and I was told that inside these crackers were dresses, kings' dresses, queens' dresses, princes' and princesses'. A band playing. Crowds of people and children and I, wild with excitement, looking, wondering whether I would have the dress of a queen or a princess.

Then someone brought me one of the large crackers and said it was mine. I put my arms around it, and whispered: "What is inside?" And the answer, I know, was "A cook's dress," and I wept and wept and wept.

I remember no more about the Christmas party, only that I was in a room alone. Someone had grown tired of telling me to "stop crying," "not to be a silly little girl." I was full of shame, and my vain little heart was broken.

My youngest brother was only ten months older than I, and we were always in the nursery together. He was a sad and nervous child, delicate and silent. He used to sit in a corner making small bags out of little pieces of cloth our nurse gave him. His aloofness teased me; my noise and energy teased him; and there are memories of tussles and trying to pull out each other's hair.

I believe I used to cry loud and long, and someone told me that when I was a few months old my nurse said to my mother: "She is not a baby; she is a tiger." The nurse had lain me down in a cupboard, so that my mother should not hear my screams. Perhaps, though still in long clothes, I knew my nurse was unintelligent.

I remember no more of these early years—the years that lie between three and nine years of age—but those things which, I suppose, all children suffer—sudden strangeness, shyness, loneliness, a sense of invisible things and people, fears born of ignorant nurses' warnings, and their own imaginings.

The loving, gentle look in my Uncle Harry's eyes remains with me throughout the years.

There was the comforting love and joy found in the pets about the house, and the passionate desire to have some day a dog of my own.   I never cared for dolls.

CHAPTER II.

I THINK I was neither a sweet, amiable, nor amenable child. I was physically strong, very affectionate, imaginative, but temperamentally alien to those around me.

I believe I was impatient with unintelligent people from the moment I was born: a tragedy—for I am myself three-parts a fool. . . .

I was about nine years old when my parents moved into Tulse Dale Lodge, a house situated between Tulse Hill and Dulwich. The place belonged to a Miss Bailey, an old friend of my mother. It was a low, grey stone house with a porch, standing in the middle of a big garden. There were stables and a large field adjoining with some fine trees. Inside the house were long low rooms, a dining room, library, a drawing room and a mysterious room always kept locked, containing things belonging to Miss Bailey—a place of shadows in my memory.

My mother's sister, Aunt Dora, and her five children, had come from India to live with us, her husband in the meanwhile having gone to Mexico to look after my father's interests out there in silver mines. The house was full of children. These cousins of mine I fancy had been spoiled by ayahs—we were a strange medley of bickering brats, and someone called me the "Ugly Duckling," and ugly I believed I was.

I have a vague recollection of my eldest sister being proud of me and dressing me up prettily. She taught me my notes on the piano. She tells me I was a very difficult child to understand, and to this day her attitude is one of bewilderment, question and concern. A tender-hearted woman and a most devoted mother, this sister of mine.

There were many happy days spent in the garden at Tulse Dale Lodge; my favorite amusement was to sit alone, high up in a tree, talking to myself and to the leaves—they were little people to me—and my friends.

> ". . . . like the talking of the trees
> And voices in the air that knew my name."

An especially naughty game of mine was to dig a hole, fill it with water, unplait my long black hair and sit in the mud bath. I called it a "Roman Bath," inspired, I feel sure, by my mother telling me the Ancient Romans taught the Ancient Britons to bathe. One day when an admirer of my elder sister called, he met a wild dishevelled child covered thick with mud, and told my sister of the extraordinary little girl he had seen in the garden; and my sister made me feel much ashamed when she told me how I had disgraced myself.

There was a day, too, when I sat on a gate watching Mr. Gladstone, who was profoundly interested in the working of a newly invented steam saw for cutting down trees.

And there was an awful day when I dug up my pet canary that had died and I had wept over; and had buried carefully in cotton wool in a Bryant and May's matchbox. I longed to see my little bird once more. I fancy that I had expected to find the box empty, that he had gone to Heaven, or had become a fairy: I never had the courage to tell anyone what I found—the blankness, the misery, of that first sight of decay.

And then there was lying on the hay in the sun, dreaming I was carried away on a cloud to meet someone, who would take me to all the beautiful places in the world.

Strangers terrified me—"the people behind the door." "They do not say what their faces say" was a remark I made when I was trying to explain my terror to my nurse. True to this day it is, only now their interest lies in the enigma.

The desire was always with me to tell a secret. It would come upon me suddenly in a crowd. I did not know what the secret was, but if only people would stand quite still and listen, then I would know right enough.

How many years afterwards did I discover that an audience inspires and strengthens, and that to "hold an audience" is a gift from God.

At ten years old I was sent to school at Brighton.

THE FAITHFUL UNCLE HARRY

Nothing remains in my memory but a dull monotony. Governesses that made me feel shy; learning that I found difficult; and the stiffness of school discipline that hurt my sensitive mind. Walking out two by two had tragically depressing effect upon me.

I was full of strange fancies, too. I used to amuse myself by putting pennies furtively in odd places, and making up passionate stories to myself of how beggars would find them, and think God had sent them in answer to their prayers. I remember not minding that I was scolded for lagging behind— that was the price I paid for my dreams.

Evidently my schoolmistress, Miss Blackmore thought my morbidity was due to physical causes— temperament was scarcely a schoolmistress' busi- ness—she called me to her private room and told me I needed medicine, and I must be a good girl and take it without any fuss. She gave me a grey powder in a cup of coffee. It made me very seriously ill. My father was sent for, and I remember his coming up to my bedroom. His face was so serious, I thought he was cross with me, and I was very un- happy. I learned long afterwards that my eldest brother had died at school after a few days' illness at the age of twelve.

I have a sinister remembrance that when I was a child I often thought grown-up people silly, and their voices ugly and their movements ungraceful: when people had beautiful speaking voices, or lovely manners, I was their slave.

Once in the holidays a cousin came to see us with her very young baby. I had never seen such a little baby before. I begged to be allowed to hold her, and someone said, "If you drop her, it will kill her, but if you sit on the ground I will put her on your lap." I sat down and the baby was put on my lap, I remember quite well the sickening fear and giddiness that came over me as I held the little bundle. I realized with overpowering tenderness the tragedy that had been suggested to my mind. "The child is fainting," I heard my mother say, "None of you understands how sensitive Beatrice is." I was made to lie down on a bed, and I was haunted miserably by a feeling that there was something queer about me.

There is a tragic memory, too, of an old nurse, Fanny, who left us when I was old enough to go to school. I used to think of her with great love and longing, often crying myself to sleep. In the holidays she came to see us, and she did not recognise me— "Surely this big girl is n't Miss Beatrice?" were her respectful words, instead of a hug and a kiss, and a jump into her lap. She did not know me, and I knew her so well, and I loved her so much. The pain I suffered at the sudden baffling of my joy is indescribable.

A year or two later, wretched terms were spent in a school at Hampstead. The mistress had cold blue eyes that stared at me—whether in admiration or disgust it was difficult for me to tell. She either painted or wore false eyebrows, which made her face funny to me. I know I was afraid to look at her—that I would have to laugh, and then she would frighten me. When she took the class and asked me a question, my mind became a blank. I do not remember learning anything at this school, or making any school friends.

I recollect one of the governesses was very kind to me; a grey haired woman, with a small, sad, tight face, and an expression that never changed. I asked her once if she had a sister, and she answered solemnly, "Yes, and her beauty was her curse." This answer filled me with awe, and for a long while gravely troubled me.

Later from Tulse Dale Lodge my eldest sister Nina married; and soon afterwards my father, with my two brothers and my Aunt Dora and her children, went to America to join my uncle in Texas. My mother, with my sister Lulo and myself, moved into a small, rather nice little house in Dulwich taken by my Uncle Harry; and Miss Catherine Bailey, my mother's friend, came back from Paris to her house, Tulse Dale Lodge.

Miss Bailey—"Aunt Kate," as I afterwards called her—attracted me strangely. She was an old spinster lady nearly seventy years of age—I was not yet fifteen—the tallest and thinnest person I had ever seen, with a very yellow wrinkled face and an austere manner. But in her youth she had been an intimate friend of Lord Byron and Tom Moore. She had seen ladies swoon with excitement when Lord Byron appeared at a party!

Aunt Kate had a pretty *apartement* at 34, Avenue de Villers, opposite the Parc Monceau. She took a great interest in me, and begged my mother to let her take me to Paris to live with her for a year, and to have lessons in music and French.

My father's financial troubles had gradually crippled him, so this chance for me to "finish my education," which indeed had not yet begun, came as a great boon to my mother.

Being at a most impressionable age, the love I had for grace and distinction developed here, where a little coterie of French and Italian people constantly came to visit her. Aunt Kate's sister had married General Count van de Meer, a distinguished gentleman, who had played a courageous part in the Commune troubles. There was Marie van de Meer, his lovely daughter, and Count Charles van de Meer and his beautiful Russian wife, Wanda, and their little girl of three, and pretty Countess Alice van de Meer, and many others whom I forget. And then there was Aunt Kate's favourite nephew, with a waxed moustache, Charles de Lorilli, a Manager in Mr. Rothschild's Bank. He used to dine with her almost every night.

I had a governess to teach me French and another to give me music lessons, and I think I was taken to every gallery and museum in Paris.

I can only remember going to a theatre once. It was to see Pailleron's *Le Monde où l'on s'ennuie.* It was as though some unexpected door opened, and for months afterwards my thoughts gazed beyond. Strangely enough Aunt Kate never took me to a theatre again.

People used to stare at me out-of-doors, and I remember feeling rather uncomfortable about my long black plaits. One day a man in passing us pushed a ticket for a box at the opera in my glove. I shall never forget Aunt Kate's face as she called him "Singe" and hailed a fiacre. I did not know whether to laugh, or cry. She would not speak to me: I felt somehow that I was to blame.

I stayed in Paris a year, getting to know a little about music, and always enjoying the novelty of the slightly artificial atmosphere of Aunt Kate's circle, where an ugly retort or an uncomplimentary truth would have been a breach of good manners. There was an atmosphere of romance about it all that filled me with delight. I fancy, though, what pleased me most was Aunt Kate's vivid manner of telling me stories of her youth, and of people she had known. Her eyes would sparkle—and she had wonderful dramatic gestures with her large Scotch hands, that impressed and thrilled me. When she told me a love story, she used to murmur "Oh's" and "Ah's," turning her eyes upwards in a most mysterious fash-

ion.   Some sad story had surely left dear Aunt Kate
a spinster.

When I was sixteen Aunt Kate brought me back
to my mother.

By this time my father was definitely ruined.
My youngest brother Edmund had come back from
America.   This brother, whom we had always called
"Max," had a genius for music, chess problems and
figures.

My dear Uncle Harry's fortune had melted away
in the general ruin.   He got some work in the City,
and took the burden of my mother, my sister, my
brother and myself upon him.   I had always loved
my Uncle Harry.   As a small child he was the one
who never frightened me, or made me shy; whose
eyes looked at me with love and understanding.
Whenever I saw him, I used to go close to him and
hold his hand, and he said lovely things that made
children laugh and feel happy.   His face was dis-
figured by smallpox, but we children thought him
very handsome, and used to quarrel among ourselves
as to which one of us would marry him when we grew
up.   He was a great reader, a student of literature
of all kinds: Italian, French, and Latin were a hobby
with him.

When I returned from Paris, I developed a passion for reading, and my mother allowed me to turn
a little box room into a study.   There were some
rapturous hours spent alone in that little room,
writing out what I particularly loved, and making

notes of what I did not understand. It was a strange medley of my uncle's books that I took into that room:—J. W. Cross' "Life of George Eliot," Lewes' "Life of Goethe," Thackeray's "English Humorists of the Eighteenth Century," "Corinne," Walt Whitman, Keats, Longfellow, Emerson, Shakespeare, Milton, Tennyson, Daudet, Balzac, and many others.

When uncle returned from the City in the evening, we would go through what I had read, and he with his gentle fun was always ready to make difficult things easy and amusing.

I asked him once: "What is Heaven really? I know it isn't a place in the sky behind the clouds." He thought for a long time: looking beyond me, he answered "Faithfulness."

Our long evenings at home were spent either at the piano or playing chess, or listening to my mother singing to her guitar, or to my uncle reading aloud. We talked a lot of nonsense, too. He was wise and witty and listened with grave eyes full of affection.

I think he knew there was something in my heart I could not speak, and he wondered what outlet I would find. We loved arguments and discussions, and there were always beloved cats and dogs and other pets.

On my return from Paris, a cousin of my father, Mrs. Eliza Hogarth, a woman of some means, heard me play the piano, and offered to have me trained, so it was arranged that I should go to the Guildhall School of Music twice a week, from Dulwich, for

my lesson. After the second term my Music Master
suggested that I should go in, with 365 other girls,
for a scholarship, which would give me three years
free musical tuition in Leipzig.   I won the scholarship: why I never took it up belongs to another chap-
ter.

The following letter from my Music Master, Mr.
Ridley Prentice, shows that I had a little musical
talent:—

"Kensington Square, W.,
September 25th, 1882.

"My dear Madam,

"I much regret to find from your daughter, Miss Beatrice Tanner, that she will leave the Guildhall School
of Music at the half term.   Personally, I shall be very
sorry to lose her as a pupil, as she is much interested in
her work, has great talent, and makes rapid progress.

"But I feel that, quite apart from my personal feeling,
it is my duty to let you know what a very serious thing it
seems to me that Miss Tanner should not complete her
musical education.

"When she came to me, she had never had any regular
musical training at all, and there was much to undo before she could really begin to make sure progress.   She
has now got over that first difficulty, and there is nothing
to stop her from becoming really a fine pianist and musician—but this of course is a work of time and labour and
cannot be accomplished all at once.

"I have no hesitation in saying that she has a very
great talent indeed, and that if she works in a proper
spirit, and is properly directed, she is sure of attaining a
very high position.   It seems to me, therefore, that it

would be a *wrong* thing if such talent were not to be properly developed, especially as in the present day no one has any chance of success who has not attained the highest possible point.

"You will see that I look on the matter as a musician, doubtless there are many other different considerations which must weigh with you, but I trust that you will pardon my writing strongly. It is not too often that one meets with real talent, so that it is all the more sad when there seems to be a prospect of its being wasted.

"Perhaps I may be allowed to add that the very great pains which I have taken with Miss Tanner give me a right to speak.

"Believe me, Dear Madam,

"Yours sincerely,

"RIDLEY PRENTICE."

During these two years of my life at Dulwich only a few friends stand out of the shadows, amongst them Mrs. Gifford, her son, and two beautiful daughters. The eldest, Maud, now Lady Gallwey, was my first girl friend. We used to have long walks and talks together. I thought her beautiful; she was interested in my year's life spent in Paris and in my music. She had a lovely figure; was always well dressed, and had heaps of admirers.

Then there was the charming Bowring Spence, and his Italian mother and sisters. He had a beautiful sympathetic voice, and used to sing Tosti's early songs. He married a niece of the Pope and became British Consul at Leghorn.

One of our most interesting neighbors was Jim

Bates (Dr. Curling Bates), a very gifted fellow, whose grandfather had been an intimate friend of Handel. He gave me Handel's snuff-box, which I still cherish. Jim Bates * was a good musician, besides being an excellent amateur actor, and he was President of the Anomalies Dramatic Club where I made my first appearance as an amateur actress.

Also there was James Nasmyth, afterwards Sir James Nasmyth, a strange creature, a friend of my musical brother Max.

I can remember no gaiety such as young people have today. Ours were the most simple of pleasures, music, card parties, country walks, cricket matches and concerts at the Crystal Palace.

There were the Urquhart girls, cousins of the Giffords, their father was a vicar at Bournemouth. The third daughter, Owney, a lovely gentle girl with a fascinating lisp, very many years afterwards, married my brother Max.

I find in an old copy book the following poems by my uncle, and one by myself written at fifteen:

BEATRICE.
HER MOTTO
VIVE LA BAGATELLE.

"A nobler yearning never broke her rest
Than but to dance and sing, be gaily drest,

* Lady Burne-Jones, who once saw Dr. Curling Bates act at Rottingdean, told me he was the best comedian she had ever seen.

And win all eyes with all accomplishment;
For ah, the slight coquette, she cannot love.
And if you kissed her feet a thousand years
She still would take the praise and care no more."

H. W. T.

"IN THEIR RIGHT PLACES."

"The Brewers should to Malta go,
The Boobys all to Scilly,
The Quakers to the Friendly Isles,
The Furriers to Chili.
The naughty little squalling babes
That break our nightly rest,
Should be packed off to Babylon,
To Lapland or to Brest.
From Spithead Cooks go off to Greece,
And while the miser waits
His passage to the Guinea Coast
Spendthrifts are in the Straits.
Let Spinsters to the Needles go,
Wine bibbers to Burgundy,
Send gluttons to the Sandwich Isles,
Wags to the Bay of Fundy.
Bachelors to the United States
Maids to the Isle of Man,
Let Gardeners go to Botany Bay,
And Shoe-blacks to Japan.
Seek out all other misplaced men,
Lest they disturb and vex us,
And all who're not provided for,
And send them off to Texas."

H. W. T.

TO STELLA'S EYES.
SWEETEST EYES WERE EVER SEEN.

'Love hath not eyes they say,
Tell me, is that e'en so?'
Said Stella, one glad day
To her fond Angelo.
Straightway her dear replies,
'By heav'n and earth, 'tis true;
For love's enchanting eyes
Were stolen, sweet by you.' "

DAWN

There is a hushed stillness through the trees.
    Dawn is breaking.
And the transient night wind greeting leaves
    The Morn awaking;
It stoops to tell the new-born flowers
    Of the Sun.
To kiss their lips with dew-drop dowers,
    Day has come.
There is a soft note of the nightingale
    Passing away
Into the sweetest melody to hail
    The break of day.
Aurora comes! with blushing pride
    She spreads her charms.
Till the pale night gently glides
    From Neptune's arms.
                            Beatrice, aged 15.

Part of a letter I find written to a cousin many years later by my Uncle Harry:

". . . During my life I have seen a great deal of Beatrice and have been with her more than with the others; and I took a little part in her bringing up, for when my brother John went away to Texas with his two boys, he left Lulo and Beatrice under my care. Some years after, when Beatrice had married, the time came when her husband went abroad to seek his fortune in 1887, and Beatrice, a year or two later, with his consent, took up the stage as a profession. She left her two dear children under my care. They remained some years in my house along with their grandmother, so my life has been always more in touch with Beatrice's, and she is my favourite. . . ."

CHAPTER III.

AT a card party at Mrs. Gifford's I first met my future husband, Patrick Campbell. His father had been manager in Hong Kong, of the Chartered Bank of India, Australia, and China. He now owned a large place, "Belmont," Stranraer, also an old-fashioned house with lawns and trees, "Ellerslie," on Sydenham Hill.

I was seventeen when I first met Pat: he was twenty, and had just left Wellington. His brother, Alan Campbell, of the 72nd Highlanders, had distinguished himself at Tel-el-Kebir.

Pat was good-looking, with unusually well-bred gentle manners, a great affection for his home and people, and a passionate love for his dead mother. His father had married again, and there were many step-children—all were dear to Pat.

A devoted old keeper at Belmont had taught him the names of birds and wild flowers—a black speck in the sky, I could scarcely see, had its name, its character, and its ways for Pat; a flower that to me was just a pretty colour, for him was a little life with its family and its home.

Pat managed a boat like a magician. I remember a wonderful long day on the Thames. Pat

34

looked only at me—the boat went without effort or sound, quick and straight.

In the locks even we seemed alone—he spoke little —the golden glory of the dawn before passion is born was between us——

We picked wild flowers together. I remember a little bird flying into my hand and Pat's words, "Even the wild birds love you."

We eloped within four months of our first meeting and were married at St. Helen's Church, Bishopsgate Street.

One thing I can never forget—my mother's face and her heartbroken cry when I told her.

After more than thirty-five years of life—with its battles, its wounds, its every ready pain—it is not easy to write of the joy of that first love.

Incapable of pause or reckoning, with the divine faith and courage of fearless children, we faced the world we thought ours, and paid the price bravely.

Slowly to me came the awakening that the responsibility of the two children, born within three years, was mine. Pat, who had never been very strong, was ordered abroad for his health. . . .

I can remember vividly a hot summer night. The moon shone through the open window and I lay trying to see into the future. At about 2 o'clock I was overcome with restless anxiety, I slipped out of bed, taking care not to awaken Pat, and, throwing on a wrap, crept downstairs and opened the door leading to a narrow garden.

I walked up and down that little garden, now and then looking up at the window of the rooms where my husband and little son were asleep until daylight, thinking and wondering what was to be done. I knew Pat was not strong enough to continue working in the city, and that *I* must help. I could not imagine what work I could do.

I had given up my musical scholarship, and so was not qualified for a musical career. My lovely baby, and another coming in a few weeks, must be provided for. I was bewildered—lost.

With the daylight something entered my soul, and has never since left me—it seemed to cover me like a fine veil of steel, giving me a strange sense of security. Slowly I became conscious that within *myself* lay the strength I needed, and that I must never be afraid.

Was it the birth of self-reliance—or that overwhelming spirit "the sense of responsibility" beating against my heart—or the call of my "secret?"—I cannot say—I know I crept quietly back to bed in the grey light of the morning with a new courage and determination.

Pat was earning less than £100 a year, and his delicate health was alarming. His mother had died of consumption three years after his birth, and I fancy this preyed on my mind. The failure of the

Old Oriental Bank had practically ruined my father-in-law. . . .

Then my girl was born—"a little queen, with such beautiful hands," my mother said.

About two months later I was suddenly asked by Jim Bates to play the leading part at the Anomalies Dramatic Club, one of the members having fallen ill. I felt very unhappy and uncertain. The idea seemed to terrify me. My friends said it would cheer me up, and amuse me.

Someone had fixed in my mind when I was very young that Art was a form of prayer, and I could not regard it is an amusement, but my ridiculous seriousness was overcome in the end by Pat, who persuaded me to accept.

The Anomalies Dramatic Club was composed of 365 members, who each paid a subscription of £3 3s. a year: the Club gave three performances every year of two plays. The performances took place in the Town Hall.

This extract from *The Stage* shows that I met with some success.*

Pat's health became worse, and at last he was ordered by the doctor to take a sea voyage. It was suggested he should go to Brisbane, where a relative

---

* *"In his Power,* by Mark Quinton, 18th November, 1886. The Anomalies are fortunate in counting Mrs. Campbell as one of their members. It was this lady's first appearance on any stage on Thursday, and her performance was therefore the more extraordinary. Mrs. Campbell possesses a natural depth of pathos and yet a power and earnestness, which, joined to a graceful, easy manner and charming presence render her a most valuable acquisition."

of his, William Ross, was at the moment. The thought of the parting was misery to us both, but the state of his health made it imperative. It was arranged, if Pat succeeded in finding work, the children and I would join him.

The day he left, my sister and I went to the station to see him off. I don't know how it happened, but we missed him. I fainted. Someone in nurse's uniform lifted my head and gave me water. I can remember well the agony I felt as I realized the tragedy of our parting.

The following telegram is among my old papers:—

"5th October, 1887.
"Good-bye, darling, did my best to see you. Dare not miss another train. Perhaps it was better.
"PAT."

Had any of us realised the sort of difficulties a boy of Pat's nature would have to encounter, with no capital and delicate health, we would never have let him go on from Brisbane to Sydney and then on to Mashonaland. He and I both believed with the optimism of children in every new venture he undertook. I was sure he would soon make enough money to send for me and the children. And in those first years our dream of the joy of reunion gave our hearts courage.

The following are a few extracts from the hundreds of letters Pat wrote to me during the six and a

half years he was away.   The world has invented
many strange stories about me, so the truth of our
young lives and struggle, may be found interesting.

"Brisbane,
"15th December, 1887.
"Fairly good news, my own, own darling.   I have got
a berth in the B. I. Company's office, £2 a week to commence with, and I think it will increase soon.   I started
to work yesterday.   Some of the fellows seem very nice;
the hours are from 9 till 5.30.   It isn't very much, darling, but anyway it is a start.

"I got all your dear, sweet letters to-day, five forwarded on from Aden and one direct to Brisbane.   My
darling, do you know what these letters are to me? . . .

"The old *Duke of Buccleuch* went away to-day.   It
made me quite sad all day.   They would willingly have
taken me back to England with them.   It took all my
strength of will not to go. . . .

"Act as much as you like.   I know you love me; that
is enough. . . ."

After Pat left England I played again with the
Anomalies Dramatic Company in *Blow for Blow,*
and *The Money Spinner*.

"Brisbane,
"8th January, 1888.
" . . . Your last letter telling me about the Governor
agreeing to stand security for the rent has taken a great
load off my mind.   Oh, darling, it is awful for me here
to think of all the worry and trouble you have at home.
It is heart-breaking to think of the long time it will be
before I see you again.   I try and keep my spirits up,

but I am utterly miserable without you. . . . Mr. Woodward has gone away prospecting for gold with two other fellows who have been most lucky. He has promised to let me know at once if they find anything good. North Queensland seems to abound in gold; they find fresh gold every day. . . ."

"Brisbane,
"14th January, 1888.

" . . . I have been over head and ears in work all the week, darling, and really have not had time to write you the long letter I promised.

"I have sent a cheque this post for £29 15s. 6d. (all I can get together) to an old friend in Kimberley, Harold Ingall, asking him to buy a demand draft for what it will fetch, payable to Mrs. Stella Campbell, and send it on to you. I have asked him to try and send it same mail as this.

"Grand reports every day about gold. . . ."

"Brisbane,
"21st February, 1888.

"My own darling,

"I have been laid up in bed for the last ten days with a touch of coloured fever, but I am all right now, only it has left me very weak. You need not be frightened, the climate seems to suit me splendidly. They say most young fellows get a touch of fever when they first come out. . . .

"It was awful work being laid up without you to look after me. I was very bad for three days, off my head altogether. One or two people were most kind. I am rather glad I have had it, as one has to go through it, and it might have been much worse.

"Nothing new out here. . . ."

Three months afterwards he wrote:—

"Sydney,
"17th May, 1888.

". . . .

"After an interval of three mails I have just received your sweet letter of 29th March. You may well say I seem miserable. I am always being haunted by the idea that you will learn to hate me, because I am so long in helping you out of your great troubles that your patience and goodness cannot last. . . .

"Should I by any chance be able to get a good berth at £35, I will then be able to send you at least £20 a month, and then, my darling, you will be able to live more comfortably. It will be a blessed day to me when I am able to write and send you the first regular remittance, and I feel sure it will only be a month or so hence now. You will think I am wasting time staying here, but there has not been a single boat going to Africa yet.

"What a pet the little girl must be. Do try and send their photos, and, my own wife, send me one of your own. I want that above everything. . . ."

"Mauritius,
"28th July, 1888.

"I feel utterly miserable. I have been stuck here for a month, no possible way of getting on to Africa. At last we are going to start in the *Dunbar Castle* to-day. I have no heart to write to you. My money has given out, and I am obliged to draw on my father for my passage from here. I can't help it. I am afraid he will be wild, but it is the only thing I could do. I have written him a nice letter, and I will pay it back as soon as I get to work. . . .

"Stella, darling, don't get disgusted with me. God knows I have done my best. . . . And then, of course, I have had no word from the time I left Sydney and shall not, perhaps find a letter when I get to Kimberley. I do hope Kimberly will be the end of our troubles.

"I cannot write more. It is awful to be the means of so much misery to you, for I worship you, my darling.

"God bless you and the children.

"PAT."

"Kimberley Central Diamond Mining Company, Ltd.,
"Kimberley,
"17th September, 1888.
" . . .

"I got your sweet letter on Saturday enclosing the one written to you by my father. I am writing him a long letter by this mail.

"You will have got Ross's cable to my father about my billet by now. I do hope, my darling, it was a comfort.

"I get £300 a year to start. My predecessor, who was only five months in the Company, and then lost the post through drink, got a rise of £50 at the end of three months. I do hope I get the same. Ross thinks I will be able to get something better soon. Things are very dull just now. The elections are on next month.

"This seems a splendid place for making money. I do hope I can only get a start. I know Ross will put me in the way of anything good. . . .

"I am so glad to know that the acting has made you happier. . . .

"PAT."

"PAT" CAMPBELL

Then Pat went on to Mashonaland, sometimes prospecting with hopes of concessions and settlements, and later I heard of his big game shooting with Selous. How he must have loved that.

Then followed many weeks and no letters, and Pat could only send money very irregularly. So at last it was decided that I should take up the stage professionally, and I wrote asking for Pat's permission. This he gave, and I started my career. I had already gained some experience and success in my performances at the Anomalies Dramatic Club.

"Central Diamond Mfg. Coy.,
"Stockdale Street,
"Kimberley,
"12th November, 1888.

"My own Stella wife,

"I received your sweet letter telling me of your rehearsals, and I long to get the long letter next week, which you have promised to send me, telling me all about the first performance, and I do hope it won't knock you up. . . .

"I have just heard of a billet going with a salary of £500 a year, and I am going to do my very best to get it.

"My life here is very monotonous, but I am getting on very well in this office, and the work is most interesting; the diamonds are simply superb. We are making a collection of curious ones for the Paris Exhibition. There is one most beautiful stone, the palest emerald green and very fiery. Some jet black ones which sparkle splendidly; others amber-coloured, orange, pink, yellow of all shades, and some of the purest water, all shapes and all sizes. One is shaped just like a man's head;

another is only half-formed, one half a pure diamond and the other a kind of milky pebble; another, a large stone, has a distinct representation of a tiny fern in it, another one is a perfectly round, flat, smooth stone, rather larger than a shilling and about twice as thick, quite clear, you can read print through it. Some of the stones are very valuable. The emerald-green one is only 8 carats and is worth about £700. Many of the white stones are worth £7 to £10 a carat.

"God bless you, my own, own blessed wife. Write always; I feel so anxious about you. Promise me not to run risks. Send me all your criticisms. I am so anxious to hear.

"I know you will be a success.

"Think as well as you can of

"DADDY."

"Kimberley,
"January, 1889.
". . .

"I am beginning to hate Kimberley; what I want is for Rhodes to send me up into the interior to Lobengula's country, Matabeleland. The general impression here is that the first fellows who are sent up will make their fortunes. I shall do my level best to get sent. . . .

"I believe this last scheme of Rhodes' will turn into a company every bit as large and powerful as the old East India Company. From all accounts the country to be opened up is magnificent, and full of minerals far superior to anything yet found in Africa. The only difficulty is transport, and Rhodes is going to run a railway to the Zambesi. There is a wonderful future for Africa, if Rhodes only lives."

*   *   *   *   *

About this time I received the following, now amusing letter from my dear old friend. "Aunt Kate," which gives a most vivid impression of the prejudiced attitude towards the theatrical profession in those days:—

"34, Avenue de Villiers,
"Paris,

"My dear Beatrice,

"Since I received your first letter I have felt almost unable to write. The shock it gave me I could never explain to you, nor would you understand it. Nor did I quite realise before *how* dear you were to me. I should hardly have believed that losing you would, after all, have caused me such infinite pain.

"Poor, unfortunate child, may God help you, if, as you say, the die for evil is cast. I can only pray, as the only chance to save you, that you make too decided a failure ever to try again.

"Good God, how could you think I could write and wish you success? *How thankful I feel* that it was not whilst with *me* that you took the wrong turning. Mrs. Hogarth is a vulgar mind—she made, too, in one of her letters, observations which decided me about her. I forget, but to the effect that it mattered little about you if you got money.

"But your mother! ! ! I should have thought her the *very last* to allow you to enter on such a path! !

"Ah, well, I do not think anyone ever loved my poor little child as I did. Although our meetings were difficult, I knew you were there—I felt I had one other tie to earth. And when you were the first-rate musician which I have never doubted your becoming, I hoped you might have played with glory at concerts, and over here, what a joy to have heard you—and your praise. For *that* would have been honest and reputable praise. Whilst gaining which you could have held up your head in any society. Oh, my poor Beatrice, you can form no idea—you have yet to learn—the shame, the humiliation of seeing yourself despised by decent people.

"Even the admiration of the mob will not make up for it to you. You have too much intelligence for that and, I had thought, too much pride.

"I now see your reason for leaving me so many weeks without a letter; you would not hint at it till too late. And yet, of course, no remonstrance would ever stop you. How could they allow and encourage your first home attempts?

"How can a woman bid with pleasure farewell to her best and happiest heritage—name, reputation, affection— to allow her every look and movement to be criticised by all the common jeering mouths and minds of the public. And this was once dear little Beatrice—the poor little girl who spent one happy year in Paris with her 'Aunt Kate.'

"What a dream it will be to you in your future riotous life. In fact I am wretched—such a sorrow and disappointment from what I thought was in store for my darling. However, let me have my own feelings alone— they are nothing in the matter; and the past is gone. I must try to forget that dream.

Should you succeed, there may at last be money; but is that all to those around you? Is your future nothing, your happiness?

"Well, Texas would have been better than this. On the receipt of your letter of six weeks back I told Charley you had some secret plan in view of 'exquisite joy.' I said, almost with bated breath, 'Is it the stage—an

actress?' He looked grave, and said I had no right to
imagine such a thing. Beatrice was frivolous, but he
knew you better than that your nature would ever let
you sink to *that,* so low. And now he has listened, but
answered not a word, and only looked doubly grave.

"Oh, think what a charm your music might have cast
on all circles where you entered. And I should have
felt my poor old heart beat with pleasure when you told
me. God forbid I should tell any more than necessary
of this, your last horrid fancy.

"A painful effort this letter is. But I would not
write until a day or two had a little cooled and calmed
me. I am anything but strong yet.

"I feel deep sympathy for Mr. Hill*—a gentleman
in mind, as you have ever described him. He must regret that his business prevents him taking his wife and
children far off and cutting entirely with her family—
for although you will naturally hide your name, bad
news always forces its way.

"See what it is to let a young child grow up without
any guidance. Parents cannot begin too young. Here is
a nature, with so much in it loving and good—which
might have been turned for happiness to herself and
all around. And now lost. Can I, who knew and
appreciated it (alas! all too late), be otherwise than sad
and miserable? Would that I could have kept you ever
here with me.

"I must bid you good-bye, Beatrice, believe me with
much sorrow and sympathy with you and your ill-gov-
erned impulses. I may have said harsh or painful things. I grieve to cause you pain, my dear, but
you rightly were expecting it must be so. You know
my disgust for that class to which you are going to ally

* My eldest sister's husband.

yourself—our disgust, I might say—and to think that one we loved, and had lately in our midst, goes and with pleasure, into such a set—to be one of them!

"Then forgive me if I speak my mind; I never could flatter or pretend what I did not feel. What I do feel most painfully is grief for you. And also much sympathy for you in the wretched life which you must have been going through.

"But my words and thoughts can matter little now—you will be in too great a state of over-excitement to think of calm lives such as ours over here.

"May your health not break down (or, who knows? that might be the best thing).

"With heartfelt anguish and sorrow and pity for yourself, dear Beatrice, also much sympathy, for you *must* suffer deeply. You cannot leave all promise of youth and kindred—all the past—for such a life—and be happy. Oh, no, I feel much for the heart, which I fancied I knew better than others did, and which I surely had found. Poor, dear child, good-bye. I cannot see for my tears. Oh, Beatrice, how could you? I loved you too truly not to grieve bitterly, the breaking of your young life, which to *me* millions could never make up for.

"Your still fond aunt,
"KATHERINE BAILEY"

CHAPTER IV.

I WAS given an introduction by Mr. F. W. Macklin—a good actor who sometimes played for the Anomalies Dramatic Club, to an agent —Harrington Baily.

Mr. Baily's office was in a street off the Strand. The idea was, that I should pay him a guinea fee, put my name down on his books, tell him what experience I had had as an amateur or otherwise; he would then make a note of my name and appearance, and let me know when he had any work to offer me.

As I was looking for the number of his office, I saw a poor cat in the gutter licking two little drowned kittens: she was mewing over them pitiably. This upset me. I found Mr. Baily's door, went up a flight of stone steps and was shown into his office. He stood up to shake hands with me. I opened my mouth to speak, and I burst into a flood of tears. I suppose I was tired and hungry, and my stout heart and stiff upper lip went to pieces at the sight of the drowned kittens—I am not sure that even now I could pass the sight unmoved—I told Mr. Baily what I had seen. He very sympathetically took me into an inner room and rang the bell for his housekeeper, ordering her to bring me some tea. Then he left me. About a quarter of an hour afterwards

49

he returned, and I remember with what a sympathetic smile and manner he told me there was a man, Mr. Green by name, in the next room, who was taking out a play, *Bachelors,* by Mr. Hermann Vezin; he wanted a leading lady, but he could only pay £2 10s. a week, and the actress was to supply her own dresses.

[I thought it a dazzling offer. I saw Mr. Green, and he seemed to me a wonderful person, for he engaged me at once. I went home to my mother with my good news. My friends gave me some dress materials, and I sat up at night making my frocks; the day-time was taken up with rehearsals.]

The following letter shows the terms of my agreement for this play:—

> "Frank Green's Company,
> "October 16th, 1888.
> "Dear Madam,
> "I hereby engage you for my tour of *Bachelors* to commence at the Alexandria Theatre, Liverpool, on October 22nd, 1888, at a salary of £2 10s. per week. Fares paid to join, and while on tour. You to give one week previous to opening for rehearsals. This engagement subject to a fortnight's notice on either side and to the usual playhouse rules and regulations.
> "Frank Green.

To Miss Stella Campbell." *

---

* It was not until I joined Mr. Ben Greet's Company that I called myself Mrs. Patrick Campbell. My father-in-law at first objected, but later we were great friends, and he was proud of my success.

I was out to fight for my two children, and to try and make enough money to bring Pat home to us more quickly.

We were rehearsed for a week at the Mona Hotel, Covent Garden, by Mr. Hermann Vezin, and then on the Sunday we started off for Liverpool to open at the Alexandra Theatre, November 20th, 1888.

The following was the cast:—

Rufus Marrable (a retired Q.C.), Mr. William Lowe,
Charles Lovelace (his nephew), Mr. Oswald Yorke.
Robert Bromley (a professor of music), Mr. Edgar Smart.
Dr. West, Mr. Bruce Henderson.
Potts (factotum at Bachelor's Hall), Mr. Sidney Burt.
Mrs. Lynne Loseby (a young widow), Miss Stella Campbell.
Emmeline Loseby (her cousin), Miss Naomi Neilson.
Mrs. Moody (landlady of Bachelor's Hall), Mrs. William Lowe.
Sophia Moody (her daughter), Miss Grace Gordon.
Susan Stubbs (Mrs. Loseby's maid), Miss Clara Marbrame.

I remember on the Monday I went out for a walk in the morning trembling with excitement. I looked in the shop windows, feeling nervous and desolate. I was standing outside a draper's shop, when a kind voice said: "You look very pale, miss; won't you come in and sit down?" It was the draper himself. I went in and sat on a chair by the counter. I told him I was going to act that night at the Alexandra

Theatre, and that it was the first time in my life that I would be acting in a real theatre. He was very interested, and cheered me by saying that he would come and see the performance. I felt I would have one friend in the house—the company were all strangers to me—and I had not left my babies before.

When I came on to the stage my first feeling was that the audience was too far away for me to reach out to them, so I must, as it were, quickly gather them up to myself: and I think I may say that this has always been the instinctive principle of my acting. Whether it is the wrong or the right principle, I leave it for others to decide.

I am sure I had no technique, and my voice was the voice of a "singing mouse." The papers praised me, and they also praised my dresses, and I was very proud and happy.

My next engagement was on tour in *Tares* with Mrs. Bandmann-Palmer.

I think my contract for this play too, may hold some interest for the young actresses of to-day:—

"To Mrs. Patrick Campbell.

"I hereby undertake to engage you for my forthcoming Spring Tour, commencing on April 22nd, 1889, at a weekly salary of £2 (two pounds) for seven performances (if required) in each week, you undertaking to play the part of "Rachael Denison" in *Tares* and to understudy and act all other parts for which you may be cast during the said tour; you to find your own dresses, you to at-

tend rehearsals in London for two clear weeks previous
to commencement of tour; and to pay your own rail
fare to the opening town, and to be there in time for rehearsal on the morning of Monday, April 22nd.   I to
pay your third-class railway fares on each journey taken
with the company after joining.

"This engagement is to be terminable by a fortnight's
notice on either side, and you are to abide by the rules
and regulations of the various theatres in which the company may be acting.

                    "Millicent Bandmann-Palmer.
    "April 15th, 1889."

How was it done?   How did we live?   And how
manage to send money home?   We *did,* and many
of us are alive to tell the tale.

Tares was a good effective play by Mrs. Oscar
Beringer.   I had lines something like these, which
received frantic applause:—

    She: "Leave my house!"

    I: "My house is truth and honour, and in leav-
ing, I turn you out."

I was very young, ridiculously thin, and fragile-
looking.   The manageress was stout, strong, and
middle-aged, and I remember in one town shouts of
"Jumbo" and "Alice."   I do not know the story of
these elephants at the Zoo, but I believe one died of
a broken heart for the other.

Mrs. Bandmann-Palmer did not like me.   She
told me I belonged to the "school of squirmers."
The company were kind, sympathetic people, and

Mr. Lyall Swete has remained a dear friend of mine to this day.

At last Mrs. Bandmann-Palmer offended me deeply and I handed in my notice.

The members of the company expressed their feelings of sympathy for me in the following letter, showing they were all my faithful allies:—

"Grand Theatre,
"Cardiff,
"2nd June, 1889.

"Dear Mrs. Campbell,

"We cannot allow you to leave us without expressing our deep regret in losing a true friend and so excellent an artist.

"We should also like to record our admiration of the way in which you have rendered the part of 'Rachael Denison.'

"We hope that the friendship we all have for you will be strengthened and renewed at no very distant date, and in the meantime we sincerely wish you everything that you could possibly wish for yourself, and remain,

"Your friendly admirers,
"Acton Bond.
"Mervyn Herepath.
"E. Lyall Swete.
"Caleb Porter.
"Charles B. West.
"Frank Worthing.
"Lucca de Rivas.
"Ida North.
"Hinnetta Faye.
"Alice Carlton.

"*Tares*' Company—Spring Tour."

They arranged a farewell supper party.   We were all to contribute a performance to the entertainment. How excited I was.   I remember I trimmed a white dress I had with a border of real green ivy leaves and arranged the dress in Greek fashion.

I recited Tennyson's "Two Sisters," pouring out my "secret" to that little company.   I felt they all believed in me, and my future, and I was full of gratitude and pride.

After this engagement I spent many weeks at home, and received the following letters from Pat:—

"Central Company,
"Kimberley.
"16th September, 1889.
". . .

"Thank you very much for your dear, long letter, telling me you had a chance of getting on so well.   It was a great comfort to me, for I am fairly down in the mouth. I can get no word from the De Beers people, and feel very anxious.   I am very well in health, darling, and much stronger than I was.   We are just getting the commencement of summer here, and it is very hot. . . .

"Rhodes has only just come up here, and I cannot get hold of him; he is so busy.   I cannot find out what they are going to do in Matabeleland. . . .

"PAT."

"Kimberley,
"14th October, 1889.
"My darling wife,
"It was impossible for me to send you money last month.   I am out of a billet, and am very miserable

about it. I do hope to have better news next week. I hoped to have got something to do by to-day, darling; it will be only for a week or two at most.

"Thank you so much for your sweet letters. I think I shall have good news for you next mail. I have got a very good name here in Kimberley, but things are very dull just now and few billets going. . . ."

"Kimberley,
"8th November, 1889

". . .

"I have news which I am afraid may frighten you. I am going to Matabeleland to-day. I had the chance offered me and, after consulting many friends who are in the know, I made up my mind to go, as I could not get a billet in Kimberley.

"There are fifteen of us going, all connected with the De Beers Company, and mostly friends of Rhodes. We are not allowed to know anything yet, and are sworn in and attached to E. Troop of Bechuanaland Border Police, with troopers' pay, about £5 a month (and all found), which is all I shall be able to send you for a month or two.

"Rhodes and all the De Beers directors tell me to go, and I shall never regret it. What I fancy is that we are to get commissions in the new Chartered Company's forces, with a good interest in the company. We shall probably know more about it when we get further up country. Everybody here seems to think that we are bound to make our fortunes, as we are being sent up by Mr. Rhodes, who is a sort of king out here. We go right through Bechuanaland, via Barkley, Mafeking, and are to receive instructions at a place called Ibili, on the Matabele frontier. We are going in one of the Chartered Company's wagons, and will probably be about six weeks or two months before we get to Ibili.

"You may think me wrong to go, dear, but I could get nothing to do in Kimberley and was getting into debt, and saw no prospects. Everybody advised me to accept the offer, and seemed to think my fortune is made.

"I will write you again when I know more.

"Good-bye, darling. God bless you. Don't think badly of me. I am doing my best.   "Pat."

*   *   *   *   *

My next engagement was with Mr. Ben Greet in his Touring Company, and this was the beginning of really fine experience for me. I was thrown, as it were, into the sea to swim. The salary was £2 10s. a week, and I to supply my own dresses.

How through the night we used to stitch! Miss Violet Ray—a lovely girl, with whom I made great friends—and I.

I remember how she used to coax me to allow her to take my little son—he was then about five years old, and used to come and stay with me for a week or so at a time—out for a walk, and insisted upon his calling her "mother" * in shops or when people passing by could overhear. She thought it so wonderful to have a son.

We played *As you Like It, A Midsummer Night's Dream, Twelfth Night, Love in a Mist,* by Louis N. Parker; and once, Ben Greet made me play principal

---

* Violet Ray some years afterwards left the stage and married Mr. Nye Chant, and had lovely children of her own.

boy in a pantomime, *Aladdin.* I remember the horror of the boy's velvet suit sent down from London, evidently for a very stout lady; the bust had to be filled with tissue paper for me.

I came down to the footlights and sang with the orchestra. The song began:—

"They say the years have swallows' wings,
But mine have leaden feet."

And the refrain was: "For you, for you, my darling. . . ."

I felt so foolish that I wept. Dear Mr. Ben Greet, whose part in the pantomime I forget, laughed merrily at me. I am afraid I gave a shocking performance—I know I was never offered a pantomime engagement again.

I often used to hear Mr. Ben Greet's voice from the prompt corner, "Don't mug, Pat," when I thought I was making a fine facial expression, or, perhaps, I was not thinking at all.

Mr. Ben Greet was a great man to me, for it seemed there was not a play he did not know from start to finish, with every bit of "business" connected with it. He was always smiling, cheerful, and courageous, whether it was a big audience or a small one, and won my love by his extraordinary kindness to my children.

There was a never-to-be-forgotten day, when Mr. Greet took my little son down to the beach, and allowed him to help some men who were filling a coal barge. How I remember the little black figure on the sands running to meet me in the evening, wild with joy and excitement.

I do not think Ben Greet ever shook my faith, that some day I would be able to act well, and that the public would love me, and if it were necessary, I should be able to educate and provide for my children.

I wish I could remember about the lodgings on tour, the landladies, my fellow actors and actresses. It is foolish of me to have forgotten so much kindness—and adventure.

I kept no diary. I lived, as it were, in front of the moment, not criticising the hour: actual events did not absorb me, for I have no recollection of disliking anything or finding anything tedious. I suppose I was so grateful for the *opportunity;* the enterprise: my mind was set on the goal ahead—Pat's return—and his pride in his children and my success.

There must have been many dreary hours—ugliness that hurt, shabby clothes, insufficient food, exhaustion; but these things left no sting.

Looking back, I remember the actors and actresses as all very kind, clever people, and so grateful to be in an engagement, their warm childish impulses unharmed by the social ambitions of the London artist. Songs in the train, brilliant repartee hurled at tired railway porters, Shakespeare quoted at weary cabmen.

Their name on a good position on the hoardings, or their praise in the local paper, took all sense of hardship and care away, and filled them with gaiety and happiness.

I recall the following incident clearly:–

I had been working very hard, living on a few shillings a week—I always sent money home out of my £2 or £2 10s., salary: in those days you could get a nice room and board for 18s. a week; and many actresses lived on £1 a week.

One night the management, to save expense, sent us on to our next town by the "milk train." We arrived at 5 a. m. on a winter's morning, and I had no room to go to. I asked a kindly-looking old porter if he knew of any rooms, and he advised me to go home with him. His wife, he said, had a little room to let. He looked a most trustworthy individual.

As a rule, one asked for addresses at the theatre, if lodgings had not been arranged by letter beforehand, but the theatre was not open at that hour. So I went along with the kindly porter. I remember the small attic under the roof. It looked tidy and clean, so far as I could see by the light of the candle.

I got into bed and fell into a deep sleep—I was worn out, I never could sleep in a train. I awoke with a start. The grey morning light came through the little window, which was almost on a level with the floor; the ceiling slanted to the top of the window. At first I could not remember where I was, or *where my children were!* I was lost in terror, and I instinctively screamed "Mother!" The sound of my voice brought me to my senses. With the loss of memory my resistance had snapped, and I knew fear.

Pat's letters came seldom. Sometimes he was out of a job, or down with malaria; sometimes succeeding for a few months, and then a cheque would come. Sometimes he was cut off from all communication with the outer world by the flooded rivers. Then I used to think he had died of fever, or that he had been mauled by a lion. Those hours numbed me and sapped a little of my young life, I think. We had both agreed that Pat should stay away until he could bring money home, or until I had succeeded sufficiently in my work for us to be together again. My uncle's and mother's sympathy and devotion, helped to keep my heart up, and there were my children's happy little visits to me; and sometimes a girl friend would come and stay with me for a week.

During this engagement a performance was given by Mr. Ben Greet of *The Hunchback,* for the *début* of Miss Laura Johnson, a pupil of Hermann Vezin and Madame Modjeska, I had to study "Helen" quickly. A straw-coloured wig was sent up for me from London, and a high-waisted pink satin dress. "Modus" was played by Mr. Ben Greet. Dressed up as I was, I enjoyed mightily the comedy scene I played with him. I discovered for the first time that when I was amused, the audience laughed. There was great enthusiasm, and I knew I was a success.

On my way back from the theatre to my lodgings, I was followed by a man, and, although I hurried till I almost ran, he overtook me, and he introduced himself to me as Hugh Moss, many years afterwards Sir Hugh Moss, of the Moss Empires. He told me that I had made a great success, that John Hare and Clement Scott had been in the theatre, invited by Mr. Hermann Vezin to see Miss Laura Johnson, but that it was I who had won their hearts. I thanked him shyly, and hurried home, as he stared after me. I never remember meeting him again.

One day when we were playing at Folkestone, Laura Johnson and Hermann Vezin thought a sea trip before the theatre would be amusing, so they went in an excursion boat from Folkestone to Boulogne, but they were late in getting back for the beginning of the evening performance.

I was sent for and told that a *Lever de Rideau* must be played. I went to the theatre, and Mr. Ben Greet said we must give a one-act play he had in his repertoire; about a boys' school next door to a convent. A boy climbs over the garden wall and makes love to a girl. A nun discovers them, and is horrified. It turns out that the boy and girl are cousins and are engaged so the play ends with a merry dance. Ben Greet told me that the parts of the boy and girl were to be played by two members of the company, who knew their *rôles,* but that I must play the nun—that I was to make a nun's dress out of some black cloth and white linen with safety-pins at once, and that *he* would say the *words* loudly from the prompt corner. All I had to do was to open and shut my mouth, hold up my hands in horror until the dance at the end, in which the nun joins. *I did so, and it was a success.*

Mr. Pinero was in front. Years afterwards I asked him if he had noticed anything odd about the performance, and he said "No."

During this tour, Mr. Ben Greet took us to give two pastoral performances for Lord Pembroke at Wilton—*As you Like It,* and *A Midsummer Night's Dream.* The company were excited at the idea of going to Wilton, the home of Shakespeare's friend, William Herbert.

It is said this family once possessed a letter—now unfortunately lost—from Queen Elizabeth, saying she would like to come and stay at Wilton for three night's and meet "that man Shakespeare who writes plays."

Lord Pembroke * was one of the handsomest men of his day. He was very tall, extraordinarily handsome, with a fine figure and hazel eyes—the colour of the water of a tarn—full of deep, gentle sympathy; beautiful features, and a short, curly beard. He had a singularly winning and sympathetic manner; in-

* The late Earl of Pembroke, whose sister, Lady Maud, and her husband, Sir Hubert Parry, lived a few doors from me in Kensington Square, and were my dear friends for twenty years.

deed, a sympathy in his whole bearing which won everybody's love.

A great many people had arrived to see the play from neighbouring houses. Two among the guests, who later became great friends of mine, Mrs. Horner * and Miss Balfour,† told me afterwards of an incident rather typical of the mental attitude in those days towards stage players.

Mrs. Horner had come over from Mells, bringing Miss Balfour with her, to see *As You Like It*. When they arrived, they were met at the hall door by Lady Pembroke, looking very excited and mysterious. She said they were not to see any of the other guests, but they were to come and be "dressed up" at once to impersonate two ladies in Ben Greet's company. Lady Pembroke would not listen to any hesitation. She rang for her maid, and said: "Fetch me some Gainsborough hats and cloaks"; and a wig, and some rouge were found.

Frances Horner, with her remarkable face and eyes, was very difficult to disguise, so it was decided to turn her into a very dissipated old harridan. I am not sure she did not have a tooth blacked out. She wore the wig and was highly rouged, and assumed an aggressive, vulgar manner.

Miss Balfour wore a bonnet, a thick veil, a long red cloak, and she, too, was rouged. She was given some queer French name. Mrs. Horner was called

* Lady Horner, of Mells Park, Frome. .
† The Hon. Mrs. Alfred Lyttelton.

"Miss Greet." When they came out on to the lawn with Lady Pembroke, their most intimate friends were sitting and walking about—they did not expect their disguise would last a moment.

Miss Balfour was introduced to Lord Pembroke, and Mrs. Horner to Lady Brownlow, and other guests, and nobody recognised them.

Lord Pembroke told Miss Balfour afterwards that he was afraid to look at her, she seemed so painted and so shy. She heard someone say: "That one is rather like Miss Balfour, if Miss Balfour were pretty."

Mrs. Horner attacked her impersonation with vigour. She declared, with a hideous grin, that her favourite *rôle* was "Juliet," and everyone shunned her except Lord Ribblesdale, whose amused tolerance of all idiosyncrasy has always helped him to be kind.

At luncheon the climax was reached. The real members of Ben Greet's company arrived, and sat with other guests at another table. Miss Balfour had just been invited by Mr. Harry Cust to go for a walk with him in the woods after the performance, and Mrs. Horner had secured the promise from the same young man, that he would take a box at her benefit, when Lady Pembroke rose hurriedly, and said in an agitated whisper: "It's no use going on; that's Frances Horner and that's D. D. Balfour, and you must be quiet about it because of the next table."

We, at the next table, only thought there were curious people at the other table.

They must have been a little surprised by our youth and prettiness; we were both of us only a little over twenty, and Violet Ray was very lovely.

I had another impression at this gathering, which surprised and annoyed me. Some of the guests spoke in a curiously patronising way, which made me very uncomfortable. I think I must have shown this, for suddenly a woman with a face full of beauty and intelligence, put her arm about me. Who of the hundreds who loved her can ever forget her, or think of her without a blessing, dear Mrs. Percy Wyndham *—"Aunt Madeline." From that moment she entered my heart, and I held her there until she died in 1920, and I hold her there still.

Ignorant of the world, as I was, easily impressed by any external grace and beauty, Aunt Madeline set a standard for me, by which I judged people instinctively; later, when I moved among the heterogeneous crowd which surrounds successful artists, I discerned those whom I thought would be worthy of her friendship, and those who would not be.

No doubt it is chiefly to her, I owe a vision of life as it is best to live it. She had no prejudices, all about her was warmth, an intelligent quickness of sympathy, and a lack of curiosity, making explana-

*The Hon. Mrs. Percy Wyndham. After her death her son, Colonel Guy Wyndham, brought me all my letters written to her during nearly thirty years. "Aunt Madeline" had kept them with her children's.

IN ONE OF HER MOST FAMOUS ROLES

tions unnecessary, leaving the sacred recesses of the heart unhurt. . . .

But to go back to Wilton; the morning had been dull and the afternoon was cloudy, but it was fine enough for us to act. The scene was most beautiful, great spreading trees at the side of a little open glade. At the back, undulating grounds.

At my first entrance as Ganymede, Lord Pembroke's pugs—he had a special breed of his own—suddenly rushed over the grass to a knoll I had reached, and barked furiously at my long boots.

I am afraid I was delighted at the interruption—I am most surely a fool over dogs—I stooped down and spoke to them in a special dog language of my own, forgetting for the moment all about Rosalind and the smart audience.

Lord Pembroke, with mingled embarrassment, courtesy, and humour, came across the ground and apologised as he called the dogs away. Perhaps the interruption made my "Rosalind" more natural. How I loved the beauty of it all.

*   *   *   *   *

In the evening, to the light of lanterns and the moon, we played *A Midsummer Night's Dream,* lying on the grass, running to and fro, the moths playing about us. The glamour of the night and the cadence of the verse, filled me with their loveliness.

The following letter from Lord Pembroke, given

to me many months afterwards by Mr. Ben Greet, is interesting:—

> "Wilton House,
> "Salisbury,
> "27th March, 1891.

"My dear Mr. Ben Greet,

"I do remember most vividly how charming the whole performance was, and how specially delightful the 'Rosalind' of Mrs. Patrick Campbell. She was the best 'Rosalind,' to my mind, that I ever saw, not even excepting Miss Rehan, admirable as she was. That very gifted and talented actress made more of the part—put more into it—but her impersonation lacked the freshness and spontaneity of Mrs. Campbell's that made hers so delicious. But comparisons are ungracious between things that are really good. If Mrs. Campbell ever acts 'Rosalind' in London, may I be there to see.

"I heard that she played 'Lady Teazle' at a matinée in town not long ago. I wish I had known of it. The part should have suited her admirably, and Beerbohm Tree told me that he had heard the performance spoken of very highly in the acting world. . . ."

It was, I believe, shortly after this performance at Wilton that a matinée of *A Buried Talent* by Louis N. Parker was given at the Vaudeville Theatre, London, by Mr. Ben Greet.

The following letter, sent me by the author, shows the success with which it met:—

A Buried Talent.

"It was on the afternoon of Wednesday, June 5th,

1890—thirty-one years ago—that my firstling, *A Buried Talent,* with you in the female part, was produced by Ben Greet at a single matinée at the Vaudeville Theatre in the Strand. I had seen you play once before in my *Love-in-a-Mist*—one of the most alluring performances I have ever witnessed—so I knew to some extent what to expect. Your fellow players were Ben Greet, Basset Roe, Roland Atwood, and Murray Hawthorne. As I only got to London in time for lunch—for which I had no appetite—I saw no rehearsal, and, in spite of my previous knowledge of you, you dawned on me as a revelation. I have just refreshed my memory by reading the play again, and that has brought your picture vividly before me. You were a pure joy. You radiated beauty and grace; and your voice was music. You represented a girl who was able to act and sing the principal part in a new opera at a moment's notice, and without a rehearsal. That can be, and has been done, but, as a rule, when a character in a play is described as having such an exceptional gift, the stalls are sceptical and the gallery boos with engaging frankness. This was not so in your case. We felt that such a *tour de force* would be child's play to you, you convinced us that you could do that, or anything else you chose; and goodness knows you have since shown us we were right. I think that, for both of us, the subject of the playlet had a curious personal application at the moment, which has kept that single performance a more fragrant memory than many much more portentous first nights. At any rate, I can speak for myself."

*   *   *   *   *

But, sad to relate, I overworked with Ben Greet. I caught chill upon chill acting in his open-air plays in the wet grass; and at last I had to go home very

seriously ill. My voice went for seven months, and
for many weeks I had to write on a slate. My singing voice never returned. It was dreadful—and I
was heartbroken. I could not speak to the children,
if I played with them I tired, and I could only take
them for very short walks. Grief and loneliness
overpowered me—I was very unhappy.

The following is Pat's letter, when he heard the
news of my illness. It will be seen that from September, 1890, to March, 1891, I had had no word
from him. My health had broken down, my voice
gone, all thought of acting had to be given up, Pat
had not been able to send money or write for six
months.

> "c/o H. H. the Administrator,
> "Fort Salisbury,
> "Mashonaland,
> "7th January, 1891.

"My own darling wife,
    "At last I have time to send you a line. I have been
on the rush ever since I last wrote in August, and have
only just reached this place. Soon after writing to you
I started with Mr. Colquhoun for Manica, went down
with him to Mutassa, where he got the treaty with the
Manica King, over which so much fuss has been made
in the papers. He then sent me post haste by myself to
ride to Fort Churter, a distance of 120 miles as the
crow flies—through dense bush, over many mountains
and across several large rivers—to take a message, re-
porting the getting of the treaty, to be forwarded to

Mr. Rhodes in Kimberley. I had then to return immediately and meet him at the Kraal of a chief named Gotos, some eighty miles away from Mutassa. This I did, and was at once sent again by himself with a Bamangwato boy to go to Mutassa and remain as the Company's representative until Mr. Colquhoun sent someone to relieve me. I had only got one day away on my way to Mutassa when a man was sent after me to recall me, owing to a dispatch having been received that the Portuguese Convention had been signed—a mistake, as it happened— Mr. Colquhoun then sent me off to report verbally to Mr. Rhodes, who had started on a tour through Bechuanaland with the Governor, as to the proceedings of the Manica Mission. In eleven days I rode a distance of 600 miles to Palapye, the chief Mangwato town, where I met Mr. Rhodes and the Governor, Sir Henry Lock. Mr. Rhodes was very kind and very pleased to see me, the first member of the Pioneer Expedition who had come down. I was three days with him, and he then sent me down to Kimberley by post cart, a distance of 700 miles, travelling day and night, to see the Secretary of the Company and report verbally.

"I was one week in Kimberley, during which I had not one half-hour to myself, being the first pioneer down from Mashonaland—interviewed by newspapers and individuals of all sorts in the very early morning, at the office all day giving information, fêted and lionised with dinners, etc., at night—sickening, I can tell you, darling, after the grand free, healthy open-air life I had been leading so long. I was really glad when I turned my back on Kimberley. On my return journey, I was delayed a week at a place called Vryburg, doing business for the Company, travelled on to Palapye by post cart, and between that place and Fort Tuli, Dr. Jamieson, the local

Managing Director, caught me up, and I drove up with him to this place in a Cape cart, and arrived here two days ago.

"Sweetheart, I am afraid this is a very egotistical letter, but I am giving you a brief outline of how my life has been spent these last four months. Next mail I hope to be able to send you a long detailed account, for I have had many curious experiences.

"I have a splendid chance of making a large sum of money in a little time. We, that is, Mr. Colquhoun's staff, have sent out two splendid prospectors, fully equipped to peg out and develop our claims. They have gone out under the wing of Mr. Selous, who is taking them to a very rich district only known to himself and Mauch, the German Geologist and Explorer, and not discovered as yet by the prospectors who came up with us.

"Splendid reports are coming in from all round about the gold prospects.

"I will give you full particulars next mail. My prospects now are a thousand times better than they ever were before, and I believe that in a year or a year and a half I shall be able to come home to you, darling, with, if not a large, at least a fortune.

"Darling, I have just had your letters (three) of September 30th, October 1st, and November 13th handed me. They terrify me to think how nearly I have lost you, my own true blessed wife. What a brute I am to leave you all alone to fight so hard a battle at home. And now I am afraid that most, if not all, the money due to me for the last six months has been paid towards my share of the expenses of our prospecting party. I have no time to find out before this mail goes, but will see what I can do next mail. I only get £15 a month now and rations. The Company will not pay high salaries at first; they promise that in a few months they shall be increased materially. . . .

"The postriders are waiting. Tell Beo * that I have seen lots of lions and tigers, too near to be exactly pleasant, but have not had to fight one yet. Perhaps I may kill one some day and send him home the skin. Tell him I have also seen some tremendous elephants and hippopotami, one of which I shot, ostriches, too, are pretty plentiful.

"One poor fellow was killed and eaten by lions the other day, and they have killed innumerable horses, oxen, sheep etc. Eight lions have been shot round about this place alone since the Expedition arrived. . . .

"This is a wonderful country. Good-bye my own.
                              "Yours for ever,
                                        "PAT.
"P. S.—Will write long, long letter next mail, and try and send some money."

This letter relieved my mind about Pat, but did not help the financial difficulties.

My people became very anxious about my serious state of health. A dear niece of my brother-in-law took me first to Dr. Butler Smyth, who found a patch on the lung, and then to Sir Felix Semon, who at that time was throat Physician to King Edward.

Neither Sir Felix nor I ever forgot our first interview, for when he told me I had phthisical laryngitis, that I must live abroad and give up my profession, I stood up angrily, saying "You must be a fool." From that moment a warm friendship

---

* Pronounced Bayo—a pet name given to my little son, by his godmother, Owney Urquhart.

sprang up between us, and his wife, Güstchen, with the singing voice of an angel, also became a dear friend of mine.

By June, 1891, I had received more cheerful letters from Pat, and my health began to improve.

I arranged with Mr. Ben Greet—through Mrs. Percy Wyndham's promise to obtain the patronage of royalty, also of many friends of hers—to give a matinée of *As You Like It* at the Shaftesbury Theatre:—

Shaftesbury Theatre,
Thursday, June 18th, 1891,
2.30 P. M.
Under the distinguished patronage of
H. R. H. Princess Christian of Schleswig Holstein.

Duchess of Abercorn	Lady Brassey
Earl Pembroke	Lady Fitzhardinge
Countess of Pembroke	Lady Alice Gaisford
Earl Brownlow	Hon. Percy Wyndham
Countess Brownlow	Hon. Mrs. Percy Wyndham
Countess Grosvenor	Mrs. Grenfell of Taplow
Countess Spencer	Court
Countess Yarborough	Mrs Grant, of Glen Moriston

Manager—Mr. Ben Greet.

More cheery letters came from Pat.

"Fort Salisbury,
"22nd March, 1891.
"My own darling wife,
"I fear you must have been very anxious not having heard a word from me for so long. We have been shut

off from all communication with the outer world for nearly three months by the flooded rivers, and the last news we had from Kimberley was dated 18th December. I sent a cheque for £30 to a friend of mine at Kimberley, Harold Ingall, on 9th January, asking him to send you a draft on London for proceeds, and I pray God it has reached you; so far as we can learn that was the last mail that got through the rivers.   I will send you some more money as soon as communication is opened.   It is dangerous sending now as the letters only lie about at one of the rivers, and are likely to get lost.

"This letter is being taken right across Matabeleland to Buluwayo with some dispatches from the Administrator to try and get communication that way.   The man who is bearing them is a Mr. Usher, who has just come through from Buluwayo, leaving there on the 12th February, bringing some cattle which were purchased from Lobengula for rations, and which we are very glad to see, I can tell you, as we are, owing to the road being closed, completely out of food, and have been living on what we could get from the natives—principally Indian corn, rice, and pumpkins, for some time.

"Usher brings very good news from Buluwayo, the capital of the Matabele; he was present at the 'Big Dance of the Nation,' when all war movements for the year are arranged, and although several of the Chiefs asked the King to be allowed to march their impis against us here in Mashonaland, he resolutely refused to allow them, saying that he was well pleased with what the English had done and he would not allow them to be interfered with.   We have also letters from Mr. Moffat, the British Resident at Buluwayo, to the same effect.

"And now, darling, I have the commencement of some good news for you.   I told you in a previous letter that

we had formed a Syndicate for pegging out the claims
we get as pioneers, and had engaged two first-rate prospectors named Arndt and Arnold.   Well, we had a letter
the other day from Arndt to the effect that he had discovered the 'Kaiser Wilhelm' goldfields, which have been
so much talked about all over the world, which have
been only seen by a few white men before, amongst them
Mauch, the German Geologist, who was most enthusiastic
about their richness.   So far as we can understand from
Arndt's letter, brought in by a native, the fields lie about
100 or 120 miles to the north-east of this place, and are
of very large extent, and Arndt says that having only
just seen the fields, he did not like to say much, but
he considered that they were of the finest formation
that he had ever seen in his experience of over 20 years'
prospecting.   So, dear, this is very encouraging news, and
everybody here is congratulating us, and saying that we
are sure to make our fortunes, as owing to the difficulties of travelling the rush which at once took place on receipt of the news of the finding of fields cannot possibly
get there for two or three weeks, and our men will have
the fields a good six weeks to themselves and be able
to take the pick of the reefs.

"Sweetheart, I pray God I shall be able to make
a lot of money to be able to come home and make you
comfortable, and give you all the pleasures that I long
to, to repay you for all the misery and discomfort I have
put you to. . . .

"To return to Mashonaland, every day brings in fresh
reports of the finding of gold, everybody here is enthusiastic, and I really think there is a grand future for the
country.   Silver has also been found, and I am told
some rich tin reefs, and the country seems to abound in
all kinds of minerals.

"Then it is a magnificent country for farming, and I think will produce everything, and as grazing land it is splendid—an undulating prairie, well wooded and watered, and with a splendid rich grass, on which cattle grow very fat. The only drawback to the country is the quantity of rain—from end of November to probably end of this month an enormous amount of rain falls, and during these months there is a great deal of malarial fever knocking about. A great many of the men have had severe attacks, and a few have died. Fortunately, I have escaped altogether. It seems healthy all the year round at Fort Salisbury on the high Veldt, but as soon as you get off the high Veldt on to the low ground it becomes very unhealthy. Most of the men have got fever from being down in the low country during the wet season. . . .

"PAT CAMPBELL."

"Administrator's Office,
"Fort Salisbury,
"3rd June, 1891.

". . .

"I received your letters of 10th and 11th March last mail, and loved them so, and my Beo's letter. . . . I told you in my last letter of our fight with the Portuguese. I have since had further particulars. We only had 47 men and a seven-pounder, and they had 100 Europeans and 300 black soldiers. We, of course, had the best position and, strange to say, did not have a man wounded. They lost two officers and 13 white men and about 50 black. We took nine quick-firing guns from them; they only managed to take two away with them.

"Some of our men had wonderful escapes; they had to go out and cut down trees under a heavy fire to get the

gun into action.   One man had his axe knocked out of
his hand by a bullet, another, Tulloch, was chopping
down a tree, and the bullets knocked splinters out of it.
Young Morier a friend of mine, son of Sir R. Morier, the
·Russian Ambassador, was leaning his rifle against a tree
to take aim, when a bullet struck the tree, knocking a
large splinter into his face, and giving him a bad black
eye.   A bullet went through the timber of the big gun
while they were all standing round working it and entered
a cartridge, but fortunately did not explode it.

"The Portuguese used the new magazine rifle, which
shoots splendidly.   They were thoroughly beaten, altho'
the fight only lasted two hours, and their officers behaved
very well, and cleared off pell-mell during the night,
leaving the nine big guns behind them.   They may come
on again, but it will be some time before they can move,
as the natives are afraid to carry for them.

"One of our prospectors has pegged out 15 good
claims, the first start for my fortune, darling.   I hope
they will turn out good.   The fighting, etc., is keeping the
country back fearfully. . . ."

After the matinée of *As You Like It,* in which I
was so valiantly helped by Mrs. Percy Wyndham,
I was engaged, on the advice of Mr. Clement Scott
and Mr. Ben Greet, by the Messrs. Gatti to play at
the Adelphi in *The Trumpet Call,* by Mr. George
R. Sims and Mr. Robert Buchanan.

On the first night of this play, in a dark scene,
my ragged black skirt fell down around my feet for
I wore no petticoat.

The momentary sounds of levity from the audience
made me glare at them in indignation: I continued

my tragic scene, pulling up my skirt and holding it together, behind me, with one hand, as I went up a narrow flight of stairs along a corridor—too lost in my *rôle* to feel dismayed.   My exit line—"Oh God, may I never wake again," I hoped had not been spoiled.*

Then there were also *The Lights of Home, The White Rose,* and *The Black Domino* by the same authors.

I was very delicate, and often out of the cast, with the return of loss of voice; once I was away for six weeks.   Eventually I fell ill with typhoid fever.

I remember how it began.   It was a Saturday; we had played two performances; during these performances I kept feeling a strange icy sensation on the top of my head, gradually creeping down my spine.   I said to some of the company, "Don't come near me, I am sure I am going to be very ill, and it may be something catching."

When I went back to my rooms after the performance, these shiverings became worse.   I lay awake all night longing for the daylight.   I felt, if the day did not come quickly, I would be too ill ever to get home to my children, and to my mother.

When the landlady came to my room in the morning, she helped me into my clothes.   I could scarcely

---

* It is characteristic of a certain side of human nature that I received more than one anonymous post-card, saying the writer was sure I had arranged the *dénouement* to make certain of a success.

stand or see. She called a hansom cab, helped me into it, and told the man to drive to "Newcote," my uncle's house in Dulwich.

The drive seemed interminable, and my eyes shut against my will. When the hansom cab arrived at the gate, I couldn't move my hands or body. The man got down from the box and rang the bell, and the servant and the man helped me out. My mother came into the hall with the children. I remember saying, "Mother, I am ill," and the feeling of not being able to stoop down and kiss the children.

Then dark nights followed, people sitting near my bed, shaded candles, doctors standing over me—nine days uncertainty—and then typhoid fever pronounced. I can see the frightened faces that depressed me, and made me angry. I had a desire to sing as loud as I could to keep alive; and then to listen proudly to myself as I shouted. I was in raging delirium for days and weeks. At last there was a long silence, and I heard a voice quite close to me say suddenly the words "She is sinking." At the sound of those words something flared like a flame of fire through me; the thought, "I cannot die, there are the children," filled my brain.

I was told the doctor did not hesitate, he noticed a change and poured neat brandy from the bottle down my throat. They told me I struggled, fighting back to life, and I am sure this is the truth. I remember the struggle.

Then I began to get better. I slept for hours and

hours. Gradually I noticed the worn expression in the faces of those who had nursed me. What, indeed, must my mother, and my dear uncle, and others of the family not have suffered? I was little more than a girl; my children scarcely more than babies; my husband in Africa, not able to send me money. My uncle earned under £200 a year; my mother had no income of her own; and all thought of my career seemed over.

My bodily strength returned, but my nerves were never again the same: something snapped that never mended. The sweetness and the calm strong faith of youth, and the belief that I could depend upon Pat had gone forever. The months and years of parting from him, the hard work, insufficient food, insufficient rest, and the strain of my long illness had killed it all.

I realised, too, the closeness of death, and the responsibility of my children tore at my heart.

Four months afterwards I played *The Second Mrs. Tanqueray,* which play, I suppose, is the most successful modern English play of the century.

CHAPTER V.

IT was necessary for me to act again as soon as possible. I was still physically feeble, white and fragile—my hair only just beginning to grow again—but I could not refuse the Messrs. Gatti when they sent for me to play the *rôle* of "Clarice Berton" in *The Black Domino,* at a salary of £8 a week.

The play was badly reviewed, the Messrs. Gatti attributing the failure in great part to me. They said my voice was weak, my gestures ineffective, and nothing I said or did "got over the footlights": and they gave me my fortnight's notice. This was a most tragic moment for me; money was urgently needed, my illness having cost so much, and the load of debt to doctor and chemist had to be lifted.

Circumstances were fiercely against me, but it will be seen Fate lent a hand to fight for me.

On a certain evening Mrs. Alexander and Mr. Graham Robertson came to the Adelphi Theatre. Mrs. Alexander knew that her husband was searching for an actress to play the part in Mr. Pinero's new play *The Second Mrs. Tanqueray.* It may have been chance that sent these two to the play that night, or Mrs. Alexander may have read in the paper that I was "beautiful," and "had a rare distinction, elegance and power"—I still thought myself scraggy and plain—this I cannot say. But in spite of my "weak voice" and "feeble gestures," personality, or my looks, or some histrionic talent I possessed, came across the footlights, and sent these two back to Mr. Alexander, with the news that an actress exactly suited to the new play of Mr. Pinero was to be seen at the Adelphi Theatre.

Mr. Alexander wrote making an appointment for me to meet both him, and Mr. Pinero, at the St. James's Theatre.

I think my resolution was strengthened by the bitterness of my disappointment at having received my notice at the Adelphi. The mixture of fearlessness and fragility, the whiteness of my face, some strange and elusive charm, owing to my Italian strain no doubt, interested my future manager.

I dressed carefully—I remember only my little yellow straw bonnet trimmed with cherries and a narrow black velvet ribbon under my chin tied under my left ear, with long narrow ends accentuating the length of my neck.

In those days most women hid their throats in folds of écru net in the fashion of the lovely Marchioness of Granby. My throat was always bare, or in American journalistic language "sprang visibly from between her shoulders proud to bear her lovely head." I was tall and exceptionally slight.

After a few questions as to what I had done in the way of theatrical work, Mr. Pinero read the play to me, *beginning* at the famous moment when

Paula enters after Mr. Tanqueray's farewell dinner to his friends.

The reality of the play after the melodrama I had striven with at the Adelphi, made my heart bound with joy, and no doubt I showed some intelligent and vivid appreciation, though I did not at this reading, for a moment understand what Paula's life was.   Did I ever grasp it in my interpretation: I wonder? . . .

Both Mr. Pinero and Mr. Alexander seemed anxious to engage me.

Full of enthusiasm I went back to the Messrs. Gatti to tell them of my good fortune, and of the wonderful new *rôle* offered me.   I remember the worried expression on their kind faces and my sinking heart as they said, "What's good enough for Mr. Pinero is good enough for us."   They withdrew their notice, and my contract with them bound me to continue playing my part at the Adelphi in *The Black Domino*.

The days dragged on, the play at the Adelphi remaining a failure: at last the Messrs. Gatti definitely resolved to take it off.   They sent for me again and said, "If you are still wanted at the St. James's you can go at the end of a fortnight."

Then followed another interview with Mr. Alexander, who told me it was too late; my friend Miss Elisabeth Robins had been engaged for the *rôle* of "Paula Tanqueray."

But Mr. Pinero was determined to get me if pos-

AS CLARICE IN "THE BLACK DOMINO"

sible. The matter was put by them both frankly to Miss Robins, who, with the most remarkable and characteristic generosity, which is shown in the following letter, surrendered the *rôle* to me:—

"May 2nd, 1893.

"Dear Stella,

"I suppose Mr. Alexander has told you of what occurred Sunday and yesterday. I congratulate you upon your splendid fortune in having *The Second Mrs. Tanqueray* to play.

"From what I heard read of the part, it is the kind of thing that comes along once in an actress' lifetime, seldom oftener, and that it has come to *you* is my best consolation for having lost it myself. You will play it brilliantly and your loyal service in less congenial *rôles* will find its reward in this glorious new opportunity. There is to my mind no woman in London so enviable at this moment, dear savage, as *you*.

"Keep well and strong.

"Yours affectionately always,

"E. R."

I had met Miss Robins first at the Adelphi, where she played the leading *rôle* in *The Trumpet Call* with me. I delighted in her seriousness and cleverness. She was the first intellectual I had met on the stage.

The peculiar quality of Miss Elizabeth Robins' dramatic gift was the swiftness with which she succeeded in sending thought across the footlights;

emotion took a second place, personality a third.

I thought her finest performance was in *The Master Builder,* and it was the most intellectually comprehensive piece of work I had ever seen on the English stage.

Most successful actors and actresses are entirely dependent upon personality for their effect, aided as the case may be, by the charm of their diction or their natural grace of gesture, or personal beauty. Mediocre artists have risen to a considerable position on this quality of "personality." They never transcend it. Plays are written around it, and many plays have been sacrificed to it. In an Ibsen play it is a very great misfortune, imprisoning the artist in his own narrow circle of individualism.

I was engaged at a salary of £15 a week, at a fortnight's notice, and to rehearse *on approval.* So I can scarcely flatter myself that either Mr. Pinero or Mr. George Alexander thought anything of me beyond my looks. The salary seemed very generous to me after my £8 a week at the Adelphi.

Both author and manager were worried and anxious at rehearsals. I heard afterwards that more than one management had refused *The Second Mrs. Tanqueray,* considering the play too *risqué.*

I was an amateur so far as trained technique went. And I was wilful, self-opinionated, strangely sensitive, impatient, easily offended, with nerves strained by illness. No doubt they hoped I was teachable.

The first rehearsals were very difficult for me. A certain cold "official" manner, which was the peculiarity of Mr. Alexander's style, was very unsympathetic to me, whilst my unreasonable ways, wanting always to do, instead of to listen—feeling their wishes hindered my own imagination—must have been tiresome beyond words.

At first they treated me as a child that must be taught its A B C. I was given no free rein. My passionate longing for beauty, my uncontrollable "sense of humour"—or whatever it was that made me quickly recognise the ludicrous and artificial—was snubbed. A snub shattered me, unless at the moment my spirits were high enough, to give me the courage to go one better.

Such remarks as "Don't forget you are not playing at the Adelphi now, but at the St. James's," gave me a wild desire to laugh and play the fool; always an element in me that had to be reckoned with in those days, and which surrounded me in a sea of extravagant anecdotes.

The Company included among many distinguished artists the lovely Maude Millet, with her rare and sweet nature and eyes "like the heavens in June"— every Eton and Harrow boy of the time could show you a picture of her pretty face as she looked in *Sweet Lavender*. I believe she made the fortune of W. Downey, the photographer,—Cyril Maude, sympathetic and chivalrous, and dear Nutcombe

Gould,* the most gentle and refined of creatures, who in old clothes and patched boots looked the most distinguished man on the stage.

Perhaps my youth, my lack of professional tricks, my disposition to laugh and say funny things endeared me to the company. I know they were all affectionate, kind, and friendly.

Artists always feel eager and interested when they come across original work.

I remember years later an actor † at a rehearsal I was taking saying to me, "Yes, yes, quite so, thank you, I understand," for at least a quarter of an hour, then my impatient, "Well, why don't you do it?" and his very polite reply, as he looked at me through an eye-glass, "I wonder if you would mind my showing you for one moment what I myself would like to do?" And then he showed me. I remember our eyes met, and how merrily I laughed in happy recognition of his skill. There being no part for him in my next production, and wishing to retain his services, I let him cross the stage as Gerald du Maurier's valet, with a coat over his arm, humming a scrap of an Irish song—he brought down the house.

I took him in my Company to America at a salary of £15 a week, and I left him there at a salary of £100, and he is there still, at a salary of £200 or £300.

* It was a principle with Mr. Nutcombe Gould never to wear new clothes on the stage.

† Mr. George Arliss.

At last the rehearsal of the third act reached the point where the stage direction reads:—"She sits at the piano and strums a valse." Now my mother had never allowed any of her children to strum. She insisted on all art being treated with reverence, and impressed upon us that the piano was not a toy. The painful trifling known as strumming was forbidden in our home. Many a time have I known the piano locked—someone had been punished.

I played rather well and with a passionate love of touch and tone, which gained me my scholarship at the Guildhall School of Music; but I am not a muscian in the true sense of the word.

I sat down to the piano hesitatingly, asking twice to be excused, until I had prepared something suitable. A voice from the stalls: "We would like to hear whether you can play." This offended me. Holding my book in my right hand, with my left I played beautifully—and with impertinence—a piece written by a girl friend of mine. This moment changed the whole temper of the rehearsals. Those who listened knew that my playing must be the outcome of serious study, and some understanding of art; above all that my playing would invest the part of "Paula" with not a little glamour.

I remember Mr. Bernard Shaw in criticising the play saying something like this:—"It was all about a poor lady who committed suicide because they wouldn't let her finish playing her piece at the piano."

I was quite conscious of the effect I was producing. I caught sight of Nutcombe Gould's face and Cyril Maude's in the "wings," and I prolonged the surprise for about three minutes. Mr. Pinero and Mr. Alexander were in the stalls; at last from the darkness an expressionless voice said. "That will do Mrs. Campbell, we will go on with the rehearsal, please!" From that moment there was a difference. It seemed to me that Mr. Pinero especially treated me with more confidence. I didn't feel "from the Adelphi" any more. He caught hold of my arm and called me "dear child," and I felt I had his trust.

It is this brilliant author's habit to think out and impose upon his interpreters every piece of characterisation—every inflection; very rarely does he allow the "business" he has conceived to be altered, many characteristic readings, and gestures, which have been attributed to the talent, and sometimes it must be admitted humbly—to the want of sensitive good taste of the actors—have been carefully taught them by the author. It was, therefore, a remarkable evidence of some good impression I had made, when at a certain moment of the play Mr. Pinero said:—"Here in your anger, you sweep off the bric-a-brac and photographs from the piano." I replied in horror, "Oh, I could not make her rough and ugly with her hands, however angry she is." He looked at me gently and replied, "All right, my child, do as you like."

The memory of the awful fatigue of the rehearsals remains with me. I used to get in a state of

alarming exhaustion, a sudden condition that over-
came me at times for some years afterwards.   This,
I suppose, had something to do with the effect on
my heart of the typhoid fever.   On one occasion Mr.
Pinero brought me Brand's Essence of Beef, not
forgetting the necessary spoon, and stood by me
while I swallowed it, treating me with ever-increas-
ing gentleness.

The dressing of the part was an important one;
the stiffish fashion in which Mrs. Alexander insisted
on my arranging my hair was dreadful to me.   I
argued that no woman could go through four acts of
such tumultuous passions, eventually committing suicide, with a tidy head, unless she wore a wig.   Fortunately my hair as the play proceeded, behaved as
it chose.

The dresses were beautiful of the time; I could
feel natural, and move naturally in them.

The rule of the theatre was to wear a cotton wrap
over you, until your cue for entrance.   It fidgeted
me, having a candlesnuffer effect upon me.   I was
permitted not to wear it, to the amusement of the
others.   Indeed, I was a most spoiled and difficult
creature.   What a National Theatre would have
done with me I cannot imagine.

Then came the first of the two dress rehearsals,
no one being permitted into the auditorium except
Mr. Pinero, and he was to sit alone in the dress
circle with a lantern, a notebook, and a pencil.

I implored him not to speak to me, and I would

play the part for him. I kept my word, and to that dark, silent house and that solitary man I poured out my "secret" with the fire and feeling of my temperament and imagination. I wanted to plead for "Paula," I wanted her to be forgiven and remembered. Cyril Maude and Maude Millet implied by a furtive squeeze of my hand, now and then, that I was doing well. Mr. Alexander's official dignity was of priceless value to the play.

I tried from the beginning to lift "Paula" a little off the earth, to make her not merely a neurotic type; to give her a conscience, a soul. I think it will be admitted that after the play had run many weeks, I played "Paula" better from this point of view.

Some members of the Garrick Club will remember how Mr. Pinero arrived there after this rehearsal, and said wonderful things of "the fragile creature of Italian origin." I knew nothing of this at the time.

A second dress rehearsal was called. This time there were other people sitting in the stalls, scattered here and there. With some strange professional instinct of self-preservation, I knew I was too nervously exhausted to act the part again before the first night. I was spiritless, flat, dull, and everyone was depressed. The actors seemed to understand, and smiled encouragingly as I grew duller, and still more dull and flat. Mr. Pinero did not come near me. He knew that I was worn out, and that so far as I was concerned it was a "toss up."

When I went back to my rooms in Devonshire Street I slipped into bed in misery, knowing that everyone was disappointed in me, and *I* could not help it. I lay awake wondering how it was that just physical fatigue made it impossible for me to give of my *best*—why there had been no radiance, no charm, no swiftness; and I said to myself, now I know why some actors drink—and I had a tragic sense of the snare—of the trap of it all. I wondered what would happen if that awful physical flatness came over me on the first night. I had forgotten, or not counted upon, the inspiration and encouragement of a first-night London audience!

Towards morning I fell asleep and had a childish dream. There was a door opposite my bed, and I dreamed it was pushed slowly open, and, up near the top, a little black kitten put in its head. I awoke laughing, and when my two children came into my bed, I told them about my lucky dream. And, indeed, if a black cat walking across the stage, entirely ruining a scene, can be regarded by all actors as a most lucky event, how much more should a black kitten poking its head high up through a door in a dream on the morning of a "first night" augur success.

One other sign of good fortune had also come to me from my pet dog. I had a pug at the time called "She," a devoted creature. One day—while I was studying the part of the play, where "Paula" bursts into a fit of weeping, I could get neither shape nor form into my sobbing. I was so eager that the audience should feel that "Paula's" words, "Give me another chance," were a cry from her awakening soul to God; not merely a woman weeping to her husband—the empty noises, the moans and snuffles I made were all false and silly. After much striving I thought of "breaking up" the sounds by a natural blowing of my nose. This so affected poor "She" that she howled and howled, and I could not stop her for quite a long time—I felt perhaps I might move a human audience.

Then came the first night. I put my children to bed, leaving them in the care of the landlady. They had covered me with their hugs and kisses and wishes for success, and remembering the black kitten and the pug's tribute, I went down to the theatre with "She" in my arms, and my nerves strung up with that glorious sense of a battle to fight.

"How unnecessarily noisy the audience is," I thought, as the play proceeded. After the scene at the second act, it irritated me not a little.* I thought they would have been more silent, if they had been more deeply moved and interested.

This is how someone has described the first-night impression in the theatre:

* *The Globe* (May 28, 1893) said: "A new custom seems to have sprung up amongst first nighters. At the fall of the curtain on the second act there was a tremendous outburst of applause. The curtain was raised again and again. Mrs. Campbell had taken the house by storm. Then there were loud calls of 'author!' Mr. Pinero's appearance, however, was not made until the final fall of the curtain."

"From the moment of 'Paula's' entrance in a beautiful cloak she held the audience in a spell—her naturalness, her truth, her intelligent quickness, her beauty made a marvelous combination—and an utterly unexpected one to the greater part of the audience, and the effect was cumulative. The character built up by innumerable small touches, both by the author and the interpreter, quickly emerged into a *living* creature.

"As the great moments of the play were reached the audience and the actress were carried beyond imaginative sympathy, into the reality of a human crisis, and into the very heart of passionate emotion."

I expect this is what happened that first night; gradually the audience realised the tragedy of poor Paula—how her love for "Aubrey Tanqueray" had lit up the dark recesses of her nature, illuminating her soul—how in her struggle to subdue her jealousy, her boredom—to forget—to begin life again—she at last, in that terrible moment when she looks at herself in a mirror, and cries out that her past life is written indelibly on her face, and that her husband will always see it there—realises in a flash, her life has unfitted her forever to grasp and hold the simple happiness which her love for "Aubrey" puts within her reach. Her soul is horror-stricken, and because her higher control has been rendered helpless, she, in her anguish, destroys her body.

The ovation when the curtain fell, incredible as it may seem, was lost upon me. The tremendous applause stupefied me, and I never for a moment thought a share of it was mine. Had I not been

playing only a fortnight before at the Adelphi—
there had been no enthusiasm then, only my notice
from the Messrs. Gatti for "my weak voice" and
"feeble gestures." I felt it was all for the author
and his remarkable play.

In spite of my gratitude to Mr. Pinero I did not
realise what his play had done for *me*—the tremendous opportunity it had given me.

Crowds of people flocked on to the stage; shy and
terrified I ran up to my dressing-room, dressed
quickly, picked up my dog, and went back to my
lodgings worn out by fatigue.

The next morning my two children climbed into
my bed. I told them all about the applause, and
that I was sure the play would have a long run;
we remembered about the black kitten, and we had
breakfast in bed for a treat, where later Mrs. Alexander found us. She asked me why I had left the
theatre, and told me I had made a great personal
success and my name famous.

Mr. Pinero tells me that after the first act he went
into his wife's box, and asked how I had done; she
shook her head and told him to encourage me; then
he came to my room and said I had done well, and
to keep it up—that I stared at him, looking bewildered, and that before the second act he caught me
putting a little picture in my bosom. He asked me
what it was, and I showed him the photograph of my
little son taken when he was two years old. How
many a first night has it lain against my heart, and

given me the courage I needed in those days.

Sir John Poynter told me months afterwards that when I said Paula's first word, "Dearest," he leant back comfortably in his stall and *knew* I was going to be all right.

The following little letter from Miss Bessie Hatton, who was playing at the Adelphi, was the first letter of congratulation I received:—

"...

"30th May, 1893.

"Dear Mrs. Patrick Campbell,

"You certainly have walked over all the swells. Bravo, your fortune is made. I must quote a little song which I think peculiarly applicable to your case. A little dirty boy was singing it in the street:—

> They knocks 'er down
> And they blacks 'er eye;
> But she gets there
> All the sime.

"I don't believe the Adelphi is going to open for some time.

"Kindest regards and best congratulations on your triumph.

"Always yours sincerely,
"BESSIE HATTON."

Out of many hundreds, the letters that follow may be of interest to the reader. I publish them with apologies and blushes.

"Box F.

"Dear Mrs. Campbell,

"Mr. Aubrey Beardsley, a very brilliant and wonderful young artist and a great admirer of the wonder and charm of your art, says that he must have the honour of being presented to you, if you will allow it. So, with your gracious sanction, I will come round after Act III. with him, and you would gratify and honour him much if you would let him bow his compliments to you. He has just illustrated my play *Salome* for me; and has a copy of the *édition de luxe* which he wishes to lay at your feet.

"His drawings are quite wonderful.

"Very sincerely yours,
"OSCAR WILDE."

"63, Hamilton Terrace

"Dear Mrs. Campbell,

"A thousand congratulations on your great triumph of last Saturday night. I meant to write earlier, but I have been somewhat unwell and out of town, but please forgive me when I assure you your rendering of 'Paula' is *perfect*. We all feel grateful to you for the painstaking and kind way in which you rehearsed. You have made an enormous hit, and thoroughly deserve all the praise bestowed.

"Do try and eat nourishing food to keep your strength up, for the part is a hard one, and you must feel in robust health to tackle it!

"I hope you will come and see me sometimes. I'm at home on Mondays, and should love to shake you by the hand one Monday when you find yourself in our neighbourhood.

"MYRA PINERO."

> "Wilton House,
> "Salisbury.
> "June 23rd, 1893.

"My dear Mrs. Campbell,

"... A friend who knows my faith in your future (and I really believe that you should regard me as one of your worst enemies)—I have proclaimed it so persistently ever since I saw you act 'Rosalind' and 'Helena' here—writes on my return: 'I hear Mrs. P. Campbell is quite wonderful in *The Second Mrs. Tanqueray.*'

"I always felt quite confident that it would come— success with the great public I mean—the other you have had long ago—but circumstances sometimes retard a person's talents from getting properly known for a long time—and you became buried in Adelphian melodrama—a line quite unworthy of your powers, however much you might excel in it; and when I took the liberty of making enquiry after you last year, I was told that you were ill and had left the stage.

"Please accept my very sincere congratulations, and do not trouble to answer this letter. I do not know whether I shall be able to go and see the play, but I shall certainly do so if I can. . . .

> "PEMBROKE."

> "7, Carlton House Terrace,
> "S. W.
> "Saturday, June 31st, 1893.

"Dear Mrs. Campbell,

"At the risk of your thinking me impertinent and even fulsome, I can't help writing you a line to express my admiration of your wonderful performance, and yet I don't know how to tell you how clever I thought it— how strong and moving in the tragic passages—how charming in the touches both of comedy and of tenderness—and again how astonishingly clever.

"Of many good things, nothing was more true to nature and more completely original on the stage than the piteous flatness,* the absence of all tragic emphasis with which some of the most terrible things were told.

"And I suspect that your performance was even better than it seemed, for, in spite of the way it has been praised, the play is weak in many places. . . . Alexander quite took my breath away last night by saying that every word of it was good from end to end. . . .

" . . . Certainly a man would be justified in making *any* marriage to get rid of such friends—though he didn't succeed in shaking off the most tiresome of them all.

"Now I am fulsome. But I am expressing less than my sincere convictions, and if ever the play is run without you, you will see that I am right. So you must forgive me and accept my congratulations.

"PEMBROKE."

"Beefsteak Club,
"26th December, 1893.

"My dear Mrs. Campbell,

"I must write to tell you how deeply your performance impressed me to-day. It was even beyond what I expected—and I expected much. You get your effects with consummate ease, and the quality of your acting is entirely your own—something which you can neither borrow nor lend. I thought the play remarkable.

"With best wishes,
"I remain,
"Yours sincerely,
"HERBT. BEERBOHM TREE."

* This effective "piteous flatness" of voice was entirely Mr. Pinero's suggestion.

" . . .

"19th Feburary, 1894.

"Dear Mrs. Campbell,

"Just a line to say how sorry I am that I shan't see you to-morrow—and to say how noble your acting was the other night, just the sort of acting one dreams of, but never expects to see.

"It is the plain truth that Shakespeare's 'Cleopatra' would be the only part good enough for you, as you were on Wednesday night, when you played more superbly than any of the times I had seen you before.

"The play itself is exasperatingly thin here and there, that is why we want to see you do something where you would not have to say a word that wasn't exactly right.

"You must be fearfully tired at the week's end; I hope it won't kill you altogether. It is only those tremendous deep-chested Italians that are fit to stand the mere physical part of the strain—but you are half-Italian, are you not?

"Believe me,
"Very truly yours,
J. W. MACKAIL." *

"63, Hamilton Terrace, N. W.,
"21st April, 1894.

"Dear Mrs. Campbell,

"When you count up the minor rewards which your acting in *The Second Mrs. Tanqueray* has brought you, you will not fail, I hope, to include in them the hearty appreciation of the author. But I beg your acceptance of this little brooch, as a jog to your memory; for if you ..re

* Professor of Poetry in the University of Oxford.

kind enough to wear it occasionally, it may serve as a reminder of my indebtedness to you.

"Believe me,
"Yours always truly,
"ARTHUR W. PINERO."

"Green Room Club,
"20, Bedford Street, W. C.
"Monday Evening.
"Dear Mrs Campbell,
"We think the play should end at the finish of the third act—except that you appear again.

"We also think that you are the greatest living actress.

"LOUIS N. PARKER.
"PHILIP BURNE-JONES."

". . .

Streatham, S. W.,
"September, 1901.
"My dear Mrs. Campbell,
"I had not seen *Mrs. Tanqueray* before.

"It was exceedingly beautiful and powerful, sometimes terrible, and of extraordinary sweetness wherever a tender note was struck.

"'Paula' is like an opal of many hues and lustres, with stains of life, and wounds of passion through which the disastrous fires glow that shatter it in the end.

"There are no words in which to thank so incomparable an artist.

"Sincerely yours,
"JOHN DAVIDSON." *

* Poet, author, and dramatist.

"   .   .   .
"   Mayfair, W.,
"   10th May.
"Dear Mrs. Campbell,
"   A very old friend of mine, Lord Wemyss, has just
been here—early this morning—to rave to me about
you! He went last night to see you and says he *must*
know you. He has seen Rachel and Ristori, etc., and
none of them could touch you, and you could 'move
nations.' I hope you feel flattered. He and Lady
Wemyss are going to Scotland for a month, and after
that I must arrange a meeting, only I fear you will find
him rather deaf—at least I do—but he is artistic in
every way, and enthusiastic and sympathetic, so I think
you would like to know him.
                        "Yours very sincerely,
                        "CAROLINE CREYKE."

                        "115A, Harley Street, W.,
                        "6th June, 1913.
"   .   .   .
"You are indeed bountiful to me. I take the books
into the country, where they will give me many pleasant
hours. As to Wednesday, people are saying that you
are acting 'Paula' better than ever. The revival, therefore, I am glad to think, won't hurt your reputation.
But I know it irks you—as it does me—to retread these
old paths, and I am grateful to you for this subduing of
your spirit. Bless you.
"   If you need a testimonial at any time to your sweet
reasonableness and pretty behaviour at rehearsals don't
fail to apply to
                        "Yours faithfully and affectionately,
                        "A. PINERO."

"Marlborough Club,
"Pall Mall, S. W.,
"26th June, 1913.

"My dear Friend,
"Again I place myself at your feet. Your beautiful acting made me more than once cry like a little child. I wish my Mary had been with me.

"Yours always,
"SQUIRE BANCROFT."

"Burley-on-the-Hill,
"Oakham,
"Rutland.

"Dear Beatrice,
"I must send you an extract from a letter Edith received a few days ago. I think it will amuse you. It is not elegantly expressed, but genuine. 'I have had such a treat at last, I have seen lovely Mrs. Pat Campbell in *The Second Mrs. Tanqueray*. She gave a matinée in Clifton. How sweet she is, and her adorable voice! I did envy the people who could hug her. She has fetched me altogether. I went over like a ninepin. She looked most beautiful, but sad, and every woman in the theatre and on the stage looked like common earthworms and caterpillars beside her. I myself felt just like a slug. . . .'

"SYBIL QUEENSBERRY."

CHAPTER VI.

I WAS not yet physically fit to enjoy the triumph and gaieties of my success. The fatigue and nervous excitement of the *rôle,* with always eight, and sometimes nine performances a week to crowded critical London audiences—the play appealing to all classes—was a tremendous task so soon after my illness. Invitations to luncheons, teas, and Sunday dinner parties came from all sorts of people.

I was surrounded by what seemed to me intolerable curiosity. There were searching, thrill-seeking questions and strange, critical glances; which offended me; sometimes arousing impertinent courage on my part.

I remember a certain dinner party given for me by a well-known Jewish financier, and being asked by him at table in an earnest, curious voice, what I kept in a small locket I wore on a chain round my neck. Everyone stopped talking and listened for my answer. I replied gravely, "One hair of a Jew's moustache."

Did anyone see me as I was, I wonder? A fragile, unsophisticated young woman, still almost a girl, whose heart and nerves had been torn by poverty, illness, and the cruel strain of a long separation from the husband she loved. Brought up in a little suburb of London by a religious Italian mother—almost a recluse—adoring her children with an anxiety that was an obsession; unable to brook patronage in any form whatever, with the tenacity of an English bulldog and the tender apprehensiveness of some wild creature: passionately living in a romantic dream-world of her own.

Somebody once said of me, "You seem to feel everything from the roots of your hair to the tips of your toes."

I felt a curiously isolated being in the world that in those days surrounded the St. James's Theatre: to face it was a far less easy business for me than the stage.

Clothes began to matter, and to fuss me. To feel dressed up was misery, and to be dowdy—impossible.

No one seemed to really care who I was, or who my people were. What was my age? What did I look like off the stage? Had I a lover? Was it true that I had a husband in Africa, and that he was the father of my children?

To these people I was an accident, a sport of nature, someone who could do something that stirred and amused them. They, to me, were just a mass of people. I never realised that one was more important than another, and might be of social, artistic, or financial service to me.

They were an uncomfortable mystery to me, these people—not the mystery that surrounds art and artists, but the mystery of the mysterious knowledge of the world—of that world of which I was totally ignorant.

I did not behave quite like a dear friend of mine, who rushed upstairs to her bedroom from a smart tea party, and wept bitterly, because the people downstairs were so different from those she loved and lived amongst.

I used to feel angry and on the defensive—savage that I was.

For a long while I thought it comic that many people held the attitude—"She could not play 'Mrs. Tanqueray' as she does if she did not know something of that kind of life"—and—"Which is the real acting, 'Paula Tanqueray' on the stage, or the unworldy creature she appears off?"

I recollect a visit from a distinguished lady—dead long ago—who asked me so many questions so quickly, that I blushed to the roots of my hair. I thought she was mad. I still remember her bored expression at the end of our meeting. I never saw her again.

I like to think some sense of humour, or sense of proportion—mostly one and the same thing—kept my head a little cool in the subtle, dangerous fascination of it all.

Men made love to me, and I was accused of being a wicked flirt. I deny that. In more than one case I cared: but my first love had taught me love's true face.

Life was hideously difficult; but deep-rooted in

my bones was the instinct for true friendship founded on real affection.

Then there were the amusing people, who used to talk to me like this: "Oh, you have such an enthralling personality, Mrs. Tanq——, I mean Mrs. Campbell; one makes the mistake because you are as natural on the stage as you are off." "How can you remember all those words?" "What a memory you must have." "Do you 'make-up' before you go to the theatre?" "Do you like your troupe? You call it 'company,' don't you?" "Are you in love with Mr. Alexander?" "I think you must be in love with Mr. Pinero, and I am sure they are both in love with you."

I remember a beautiful woman leaning excitedly across the dinner table on overhearing a remark of mine, and exclaiming, "Have you a mother? How interesting."

The criticisms behind my back, I dare say, were something of this nature: "What a disappointment she is when you meet her." "She is quite childish, and rather a bore—she either could not or would not understand what I was talking about." "She does not know how to do her hair—has positively no *savoir faire*." "No, she is not common, and she is young enough to dare to look sad." "Instincts and emotions, yes; but no information, no certainty." "Her eyes are beautiful, she has wonderful hair, and her jaw line is pre-Raphaelite." "Her upper

AS SHE FIRST APPEARED IN "THE SECOND MRS. TANQUERAY"

lip is too long." "Her hands are lovely." "She isn't my type," and so on.

I remember hearing of the incredulity of a certain lady on being told that I was an ordinary married woman with two children and very little money. She had thought I was a luxurious demi-mondaine. Indeed, she had asked some of the neighbouring tradespeople—who happened also to serve me—what they thought of my reputation, and was greatly surprised by their answers.

Then there were people who thought me "divine," "exotic," "beautiful," with a "shattering personality."

Once at a sale at John Barker's someone shouted, "There's Mrs. Pat." I could not face the expression in the eyes of those who recognised me—curiosity has no feelings—I was nearly suffocated.

At the Academy, too, I was mobbed. I was with Mr. Philip Burne-Jones; he managed my escape through a side door. My portrait as "Mrs. Tanqueray," by Solomon J. Solomon, was one of the popular pictures of the year.

Later I will speak of the friends who gradually became, and have remained, dear to me.

I remember hearing an actor-manager's wife say of an actor's wife, "She is not in Society, my dear." I repeated this to a friend of mine, and this is something like the clever bit of nonsense he said in reply:—

"The death of really fine acting in this country is that

actors and actresses want to be thought ladies and gentlemen.   Artists must give themselves away.   If they want
to spit,* they must spit; curse, they must curse; love, they
must love; drink, they must drink, or their nerves will be
incapable of the necessary elasticity and spontaneity the
dramatic art demands; they will be suppressed, heavy,
ineffective."

The following two letters from the late Lord Pembroke show in an interesting way how my life at this
time struck him, also his views on the modern work
I was doing:—

"7, Carlton House Terrace, S. W.,
"August 4th, 1893.
"My dear Mrs. Campbell,
"You touched me very deeply somehow yesterday,
partly, no doubt, because you are so nice to me (for
there is a great real of self-love lurking about most of
us), but chiefly because seeing you and hearing about
your life made me realise how desperately unprotected
you are, and how constantly and inevitably difficult your
life must be.   I can't help realising that, being what
you are, and in your circumstances, you must live and will
have to live pretty constantly in a state of siege however careful you may be.

"It's an extraordinarily difficult life—and if ever men
are listened to, they cut a women off from much that is
most valuable in life, and give her a very poor compensation.

"I suppose the best safeguard for a woman placed

---

* It is said of the great Clara Morris that she used to clear her throat
and spit on the stage before the audience.

as you are, lies in her passion for her art and her career, which absorbs her to the exclusion of most other things, and makes her look on men as mere dummies or useful adjuncts in her busy life.

"I suspect this is what you would tell me. Don't be angry with me for saying so much, even if it is a trifle unconventional. If you knew the feeling that prompted it, I am sure you would not be. I cannot help understanding what the difficulty of such a life must be—and don't let it make you shy of me.

"I shall not write or talk in this strain again; it's your fault for touching me so much. I hope you will be all the better for rest and fresh air, and that we may meet again next year, if not before.

"Sincerely yours,
"PEMBROKE."

The Pembrokes were anxious that I should play Shakespearean *rôles,* and arranged to see Mr. Beerbohm Tree on the matter.

The following letter is amusing:—

"7, Carlton House Terrace, S. W.
"December 2nd, 1894

"My dear Mrs. Campbell,

"Our interview with Tree was as good as a play—indeed, better than most. He sat down in a nice, leisurely way, and was in a most agreeable mood, until Lady P. broached the subject of the sort of parts you ought to play. Then he 'smelt a rat' directly and his anxiety to get out of the house without delay was very funny.

"He agreed most amiably and hurriedly with every word we said about you, all the time hunting for his hat and umbrella. In vain I changed the subject and made him sit down again, while I told him two very pointless anecdotes in the hopes of quieting his suspicions. He was thoroughly scared, and there was nothing for it but to let him make his escape without saying anything more.

"In other words, he was very good to us in our rather presumptuous attempt, but mortally frightened lest he should commit himself to any pledge to give you a chance in a great Shakespearean part.

"But I hope it will come and before it's too late.

"I am glad you are going to study abroad a little. Nearly all English actors over-act dreadfully, and as the public won't correct them, their only chance of keeping to the proper pitch lies in the study of foreign actors. You must educate your audience in England, it won't educate you.

"Just off to Wilton.   Wishing you all good luck.
       "I am,
                    "Sincerely yours,
                              "PEMBROKE"

When playing at the Adelphi I had called on Mr. Beerbohm Tree. He was hurried and nervous in manner, and said there was no opening for me at the moment.*   I asked a salary of £4 a week.

It was not until after the *matinée* of *The Second Mrs. Tanqueray* at the St. James's Theatre on Boxing Day that he made his first offer to me—a salary of £60 a week to play in *John-a-Dreams*.

During the run of *The Second Mrs. Tanqueray*

---

* He told me charmingly many years afterwards that it was dark and he had not seen my face!

my father died in Texas in September, 1893, and the following extract from a letter of my eldest brother Edwin to my uncle shows my success had brought him happiness:—

"The day before Papa left us, when almost unconscious of all around, though there were many loving ones, he showed recognition of me alone, and then his eyes recovered their old fine brightness. Then again at times he would murmur inaudible things about England, and once just before dear Papa died I heard the words, 'Mrs. Tanqueray.' "

This letter brought me strange comfort.

Philip Burne-Jones was among the many new acquaintances my success brought me.

We soon became warm friends, and what unforgettable kindness he showed me. His talent for painting and drawing, his keen appreciation of the comedy of life, his interest in the theatre, and his genuine love of children made him a delightful companion.

All friends of Phil will remember, as I do, the almost exaggerated devotion and service he offered them.

The wonderful day came when he took me to his father's studio. I scarcely realised what was in store for me.

I suppose we all have a period in art which appeals to us in an intimate way. Perhaps because of my

Italian blood, the pre-Raphaelite School spoke to me in my own language: my very first visit to "The Grange" seemed a visit to my home. I wanted to stretch my arms in welcome to all that rich colour, pure design, and loveliness.

Sir Edward Burne-Jones—"Dearest," I called him—came a little into my life. His genius, his rare wisdom, his richly stored memory, his boundless sympathy, and his letters with their precious sketches, made the friendship he gave me one of the greatly prized honours of my life.

An unspeakable, enveloping tenderness emanated from him, as though he would shield one and all, from the pain he knew life must surely bring.

I never saw him stern, but I knew he could discern in a moment—however cunningly hidden—a monster in the human heart.

To my humble thinking, of all his pictures that I have seen, "Avalon" is the most beautiful.

Those who have not been to Walpole House and looked at this picture in quietness are to be pitied, for it speaks as only pure beauty can speak, and it fills the heart with thanksgiving.

One day I was lunching at "The Grange," perhaps I looked pale and tired, or Lady Burne-Jones, with her gentle, correct manner, was making me feel a little self-conscious; suddenly Dearest gave a quaint look at me, left the table and the room, returning in a few moments dressed as a monk, the cowl over his head, chanting absurdly from some holy book. We all broke into merriment, and the atmosphere was magically eased for me.

And I treasure this story of him: during a nursery tea with his lovely daughter Margaret and her children, Angela, a child of rare dignity, was told to stand in the corner for some disobedience. The small, proud figure, with its bowed head and its back to the bright tea-table, was a hard sight for Dearest. Late that night he came with his paint-box and his brushes. The next morning the little punishment corner was the most precious spot in the room; there was a flight of birds, and a kitten playing with its mother's tail, painted upon the wall.

Dearest always filled me with a sense of trust in myself; Lady Burne-Jones made me doubt myself; but she had a magical graciousness all the same.

Their lovely daughter Margaret and her husband, Jack Mackail, took me to their hearts; let me through the gate into their garden, as it were—my children too—and later my husband on his return from Africa.

There was nothing they did not do for me for many years, to try and ease the strain of the responsibilities, and the hard life which pressed upon me: their praise of my work was unstinted; they pulled me through many a painful doubting, and out of many a silly fault.

Jack Mackail's extraordinary serenity, his taste, his magical choice of words, his deep knowledge of literature, and his beautiful mind, made his companionship a royal gift.

The following most unfortunate incident happened about the end of the run of *The Second Mrs.
Tanqueray*. This newspaper cutting vividly describes what occurred:—

"It is extraordinary how men and women who act almost every night of their lives suffer from stage fright.
Only the other day Mrs. Patrick Campbell in the first
act of *The Second Mrs. Tanqueray* was seized with a
sudden fit of nervousness, and for the life of her she
could not remember a single word of her part.

"The prompter unfortunately was either inaudible or
absent, and Mr. Alexander was compelled to fetch the
book of the words, to which the actress referred until
she recovered her self-possession. Once the passing
terror overcome, she fairly surpassed herself and acted
superbly."·

What really happened was this:—On the Saturday I went home to my uncle's house, and my mother
told me my little son was seriously ill, and the doctor
was afraid it was diphtheria. I had played two performances; it was past twelve o'clock when I got
home. I went up to his room and sat by the bed;
and there I sat all night, and all the next day, and
Sunday night. He was too ill, and his throat was
too painful for him to speak to me.

At half-past eleven on Monday morning the doctor came and told me it was only tonsilitis, and I
need not be alarmed.

I was numb with fatigue and anxiety, but it was

Boxing Day and there were two performances to be played—trains were awkward—I arrived at the theatre just as the Overture struck up. I had the length of Aubrey Tanqueray's first scene with his friends to dress in. I scrambled into my clothes, rushed on to the stage and not one single line of the words of my part could I remember, although I had played it for seven months.

I sat on the sofa quite bewildered. Mr. Alexander brought me the book, and as he did he he murmured half to himself, "The woman's drunk!"

When the curtain came down at the end of the act I went upstairs to my room in a white rage and began dressing to go home. My understudy, Miss Granville, was in the theatre ready to go on for me, thinking I was ill.

Dear Maud Millet came into my dressing-room. I told her what had happened and Mr. Alexander's remark. All she said was, "Beerbohm Tree's in front; think of your career," and out she went next door to "Willis's Rooms" and brought back a small bottle of champagne and made me drink nearly a tumblerful. I dressed quickly for the second act and went on to the stage.

It was at this performance that Mr. Tree came round and offered to engage me at £60 a week to play with him at the Haymarket.

I then went to Mr. Alexander and told him I had accepted an offer from Mr. Beerbohm Tree; that I had heard what he, Alexander, had said; and that, though I was bound to keep my contract with him until the end of the season, I would never speak to him again.

It is quite dreadful to think of now; but there's the story! People began to say I drank, and this—added to the belief of some people that I *was* a Mrs. Tanqueray—gave me for a long time a queer reputation.

I remember at Stanway* telling this story of my sudden loss of memory to Mr. Arthur Balfour. He said that once something of the same kind had happened to him. Over-tired, he had gone a long journey to address a meeting; when he stood up to speak, not a word could he remember of what he wanted to say, until the heckling of the audience made him angry, and this anger pulled him together.

I must not omit, that some months before this, Mr. Alexander, delighted with the success of *The Second Mrs. Tanqueray,* and to show his appreciation of my share in it, had raised my salary from £15 to £30 a week.

By this time my load of debt had been a little lifted.

I had written to Pat imploring him to come home, having received a heart-broken letter from him written before he heard of my success. He had been silent for a long time, and it had greatly alarmed us; as the following letter written to my father-in-law, by my uncle, shows:—

* Stanway, the beautiful home of Lady Elcho, now Lady Weymss.

"6th September, 1893.

"Dear Mr. Campbell,

"Such a long time having elapsed since your son Pat last wrote to his wife, I began to fear lest some fearful fate had overtaken him in that wild country. I thank heaven it is not so, for Stella has just received a letter from him dated June 25th, from which I send you the following extracts:—

" '. . . I am coming home the first moment I have the money. I had collected over £20, but, as is my usual luck, got a very bad dose of fever, which has laid me up for nearly five weeks, and the doctor and medicines have taken it all.

" 'I am going on contracting on the line and shall get away soon. I long to leave Africa, where I have had nothing but bad luck. I must bring a little money home with me to start things, but it is very hard to make money—the authorities pay so badly. In fact, all over Africa there is depression and nothing doing. My life is quite monotonous—bossing up Kaffirs, making culverts, marking out banks and cuttings, etc. At night dinner, then to bed—dead tired. Sundays are the same as week-days.

" 'I fear you will find me greatly changed, . . . I pray God you won't turn from me. . . .' "

On the 31st December, 1893, Pat wrote:—

"Frontisville,
"Near Beira.

"I have just received your letters of 3rd and 17th November. Thank you, my own Stella wife, for writing such kind, loving letters; they came at a time when I was very miserable. Believe me, darling, I am coming to you the first moment I have the money. . . ."

"I wonder whether you have received my letter telling you of poor Hannay's terrible death. I think I would have been able to have got away this month, but his death has smashed up all my arrangements. . . ."

The following telegram from me to Pat, dated March 12th, 1894, speaks for itself:—

"Just received letter, reply paid whether I shall post money to you at once. Borrow on my name if possible, it will save time. Let me know, dear, where to meet you. So glad you have come.
"16, Manchester Street.   STELLA CAMPBELL."

When Pat arrived I saw in his eyes that youth, with all the belief and faith in his own efforts and his luck, had gone: his health and his energies were undermined by fever, failure, and the most bitter disappointments. Nothing had come of his hard work, his hopes, and his sacrifice. The expression in his face wrung my heart, but the old gentleness and tenderness were there—he still loved me.

His pride in his beautiful children and in my success—that was my reward.

The abnormal position in which he found himself must have been almost anguish to him: the girl-wife he had left six-and-a-half years before, now the fashionable actress, surrounded by the rush and excitement of smart friends, smart parties, smart clothes.

The curiosity, too, that surrounded the husband of "The Second Mrs. Tanqueray" was intolerable to him; also the hospitality extended to us both, which we had not the means to return. He was a great gentleman, Pat, and his position must have been most irksome to him.

He longed for his children and his wife to himself away in the country—to drink in England again—to pick up the threads of our old love and youth. He never spoke of those years in Africa, with the exception of one big-game-shooting expedition when his friend was mauled by a lion. Pat carried him for miles; he died in his arms. Pat dug his grave as best he could and buried him.

Every few days he was ill with malaria. I had eight performances a week, my two children, household cares, social responsibilities, and never enough money to go round. Dearest and Lady Burne-Jones, at Phil's suggestion, offered their house at Rottingdean to us for a week's honeymoon.

I remember how Miss Mary Moore and Mr. Charles Wyndham came over from Brighton to look at us!

Dearest wrote me a delicious letter, begging me to stay for months and months and suggesting that I should throw any books, furniture or pictures that bothered me out of the window, and that I was to order a piano from Brighton!

Lady Burne-Jones wrote saying our visit there

would be another pleasant memory for them connected with the house, it was a letter full of affection
and sympathy.

This old letter from my uncle alludes to the last
night of *The Second Mrs. Tanqueray*.

"Monday, 23rd April, 1894.

"Dear Beatrice,

"You are really a wonderful woman that you are able
to keep from losing your head under the intoxicating influence of all the applause, and praise, and presents,
and letters, laurel wreaths, bouquets, and suppers, to
which your enthusiastic admirers and friends love to
treat you.   I was indeed delighted to witness the spon-
taneous and splendid tribute of applause which the house
paid you on Saturday night.   I do believe some in the
gallery could have gone on applauding you before the
curtain 'till it were morrow.'   And you received the
hearty applause so gracefully and sweetly.   It was all
delightful.

"I suppose you heard that one young fellow in the
centre of the gallery, when all the other people had left
their seats and were filing out, remained fixed in his place
in a sort of reverie, and when told by the attendant that
he must move, cried, 'Oh, no, I am going to wait here for
The Masqueraders.' "

On March 28th, 1894, *The Masqueraders* was
produced at the St. James's Theatre, after nerve-
racking rehearsals for both Mr. Alexander, the
poor author, and myself.   Mr. Alexander and I rehearsed, only addressing each other in the words of
our parts.   How foolish it all was.

We made it up years afterwards.*

*I had recovered from a long illness. Mr. Alexander came with great sympathy to my house and said, "If you want to work again I will revive *The Second Mrs. Tanqueray,* or *Bella Donna,* or anything else you like," and he was very kind to my Stella, giving her more than one fine part at the St. James's.

CHAPTER VII.

I REMEMBER nothing about *The Masquer-aders,* excepting that my part struck me as unreal and much of the play in bad taste.

I quote from a criticism in *The Daily Telegraph.* It is amusing reading now, but at the moment it hurt.

The Daily Telegraph,
April 30th, 1894.

". . . Here we had a play brilliantly mounted, accurately presented, a marvel of production even in these days of astounding realism; and behold the whole thing, actors' work, sumptuous decoration, gorgeous mounting, and author's brilliant brain work, within an ace of being wasted because the most talked about actress of the day would not, or could not, understand one of the most beautiful, complex, and subtle studies of women that any dramatist has offered us in the whole range of the modern drama. . . .

"Dulcie is the same to everyone, incredible and inert. But even the climax kiss she does not understand. Instead of giving her patient lover a rapid, startling kiss of wilfulness and mutiny she merely pecks at his forehead like a discontented bird. (Did Clement Scott know what had happened between us, I wonder?) There is no meaning in the kiss, no sense in the scene so interpreted. The act was saved by a miracle, for the true Dulcie of the author's imagination did not exist. . . .

"The second act has ended, and the audience is in the same condition of surprise. Both Mr. George Alexander and Mr. Herbert Waring are better than ever. . . . But . . . Where is Dulcie? She should have been the gaiety and spirit of this act, its life and soul. But she is still the same dull, inert, and inaudible personality, an epitome of boredom. No feverishness, no excitement. . . .

"The better Mr. Alexander acts, the stronger becomes Mr Waring. Mr. Waring shakes, shivers, and grows pale under the excitement. . . .

"The audience cannot restrain its excitement. . . . Brilliant acting has made its mark, and why should it not? But . . . Where is Dulcie? The men have played the scene without her. Was ever a finer dramatic opportunity given to an actress? But Mrs Patrick Campbell passed it over as insignificant and beneath her notice. A Sarah Bernhardt would have leaped at it. . . ."

Other people praised me, condemning Clement Scott for treating me so "brutally, almost cruelly." Letters of sympathy poured in from strangers—how unpleasant it all was.

One foolish anecdote of this time has clung to me:—Mr. Alexander in this play by Mr. Jones had to look into my face and tell me I was beautiful and that he adored me, or some such words, and one night he said it with such a look in his eyes, as though he would willingly have wrung my neck, that I burst out laughing. When the curtain fell, his stage manager came with pompous dignity to the door of my dressing-room and said, "Mr. Alexander's compliments and will you please not laugh at him on the stage?" I replied, "My compliments to Mr. Alexander, and please tell him I never laugh at him until I get home." I was a most horrible leading lady, surely!

The following letters from friends show that I had my champions. The first from Lord Pembroke on the fair wig I wore as Dulcie; and the second from him gives his frank opinion after reading the play; also a letter from Sir Edward Burne-Jones filled me with courage and delight.

"73, Hertford Street, W.

"My dear Mrs. Campbell,

"Your letter was full of good news, especially as I detected, if I am not mistaken, a note of real contentment in it. Since I have been lying here my two best girl friends have got themselves engaged to be married, and now you have got your husband home again, and it gives me a queer, foolish feeling that if I only lie here a little longer everything in the world would settle itself.

"I'd like to hear your story very much when we meet, which I hope we may do before long, especially as I shall probably hear some fiction from others.

"I am still in bed most of the twenty-four hours, but get out for a drive in the afternoon. I shall probably leave this soon, as I fancy I have got all the good out of it that I can get. I'm out of all patience with myself being so long in getting well. I am afraid it's not likely, but it's not absolutely impossible at this moment that I should come to your first night on the 28th. I

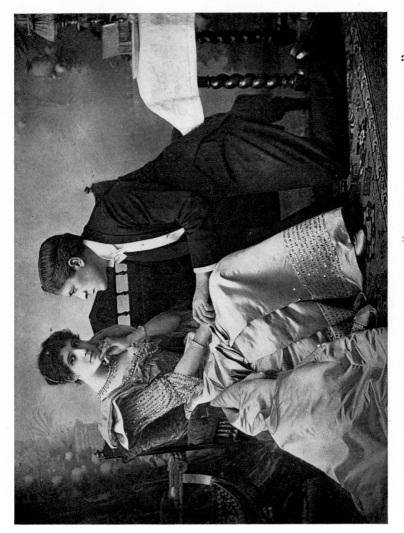

WITH GEORGE ALEXANDER IN ACT I OF "THE SECOND MRS. TANQUERAY"

may pick up a bit before then, and I should dearly like to come.

"Certainly a sweet, good woman in a fair wig* is satisfactorily unlike the 265th Mrs. Tanqueray. Why is it that in stageland fair hair is essential to goodness? It's rather the other way in real life. . . .

"Always yours,
"PEMBROKE."

"7, Carlton House Terrace, S W.
"May 8th, 1894.

"You faithless Lady,

"Why didn't you turn up on Sunday? I had been reading *The Masqueraders* and wanted to talk to you. It is full of crudities, absurdities, and anachronisms, with some palpable imitations both of Pinero and Ibsen, but it has some cleverness and go, and is likely, I should think, to please the populace. Nor does your part seem to me altogether a bad one (except that I can't conceive how you get through the 'Yah, Yah, Yah' business without sending the audience into convulsions) if *Mrs. Tanqueray* had never been written. As it is, it is really cruel—Dulcie is only a weak edition of Paula under different circumstances, several shades sillier, and slightly more hysterical, and the only possible result of your acting it, as it is evidently meant to be acted, would be to make the public say that it was only Mrs. T. over again in a slight disguise.

"This is really too bad, and I sympathise sincerely.

"Always yours,
"PEMBROKE"

Sir Edward Burne-Jones wrote giving me the

---

* Referring to Dulcie Larondie in *The Masqueraders*.

fruits of his philosophy, and saying that he did not waste precious life on reading what the critics said —and that to real artists only one critic mattered— "one's own savage, bitter self."

He also warned me of the greater peril to come, when "everything we do is praised" which, he affirmed, would follow my "unparalled success."

At the end of the run of *The Masqueraders* my contract with Mr. Alexander finished, and I joined Mr. Beerbohm Tree at the Haymarket for *John-a-Dreams,* by Mr. Haddon Chambers. I believe I was not a failure in this *rôle,* but the play did not run, and Mr. Beerbohm Tree went to America, lending me to Mr. John Hare.

Mr. Hare produced *The Notorious Mrs. Ebbsmith,* by Mr Pinero, at the Garrick Theatre on the 13th March, 1895.

The *rôle* of Agnes Ebbsmith and the first three acts of the play filled me with ecstasy. There was a touch of nobility that fired and inspired me, but the last act broke my heart. I knew that such an Agnes in life could not have drifted into the Bible-reading inertia of the woman she became in the last act: for her earlier vitality, with its mental and emotional activity, gave the lie to it—I felt she would have arisen a phœnix from the ashes.

That rounding off of plays to make the audience feel comfortable is a regrettable weakness.

To me Agnes was a finer woman, and the part a

greater one, than Mrs. Tanqueray. In those days, not so long ago, she was a new and daring type, the woman agitator, the pessimist, with original, independent ideas—in revolt against sham morals.

Agnes believes herself freed from the influence and power of sex; and that she loves Lucas as one loves a friend. Lucas does not admit his sensual love; but in reality he longs for her to assume some of the graces and allurements of her sex. He orders for her a smart and very *décolleté* evening dress. When she puts in on she feels ashamed. It delights and excites him. Agnes realises with horror that she loves him—just as any woman may love a man—and she surrenders.

Later the worldly ones arrive upon the scene, with the compromise suggested by their wisdom—Lucas shall have a sham reconciliation with his wife, on the tacit understanding that his relationship with Agnes will be continued, protected, patronised, even approved. A fine subject for a drama—the resurgence of ordinary passionate humanity through theories, bloodless schemes and thin ideals.

Agnes consents, burning the Bible in symbolism of her destroyed ideals; but again, in a moment, pulling it out of the fire.

It was the realisation of the truth that freed Agnes —that through the agony of human passion spiritualised, lies the path of freedom—not through denial or indulgence.

A fourth act—I wanted—with Agnes preaching

the doctrine of selfless, unexacting love; stern and un-
yielding only when baseness, lying, and fear in-
vade its purity—her conversion, a sudden revelation
of the Love of God; not a mere creeping back into the
shell of a narrow morality—how I should have
loved to speak that harangue in Hyde Park if only
it had been written.

Did Sir Arthur Pinero miss an opportunity, or
was he right, the time was not yet ripe? The suffragette, with her hammer in her muff, had not yet
arisen on the horizon.

I played *The Notorious Mrs. Ebbsmith* in
America, and its success there was quite extraordinary, people came round to my dressing-room—
friends and strangers—and stared speechless with
the thoughts Agnes Ebbsmith had inspired.

Mr. John Hare's performance in London, as the
Duke of St. Olpherts was a gem; his delivery of the
line, "I can't approach women—I never could—in
the missionary spirit"—said with a most profound
and impressive courtesy—for a moment eclipsed the
tragedy of the poor heroine's situation.

Mr. Hare had a delicious way of looking at you
on the stage with an absolutely sane eye. How I
admired that steady gaze.

Mr. Beerbohm Tree's tour in America had been a
financial failure; he returned, claiming me for a
production of *Fedora* at the Haymarket. I was
bound by my contract, and he refused to let me break
it. And this most brilliant and successful play, *The*

Notorious Mrs. Ebbsmith, unfortunately did not survive the change of cast.

I played Agnes Ebbsmith eight times a week for a fortnight whilst rehearsing *Fedora.* It was an impossible feat. I had only time to study the last act —the death scene—of this more than exacting *rôle.*

After a fortnight the work told on my voice and I was dumb and Mrs. Tree took up the *rôle.*

From many hundreds of letters referring to Agnes Ebbsmith, these from Mr. Mackail and Mr. Edmund Gosse made me very proud.

"14th March, 1895.

"You are with the Immortals now. I can't begin to talk about it; it seems like an insult to praise it; it was like the inner flower of fire.

"I am coming to see it again to-morrow night, and Margaret and I on Wednesday. The splendour of you!
"J. W. MacKail."

"29, Delamere Terrace, W.,
"1st April, 1895.

"My dear Mrs. Campbell,

"What I thought of the play? Well, I have a great difficulty in saying, for, to tell the truth, you swamped the play for me. The play was—you. I tell you without exaggeration that I never saw on the English stage a piece of acting which seemed to me so brilliantly sustained, varied, and vivified. Almost the only thing which seemed to me wrong was the whole 'business' about the Bible. What was that book doing *dans cette galère?* It jarred upon me as an incoherent and stagey and, therefore, disturbing element in an otherwise splendid mental and interior drama—I mean the drama of Mrs. Ebbsmith's inward movings—vicissitudes, apprehensions, whirlwind of battling instincts—all mirrored and translated by you in a manner transcendently poetical and thrilling. When it dawned upon you that Lucas was no real comrade, and the project of retaining him by commoner attractions was floating in your mind— now repulsed, now again projected—your acting was so magnificent, the strain of it on me was almost maddening, I wanted to scream. In this (I think that I am no dramatic critic, only a recorder of personal impressions) your greatness lies.

"You can interpret— you alone on our present stage— the flash and gloom, the swirl and the eddy, of a soul torn by supposed intellectual emotion.

"What did I think of the play? I am afraid I was thinking only of you. . . .

"Edmund Gosse.'

"63, Hamilton Terrace, N. W.

"My dear Mrs. Campbell,

"I saw the play last night, and it was a revelation to me. I enjoyed my evening thoroughly. I can't say more to you, dear, about your performance than I have already told you. It's the *finest bit of acting* I have ever seen. Now, dear friend, may I venture to chide you? Your acting is perfect, your appearance is perfect, but your voice showed weary fatigue now and again.

"May I implore you to take every possible *care of yourself*, rest as much as possible, and sacrifice pleasure for your art's sake. You are so gifted and have made such a gigantic hit. I don't want your voice to show wear. You can't act a part like 'Agnes' and keep late hours, too. The late hours are bound to tell, and then your great creation will become weakened from sheer physical fatigue.

"Forgive me, dear; it's for your good. I don't want people to say a word against your acting or strength of voice. It struck me last night you were *tired*. Am I right? Do give up late hours and rest all day if you can. . . .

"MYRA PINERO."

After *Fedora* I went from the Haymarket to the Lyceum, and opened with Mr. Forbes Robertson in *Romeo and Juliet* on September 21st, 1895. With the exception of "Rosalind," "Helena," and "Olivia," which I played with Mr. Ben Greet in his Pastoral Players Company, I had no experience in Shakespeare.

It must be remembered that before my first appearance on any stage, I had been to the theatre but three times in my life; and, not coming from a theatrical family, I had no traditional knowledge to guide me.

The "Phelps School" meant nothing to me. Mr. Robertson's work, on the other hand, was built upon it, and upon the influence of Sir Henry Irving; also, he had played Romeo many years before with Madame Modjeska.

I played Juliet simply, unpretentiously; I hope with the wonder and the rapture of a romantic, passionate child.

In those days, as in these, a declamatory style, exaggerated gesture, rhodomontade in any form, were to me ridiculous. Pomposity, a sense of one's own importance—slow music, gradually getting louder as the artist appears—the unnatural lifting of the voice at exits, compelling the audience to clap their hands —any meretricious form of stage effects exasperated me. I wanted nothing to interfere with the fundamental atmosphere of beauty, simplicity, and truth. Whatever the gamut, it must be within reasonableness; and the "bottom rock sane."

Want of experience, and physical fatigue, many times rendered my performances ineffective; that was unavoidable.

The fag of stage life was not in my blood; an untidy dressing room; a dresser who called me "my dear," smelt of beer, and scratched with a hook down my back until she happened to come across the eye, wore me out.

Oddly enough, I have never been known to weep at rehearsal, however heart-broken and weary I have been.

But I am running away from "Juliet."

The following article, signed by A. B. Walkely, shows much sympathy with my efforts:—

"*The Album,* Oct. 7th, 1895.
". . . . 'Juliet is a child of fourteen, but eleven years weaned Lammas,' says the nurse. . . .

"The whole spirit of the play implies that Juliet is encountered by Romeo as a child at an age when, as the French say, 'The heart has not yet spoken,' but is quite capable of speaking; and the age of fourteen in Italy is

approximately chosen for this now and then.   It has been
said that Mrs. Patrick Campbell looks older.   To me
she certainly does not; her figure is slim and girlish, her
ways are the ways of a child.   Throughout the play it is
the naïve simplicity, the trusting, childlike nature of the
girl upon which she dwells.   Even when the hot passion
wells out from her heart in the balcony scene she is absolutely näive.   A trace of self-consciousness in her refer-
ence to 'a maiden blush,' of coquetry in her 'I have
forgot why I did call thee back,' and the scene would be
ruined; but there is none.   When her father rates her
and her mother turns from her and the nurse trifles with
her, she is numbed and bewildered—a child who cannot
understand.   Before she drinks the sleeping draught she
shows all the child's natural terror of playing with death,
of the dark, of tombs, of ghosts.   When she drinks the
potion it is with simple obedience—a child who does what
she has been told.   That Mrs. Campbell should give us
with such tenderness and delicacy the child in Juliet is
no surprise to me, for it was the remnant of the child
she showed us in Mrs. Tanqueray that was more than
half the charm of that performance.

"The actress's temperament naturally inclines her
that way.   She has taken her own temperament as her
sole guide throughout, discarding 'the traditions' of the
part.   'The more's the pity' says Mr. Archer, apparently
because this and that 'tradition' would have helped her
to greater emphasis and variety in certain points, and
in the cajolery of the nurse and so forth.   For my part,
I will confess I care little or nothing about these minor
points, even if it were proved, which it is not, that a
study of 'tradition' would have helped Mrs. Campbell
to a better understanding of them.   I look for an impression of sincerity and beauty from the character as

a whole, and I can only say that Mrs. Campbell gives me this impression in a 'high degree. For me, her Juliet is from first to last an exquisitely truthful and moving performance."

I quote, too, what Mr. William Archer wrote in *The World*.

"October 21st, 1895.
". . . . My article was written before I had seen other criticisms and without any foresight of the extraordinary divergence of opinion to which Mrs. Parick Campbell's Juliet has given rise. It was easy enough to foresee that some critics would be readier than others to accept her beauty and charm as compensation for the evident lack of power and apparent lack of understanding and feeling with which she treated the intenser passages of the play, but it did not for a moment cross my mind that anyone who had ever seen a great Shakespearean performance or a great performance of any sort would call this a really adequate and competent, much less a poetic and perfect, Juliet. What was my astonishment to find that the majority of critics went into unmeasured and evidently heartfelt raptures over an impersonation in which, after the balcony scene, I have been unable to discover a single luminous ray or a thrilling moment! We have here no ordinary difference of opinion over which one can only shrug one's shoulders and say: 'There's no accounting for taste!' . . ."

Mr. William Winter's—the leading American critic—point of view is also interesting. I was, indeed, up against tradition with a vengeance.

"Theatre,

"December, 1895.

"Mr. William Winter has returned from England to New York with some exceedingly definite impressions as to Mrs. Patrick Campbell's Juliet. He found her possessed of certain sensibility and personal charm, although she was of an obviously mature, conventional drawing-room order of mind and manner. In the tragic phases of the *rôle* she was limp and powerless, and from the potion scene to the close her acting had neither purpose, form, continuity, coherence, visible passion, impressiveness, nor dramatic effort."

One night during the performance this scribbled note was sent round to me from the front of the house from Mr. Edmund Gosse:

"I have not dared to come and see you here before. I was afraid of shattering my idol, but you surpass yourself. Your Juliet is an incarnation of girlhood as a poet dreams of it."

J. W. Mackail wrote. "The more I think of your Juliet the finer and more delicately beautiful it seems, and the more eager am I to see it again."

The following letter from a girl friend, Diane Creyke,* to her mother, shows a little, what I thought of my performance—or was it the expression of my mother's anxious face that made me want to make her smile? I do not know.

"It was very amusing watching the people arrive, only

* Mrs. Ker Seymer.

I didn't know who they were. One woman was tremendously applauded by the gallery, and got up from her stall and bowed. The curtain went up at eight, and when Mrs. Pat came on there were tremendous cheers. It was most exciting. She looked excessively young, with her hair down and a wreath of flowers. Her ball dress was lovely—a mixture of flame colour and cloth of gold with angels round it. She didn't seem a bit nervous, but her voice was not very strong. The audience was tremendously enthusiastic, but I was rather disappointed there were so many scenes, and it seemed disconnected. But Mrs. Pat, except for not speaking loud enough, was perfection.

"Mr. Pat came and talked to me between the acts. Mrs. Pat made me go back with all the family to Ashley Gardens to supper. Her sisters were there, and Beo and Stella, Mrs. Pat's mother, uncle, two ladies, Irene Vanburgh, and myself. We had supper without Mrs. Pat, as she was kept at the theatre, but she arrived in white muslin with her hair down; rushed at her mother, saying: 'Oh, mamma, your daughter has been making such a fool of herself.' Irene* drove me home and was very nice."

This letter was written to me after Lord Pembroke's death by Lady Pembroke:

"Ashridge,
"August 25th, 1895.
". . . .

"This of your acting Juliet is very sad. He wanted you so much to do it, and how interested he would have

* Irene Vanbrugh played with me in *The Masqueraders,* and helped me with her sympathy through my difficulties.

been—and now he has gone.   Perhaps he does see.   I
am so glad you have Shakespeare's words to say. . . .

"I wish I could make everyone feel how near the
spirit world is, and how individuality exists and cannot be
changed.   You have imagination, and can realise this.
How the great spirits, as it were, call on us to fit ourselves to join them.   You said in one of your letters you
were not happy.   I wish I could help you.   I
would . . .

"I feel it very blessed to be intensely quiet here and
let the sense of the belief that he is waiting for me enter
my soul.

"Yours very sincerely and affectionately,
"G. PEMBROKE."

"Milford House,
"Godalming.

"Dear Mrs. Campbell,
"I went up last Thursday and saw the play.   I was
too shy to go and see you afterwards, or to send you a
message, though my friends laughed at me for it. . . .

"I must tell you how much your Juliet enchanted us.
I wish I could tell you or write you the way it interested
and thrilled me.   I wish I could write it in a way that
were worth reading, for I haven't seen yet an adequate
notice of it.

"You were wonderfully good, by far the best Juliet
I ever saw, and I so much admired the *quietness* of your
beginning before the trouble came, and then, when sorrow gathered round the poor lovers and everything goes
against them, the way in which you steadily rose with the
occasion, more pathetic, deeper, grander, as a fine nature
does under trial until the scene of the sleeping draught
comes, and there you were *splendid* and *thrilling*.

"Your face in those last scenes of grief, passion, despair, haunts me, and, do you know, you are so like a Madonna by Murillo, with your loose, dark hair, simple, sensuous, and passionate (as I think someone says in poetry).

"Well, if it gives you any satisfaction to know that you made people cry and drive home with aching hearts and too excited to sleep, you may have it.

"   . . . .

"BARBARA WEBB."

It was during the run of *Juliet* that Mrs. William Morris gave me a lovely photograph of herself, taken by Dante Gabriel Rossetti in her garden. I saw her first when her hair was white; her beauty and her grace took my breath away.

I sent her some little seed pearls for her needlework. I wonder into what work she wove them?

I find in my own handwriting across a picture of the balcony scene: "Three months' run, and I so miserable at not having played better on the first night."

How well I remember the difficulties at the theatre. Sir Henry Irving had let Mr. Robertson have the Lyceum if he "could get Mrs. Patrick Campbell. . . ."

The flattery of my manager was misleading—I was accused of flirting.

What matter, *Juliet* was over for me, forever!

CHAPTER VIII

THE next production at the Lyceum was *Michael and His Lost Angel.* Mr. Robertson begged me to come and hear Mr. Henry Arthur Jones read this play, and so far as my memory can be trusted, this cutting from some comic paper is the true story of what took place, excepting that I *did* attend a rehearsal or two to please Mr. Robertson.

"I won't say that," said Mrs. Pat,
A-pointing to the book,
"These words must stay," said H. A. J.
The lady took her hook.
Sweet Marion T. said "Oh, dear me,
These words are in a measure,
Not 'comme il faut.' "
Said Jones, "Quite so,
I'll cut 'em out with pleasure."

I felt my part in this play was vulgar, and it did not interest me, but I said I would try and play it if some of the lines were cut. Nutcombe Gould, also a member of the company, disliked the play and resigned his *rôle*.

The play was not a success, and I was very severely criticised for having resigned my part in it.

141

I did not like forsaking my manager, or offending Mr. Jones, or foregoing my salary; but there was something in that play I could not stomach.

This letter from Pat to me—in the country—shows I was not alone in my uncomfortable feeling.

"My darling,

"Thank you so much for all your kind thoughts about me. I was obliged to go to the office to-day. I think it is a touch of influenza I have. Dear, I cannot tell you how pleased I am that you are not playing in Jones' play. . . .

"All my love to you, my own darling wife,

"DADDY."

The next production was *For the Crown,* done into English by John Davidson from the play *Pour la Couronne,* by François Coppée, produced at the Lyceum under Mr. Robertson's management on February 27th, 1896. It was a fine play and had a fine success. The little part, Militza, appealed to me, and I believe I played it well.

During the rehearsals at a moment when an actor delivering a rather big speech "let himself go," John Davidson catching my eye, turned to me and said under his breath, with his grave manner and inimitable Scotch accent, "Now, if he were to behave like that in Piccadilly, he would be arrested." My merriment at what I could not explain to the company, caused some disturbance.

How excellent Miss Winifred Emery was in her part, and how well Mr. Robertson played—altogether it was a splendid production.

John Davidson and I were very friendly, and I remember I talked much to him about Racine's *Phédre* and what Sarah Bernhardt's performance of *Phédre* meant to me, and I commissioned him to translate it for me. This he did, but I have never produced it, for he expressed a wish in writing, found after his tragic death, that no work of his should ever be presented again. I do not think he realised his gifts—or perhaps he did—and others did not.

There was a little poem, "Butterflies," in this play of Davidson's, that he let me recite instead of singing. The effect, I believe, was good, and pleased people.

"BUTTERFLIES."

At sixteen years she knew no care,
How could she, sweet and pure as light,
And there pursued her everywhere
    Butterflies all white.

A lover looked, she dropped her eyes
That glowed like pansies wet with dew,
And lo! there came from out the skies
    Butterflies all blue.

Before she guessed her heart was gone
The tale of love was swiftly told,
And all about her wheeled and shone
    Butterflies all gold.

Then he forsook her one sad morn,
She wept and sobbed, "Oh, Love, come back!"
There only came to her forlorn
    Butterflies all black.

Friends who loved me sent little cuttings from papers to cheer me, such as these:—

"FROM A WOMAN'S STANDPOINT.

"By Clara Lemore.

"Mrs. Patrick Campbell.

"It is a wonderful voice—not wonderful because of its sweetness only, but because of its power of suggestion, because it seems always to be saying so much more than the bare words set down for it. As you listen to the soft, bell-like vibrations, all sorts of sad possibilities present themselves to your mind—possibilities of an intense capacity for suffering, possibilities of much silent heart-bleeding in the past, of some long-endured sorrow in the time gone by, which has left its echo still ringing in the tones of to-day.

"This seems to be the dominant note in Mrs. Campbell's individuality, this capacity for acute feeling. And when one comes to look into the thing, it is to be easily understood of all men, for is it not this very impressibility which gives her her stronghold over her audiences?

"THERE WAS A LITTLE POEM IN THIS PLAY, 'BUTTERFLIES,'
THAT HE LET ME RECITE"

"Quick to feel herself, is it to be wondered at that she should quickly raise feelings in others. Out of the soul's experience the tongue gives forth its interpretation; and so, one queries, with a sharp, hot quiver of instinctive sympathy, what has been the sorrow in this gifted woman's life, that it should have produced this curious power of passing on its sense of suffering to her listeners.

"And, after all, maybe this suggestion of an old-time grief is but the perfection of her art. It may be that she is of a buoyant nature, that she has a temperament which creates an atmosphere of unbroken sunshine for those fortunate ones who share her daily life!

"It may be, but one finds it hard to imagine. Self-sacrificing beyond even the limits of womankind she may be, intense in her affections she should be, tender in her sympathies she must be—but joyous?

"That one can hardly conceive of her."

On June 2nd, 1896, Sudermann's *Magda,* * translated by Louis N. Parker, was produced, and proved a failure: I was bitterly disappointed.

In a theatre of a more intimate size, and not burdened with the traditions of the Lyceum; the play not produced on Derby Day—the day on which this production was made—would have had a good run, as was eventually proved.

"Pastor Hefterdinck," played by Mr. Robertson, was a small and monotonous part. Audiences do not like their favourites in minor *rôles.*

---

* The play had been bought by Mr. George Alexander, and he had handed it on to Mr. Forbes Robertson.

Then again the Lyceum audiences were not used to the psychological drama. And a curtain rising for three acts on the same scene—a room with a stove, armchair, table, a bowl of goldfish, a desk, a horse-hair couch, and a few horse-hair chairs—after all the pageantry and show they had been accustomed to at this theatre for years—was not their "money's worth."

At the Royalty in 1900 *Magda* ran for many months. In America it was the play I opened with at the Opera House in Chicago, and played in every town during my long tour. The play was well known, and had been played there in German, English, French, and Italian.

Such is the battle of the theatre.

Should there be any who do not know the play, it may be interesting to give a short account of it, for this play is loved by Sarah Bernhardt, Eleanora Duse, and many others.

Magda has run away from her home in a little German town: she has become a famous singer. Her father, a retired colonel, never allows her name to be mentioned: her stepmother and younger sister have given up speaking of her.

They hear of the visit of a Prima Donna to the town, and realise that this is their Magda.

Magda calls to visit them in her rich clothes, bringing her scent, her flowers, her triumph, and her assurance into their spare home.

Her father is quite unimpressed by her success, and

looks upon her as an erring daughter who must be rescued.

Magda loves her little sister and wants to take her back with her to her hotel, but her father and step-mother expect Magda to come and stay with them.

She tries to give them some idea of the way she lives, with servants, courier, and secretary; but the Colonel is so deeply hurt that at last she consents.

Then a local magnate calls with a bouquet for Magda. He was her first lover and he deserted her: he did not know she had a child by him. She tells him this, and scorns his offer of marriage in reparation. Marriage, when she was young, would have saved her from shame and many struggles, but now——

Her father hears of this. He is extravagantly grateful to the Counsellor, holding the view that a man owes nothing to the woman he has ruined; or to the child she has borne him; and that it is an act of great generosity on the part of the Counsellor to try and make amends for what he has done.

The father's hand shakes incessantly; Magda, realising that it was her revolt against her home which produced this infirmity, gives way.

A message is sent to the Counsellor. He comes back full of fatuous joy and glowing with self-gratification over his own nobility.

This is intolerable to Magda. Finally he tells her she must be separated from her child. It would ruin his career to have a child in the house.

Then comes the final scene. Magda indignantly takes back her consent. Her father enters. She tells him of the sacrifice she is asked to make.

The father quietly bows the lover out of the room, saying he will speak to his daughter alone. He gets out his pistols, determined to shoot Magda if she disobeys him.

He talks of honour saved, and reputation restored. Until he at last goads Magda into asking him what he would say if he found that the Counsellor had not been her *only* lover. Her father calls her "strumpet," lifts his pistol to shoot her, and falls dead in a few moments from a paralytic stroke.

The characters, all except one, are highly coloured, almost to the point of caricature; but Magda herself in her revolt against a narrow society, with its crude code of morals, is a *rôle* vibrant with life.

London had seen a German company in the play, and the critics had condemned it. Sarah, too, had played it brilliantly—still they condemned the play.

The Telegraph called the play "hopelessly dull, verbose, and commonplace," and said:—

"Unfortunately, as we understand the play and the part, Mrs Patrick Campbell totally misunderstood both. She substitutes peevishness for passion, and petulance for force. . . .

"There is nothing disagreeable or unlovable or nerve-splitting in the 'Magda' as we understood her, and yet Mrs. Campbell in every line and accent suggests a revolt, a tirade against constitutional society."

Referring to the final scene, this paper says:

"It is all noise, noise, noise. In all justice, however, let it be said that the clever English actress must not be held wholly accountable for a poor, dull play, and what is after all a wretchedly bad part. . . . Never was such cheering heard in a theatre. Mrs. Campbell was called half a dozen times . . . a dull German sermon!"

These letters comforted me:

"Kensington Square,
"17th June, 1896.

"   . . .

"In the cold blood of next day I still think your 'Magda' last night was the ablest and finest thing I have ever seen you do. I cannot regret on any account that the play was produced.

"   . . . . . .

"JACK."*

"33, Brompton Crescent, S.W.
"My poor Disheartened One,
"I know too well all you are feeling about 'Magda.' No one can sympathise with you better than I, and I feel another blow for *myself,* for to my mind your performance was splendid, and as the best authorities say it was not, then maybe I am wrong. Oh, it's a delightfully simple profession! I only wish the critics would come and play the parts, for it seems to me they are the only people who know how they *should* be played.
"Well, I am aware I am not clever, but I am pigheaded sometimes, and stick to my opinion, and nothing will change my opinion of your *Magda* that it was ab-

* J. W. Mackail.

solutely true in every phase, and I admire your performance only second to your *Paula Tanqueray.* 'Them's
my sentiments!' Bless you!

> "Yours affectionately,
> "WINIFRED MAUDE."*
> "My love to 'Buttons,'† please!"

And this letter was written by that very clever
actress, Miss Rosina Filippi, after the revival at the
Royalty Theatre in May, 1900:—

"Dear Mrs. Campbell,

"Please let me add my cry of enthusiasm to the many
hundreds which have reached you to-day. You are
great—grand—in *Magda.* The higher the emotions,
the higher you rise to them. It is glorious, and I am
very grateful to you for having given us all such a
triumphant performance. I hope all London will see
you and that it may be many and many a day before
you piffle again in such horrors as *Moonlight Blossom,*
or even *The Canary.* Lord! to think that you have
Magda in your soul, and that you give us *Mrs. Temple
Martin!* Never, never, never do it again.

> "Yours affectionately,
> "ROSINA DOWSON."*

According to the notes in front of me, I played
Lady Teazle in *The School for Scandal,* at the
Lyceum, seventeen days after *Magda.* It is true the
part was not new to me. I had played it at a *mat-*

---

* Mrs. Cyril Maude.
                    † My little griffon.
    * Miss Rosina Filippi.

inée four years before.   Mr. William Farren—over eighty years of age—played Sir Peter with the traditions of his father and grandfather in the part in his bones.

Never once did Sir Peter address himself to *me*. The audience was his friend, his companion, and to them he confided his emotions.   There were in the cast others of this fine old school, and their traditional method "sat on my head"—a green baize over the singing bird's cage.

I was tired out, too, the collapse that came later was well on its way, and my work was becoming demoralised.   I let things go.

The following letter from my dear uncle alludes to my state of mind:—

"Sunday.

"Dear Demoralised Thing,

"No, *not* demoralised—never be that.   Be different from all others, be *the one*.   If Art has pushed too many over the precipice as being creatures of wretched, lumpish clay, spite of all their pretended aspirations, still *you,* walk you safely, securely along the edge; a true goddess, not less human than they, with every fibre of mind and body as sensitive as theirs, but possessing within yourself an element of supreme fineness, a dignity, a splendid individuality, to which only the *truest,* the *highest,* can attain.

"Of one of his great knights, Ariosto says, 'Natura el fare, e poi ruppe la stampa'—'Him Nature fashioned, then broke the mould.'   A peerless knight, the like of whom was never, never to be seen on earth again.   Why not *you as peerless* in your own sphere? You can be. Art has placed in your hair the undying laurel. What will you do for the honour of Art? Lay upon her shoulders the golden robe? Or cast over her incomparable form the rumpled drapery, the chiffonage of demoralisation.

"At least two things remember—do not allow yourself to deceive yourself. Then you can surely pack off demoralisation with her bedraggled skirts back across the Styx into her horrid steaming lair—forever.

"But perhaps I have not rightly understood your meaning of demoralisation. If so, then forgive this rhapsody.

"   .   .   .   .   .   .

"UNCLE."

In November of this year I went to the Avenue Theatre, then under Miss Elisabeth Robins' management, and played The Rat Wife in *Little Eyolf,* thankful for the chance of being able to do something for her.

Uncle wrote on November 12th:

"I understand exactly your feelings. I knew what a gratification it would be to you to do a service to Miss Robins."

Miss Janet Achurch, who played the leading character, fell ill, and I was asked at a moment's notice to play her part of Rita in this play. It was an alarming ordeal, for I was unable in the time given me to learn the words—I believe it was only a day.

I tied the book by a ribbon to my waist and practically read it.

I remember Mr. Asquith was in the house and warmly congratulated me, and the following letters show I got through with credit:

"4, Whitehall Court, S.W.

"My dear friend,
"You were divine and the book was scarcely noticed. Mes félicitations! You have scored a triumph, and I know you deserved it.

"Yours most sincerely,
"WM. HEINEMANN."

"Avenue Theatre,
"Northumberland Avenue,
"10th December, 1896.

"My dear Mrs. Campbell,
"Being unable to do so personally, I send these few lines to endeavour in some way to thank you for your splendid and timely assistance in coming to our rescue to-night. You are indeed 'true blue,' and should the opportunity ever arise of showing my appreciation of your good nature and courage, I shall gladly welcome it.

"Trusting your extraordinary exertions to-day will not produce any ill-effect, and again tendering to you my sincere thanks,

"Believe me,
"Yours very truly,
"F. J. HARRIS."

I find also a letter from Mr. Archer praising my performance of The Rat Wife in this play and his views as to my playing Rita at so short a notice:

"34, Great Ormond Street, W.C.
"Dear Mrs. Campbell,

"Mr. Heinemann gives me to understand that you wanted to hear my view as to your playing Rita. They are entirely favourable to your doing so. Of course, I cannot pretend that I don't regret the circumstances which have thrown the part open; but since they have occurred, I, for my part, can only rejoice in the prospect of seeing you in the character. I have always felt that it is one of the greatest parts ever written, and your rendering of it could not fail to be enormously interesting and attractive. If you see your way to undertaking it, you will certainly have all my good wishes.

"Let me once more congratulate you upon The Rat Wife. My own feeling about it you already know, but I don't think I have ever heard any performance talked of with such unanimity of admiration.

"Wherever I go I hear no dissentient voice.

"Yours very truly,
"WILLIAM ARCHER."

In February, 1897, Pat introduced Mr. Robertson to Mr. Horatio Bottomley, who interested himself, I believe, in financing *Nelson's Enchantress,* a play Mr. Robertson put on at the Avenue Theatre. It was unconvincing, and was not a success.

Then the fatigue that had been gradually threatening me for many months reached the climax. *I could not work any more.*

The thought of "giving in" was unbearable to me,

but I was persuaded by my husband, my people, and my friends to stop work altogether for a time.

My loved friend, Margaret Mackail, persuaded me to go into a nursing home, and she smiled away my despair at my "nervous breakdown."

As the doctor held my pulse I laughed, with tears pouring down my cheeks, declaring I was all right. He said gravely, "All the acting has done this."

Oh, that queer feeling when I was just falling off to sleep, that awful apprehension that "something most important was left undone." That horrible start!—and then the long, wakeful nights, and the everlasting tears.

What an odd experience it was. They put me into a little room, with a window out of which I could only see the sky; the door was left wide open, and a nurse or the doctor sat by my bed alternately, I, turning and tossing about, unable to rest. No medicine was given me, only massage, which I could not stand; no letters, no friends, no name of anyone belonging to me mentioned. The doctor—Dr. Embleton, now dead—was an extraordinarily gentle, kind man; he used to hold my hand and tell me I had "worked too hard, and felt too much," and that all I needed was sleep; if I were lonely I could get up and dress, go downstairs and go out. I do not exactly remember what happened. Either they thought me cured, or they were afraid to continue longer such strict quiet. After eight weeks I came away.

Perhaps if I had been trained in the Dramatic Art, I would have known how to spare my emotional temperament, and to depend a little on skill, technique and "tradition"—that awful word—I wonder——

The doctors ordered me to Malvern. Then my dear friend, Mrs. Percy Wyndham, hearing of my illness, wrote saying that Lady Queensberry was going abroad and would be delighted to lend me her little house at Salisbury—lovely Hatch House—its beautiful walled garden. with the postern gate— Queen Elizabeth, as a girl, had walked in the rose garden there.

Sybil Queensberry left her servants to take care of me; and her carriage for me to drive about in this most beautiful part of England; and she said my children must join me there, and my dogs, and any friends I liked. What a dream of beauty and peace it was.

The following letters refer to this time, and show, too, that my spirit was sorely troubled:

"It was really comforting news, dear, to hear that you are well enough to write and to receive letters. Your deep seclusion created a cruel blank in the world, that was becoming absolutely painful. If, however, it has helped to give you back to certain health and to calmer and happier views of life, it deserves and it will receive our sincere and heartfelt commendations. The wish in our hearts, however, was that your eight weeks' retirement might be succeeded by the invigorating sweets of a sea voyage. Think what store of health and strength the sea change would endow you with, and you would return from it to your profession and to the stage, really and truly a 'new woman' indeed, in the worthy sense, of course, not in the 'fin de *sickly*' signification of the phrase. . . ."

". . . . Of course I understand about your struggle; it could not be otherwise, but I felt sure of you, and that whatsoever fight you might have to fight, you would come out of the struggle, conquering and not conquered. . . . Only be brave. . . ."

"Uncle"

"Dearest Uncle,

"You have been right, you always said I never saw people and things as they were, that I lived in dreams—now I see, now I know, and I think the knowledge has nearly finished me.

"Where did you get all your philosophy and unselfishness?

"I am quite strong again physically—nervously, perhaps, not quite right yet. There are so many things I cannot bear to think of. . . .

"A big dose of my dear Beo and Stella at Hatch House will do me a lot of good.

"I do understand about the 'depressing feeling.' You wanted to help me, and you felt you could not, and it made you wretched, but you did help me, all the same.

"I wish you were here with me. Don't grudge me letters, say, ask what you like.

"I had a long bicycle ride alone yesterday afternoon all through lovely lanes. I found a pretty church built by Earl Beauchamp and went in to rest. Presently the clergyman came, and five people, and there was evensong.

The doors were all open and the birds chirping. The painted window, his droning voice, it was cool and restful. . . .

"BEATRICE"

Pat at this time was working hard in the City and trying his best to help me in my collapse.

"Dearest Stella,
"Of course if you feel you are able, I think it would be best for you to join Robertson again at the Lyceum. London will be very glad to have you back. Do not start with Shakespeare; cannot Robertson get a new play or a translation from some really good French play?
". . . I am so glad you have the children with you, they are such dears.
"God bless you all.

"With love,
"DADDY."

Mr. Forbes Robertson had written to me saying he was taking the Lyceum in September to open in *Hamlet* and offering me Ophelia. I felt very nervous. I knew once more I would be up against "tradition": but, I could not afford to refuse.

"Killarney House,
"Killarney.
"Dearest Beatrice,
"This is only a line of blessing to you and good wishes for you and your health and for your success in what you are now doing. I hope you are feeling the benefit

of your rest at Hatch; dear, lovely, restful little Hatch.

"I did so enjoy seeing you there, and wish you had had a little bit more of it, but again I say, I think you will feel better when you are working, and you must give your whole heart and soul to it, so as to make the best Ophelia that has ever been! For it is so touchingly beautiful, and your part will not be very long, and you can get away early from the theatre, and *early to bed will be the thing for you* for some time to come.

"Keep your spirits up.

"I believe in an awfully good time to come for you. I prophesy it.

"Ever yours most affectionately and believingly,
"MADELINE WYNDHAM."

One paper, probably *The Telegraph,* said I had "distinguished" myself, because I was the first actress who had ever made a failure of Ophelia.

I remember Mr. George Wyndham* saying he thought I was the best Ophelia he had even seen, and Mr. Sargent, too, paid me many compliments.

There were bad notices and good notices and many letters of fulsome praise.

One night I was very naughty—egged on by the continual criticism of playing Ophelia in my own hair, I played half the part in my dark hair and half in a fair wig. Miss Ellen Terry was among the audience—I wanted to know which she liked best— I never heard that she alluded to it.

* The Rt. Hon. George Wyndham, M.P.

It was odd to me that my singing was much praised, just as my dancing was praised in *Juliet*—for I can neither sing nor dance—

When Sir Henry Irving came onto the stage after a performance, he put his arm round me and said, "Beautiful, my child, beautiful." But the real truth was that Miss Terry had given such a lovely Ophelia to the world—still fresh in everyone's memory—there was no room for mine.

"Clouds,
"Salisbury,
"October 21st, 1894.

"Dearest Beatrice,

"Thank you so much for your dear, kind letter. Think of your being made happier or better by my appreciation of your work—ridiculous! But it comes from your affectionate heart and nature; you place my power of judging far, far too high, as it is only formed on 'a certain instinct, more than on knowledge or learning! To be of any real use in the world, to be a 'good or useful critic' (how I hate the word), one ought to have both—instinct for the beautiful and the knowledge of it. Had I to choose one only, I should choose the first—instinct for it—as beauty is the only thing in this world almost, that can be enjoyed without the other! but can be of no use to others, without learning! One cannot pass it on, knowledge and learning cannot teach it, or make one possess it. But instinct can make one enjoy it. One may read about beauty and learn about it till one is black in the face; but without the instinct for it, never enjoy it. That my simple enjoyment of your work should please and encourage you touches me more than

I can say!   I wish my opinion were more worth having, yet, as I have been trying to say, I believe in *instinct* on such matters in all things beautiful to be the true and a more trustworthy thing than mere knowledge.   'A little knowledge is a dangerous thing,' a true instinct a reliable thing!   And I am sure I am right in my opinion of this giving of *Hamlet*.   I cannot help feeling flattered, yet more than ever humbled, for I know what you find in me, all comes from yourself, but I thank God, all the same, that He has put something into me that makes it possible to be as it is, that those who are so far above me in intellect and power should find a resting place in my sympathy for their souls. . . .

"Your loving
"MADELINE WYNDHAM."

CHAPTER IX.

I HAVE an idea that it was again Mr. Horatio Bottomley who helped financially with the revival of *Hamlet* at the Lyceum; also with the next interesting venture—a tour Mr. Forbes Robertson made in Germany.

I had a great treasure in my pocket—Maeterlinck's play, *Pelléas et Mélisande.* I accepted the offer to accompany Mr. Robertson, if on our return he would produce *Pelléas and Mélisande;* this he agreed to do.

The plays we took to Germany were *Hamlet, Macbeth,* and *The Second Mrs. Tanqueray.*

There was some talk to the effect that Queen Victoria had requested the Emperor not to patronise with his presence this play of Mr. Pinero's. I do not know if it was true, but he certainly did not.

During *Macbeth* the Emperor sent for us and gave us gifts—to Mr. Robertson a scarf pin, to me a bracelet.

In the middle of *Macbeth* there was a long entr'-acte whilst Royalty ate a meal: how hopelessly disconcerting to the sequence of the performance.

I was struck by the Emperor's personality: the impression of intellectual force, the powerful voice—the heavy moustache turned up at the ends—pierc-

ing steel blue eyes—and the little withered hand—
a gold bangle on the wrist.

I remember he said to me, "I wish you would
teach my actors not to shout."

The German criticisms were interesting: they
called us "nerve aristocrats"!

Also this letter from Lady Edward Cavendish:

> "British Embassy,
> "Berlin,
> "16th March, 1898.

"Dear Mrs. Campbell,

"I was sorry to be out when you called on Sunday, I
should have liked to have told you what a pleasure it has
been to see you. I thought *Macbeth* altogether beautiful, and it was a great pleasure to see it so wonderfully
given. Besides the great enjoyment of seeing such acting, your gowns were gorgeous and lovely, and I must
congratulate you heartily on the great success you have
had. . . .

"The Emperor has just been with my brother. He
is loud in the praises of you and Mr. Forbes Robertson. . . . He thinks the rendering of *Hamlet* and *Macbeth* were the most perfect he had ever seen, and he was
full of admiration.

> "   . . . .
> "EMMA E. CAVENDISH."

On our return to England Mr. Robertson produced *Pelléas and Mélisande* at the Prince of Wales
Theatre on 21st June for nine matinées.

Maeterlinck's play came to my notice in this
way:

One day Jack Mackail brought me as an offering his translation of this lovely work, written out in his own fine hand.

This archaic poem of beauty, passion and loveliness, unthumb-marked and un-dog-eared by "tradition," gave me peace and certainty—I had come into my own.

I *knew* Mélisande as though she had been part of me before my eyes were open.

I *knew* I could put the beauty of the written word into colour, shape, and sound.

Mr. Robertson thought the play weak and morbid: his brother, Ian Robertson, said, "Why do you want to make such a damned fool of Forbes?" I was adamant: the contract had to be kept.

I cannot remember Mr. Mackail coming to any rehearsal; but with letters of advice, sketches and suggestions he guided me. And the lovely gold dress I wore was suggested by Sir Edward Burne-Jones.

I battled through at the theatre, arguing and insisting; warmly supported in my enthusiasm and feeling by Mr. Martin Harvey's full understanding, and appreciation of the beauty of the poem.

The incidental music needed was a most important element. I felt sure M. Gabriel Fauré was the composer needed. My friend, Mr. Frank Schuster, arranged a meeting between us at his house in Queen Anne's Gate. I had not spoken French since my

IN "THE SECOND MRS. TANQUERAY"

visit to Paris seventeen years before, but I stumbled
through somehow, reading those parts of the play
to M. Fauré which to me called most for music.

Dear M. Fauré, how sympathetically he listened,
and how humbly he said he would do his best! His
music came—he had grasped with most tender inspiration the poetic purity that pervades and en-
velops M. Maeterlinck's lovely play.

Mr. Martin Harvey's melancholy face, his curious
timbre of voice, his scholar's delight in cadence,
helped him to invest the part of Pelléas with an unearthly glamour; and Mr. Robertson's classical pro-
file, manly voice and general distinction were invaluable.

It will be remembered that the whole of the action of this play takes place in one of those gloomy
ancient castles, by the sea, which Maeterlinck has
always used as symbolical of the prison life is to the
soul; their ancient impregnable walls, their long
tradition of sorrow, crime and tragedy, stand for
life in the flesh: and the sea, the illimitable sea, is always there to speak of eternity, and the wild sea birds,
of freedom.

Mélisande's ignorance of her own birth—her sense
of exile—her grief by the pool where she has lost
her crown—are all symbolic of the soul in life.

Then comes the contact with man's desire, Golaud's
love born of passion; a contact which teaches her
nothing: which awakens no love—only fear.

As the play proceeds, Pelléas and Mélisande draw

nearer and nearer, each finding in the other the yearning of their soul's fulfilment, and in their very purity, deceiving themselves into the shadow of death.

Mélisande leans out of the window of the tower:—

> My long hair falls over, all down the tower,
> My hair waits for my lover, hour after hour,
> St. Daniel and St. Michael,
> St. Michael and St. Raphael,
> I was born on a Sunday, on a Sunday at noon.

Pelléas hears her, and comes under the window; as he tries to touch her hand, her hair becomes entangled in a bough—human love has caught her—her being is awakening! . . .

A scene of extreme beauty is when she goes to meet Pelléas in the wood and he tells her he is going away. Again the two lovers have escaped from the gloom of the prison to say good-bye, and under the moon and stars they cling to one another; they are free, they live, they love.

> Pelléas: "Tout les étoiles tombent sur moi."
> Mélisande: "Sur moi aussi, sur moi aussi."

But their shadows are still in the world, and Golaud stands at the edge of their shadows in the wood, and all the jealousy and mad lust of a man possess him, and he kills his brother, Pelléas.

The end is all pity, pity for Golaud who does not

understand: for Mélisande who has brought his child into the world and is dying: for Pelléas who is dead. The play ends with the birth of another soul.   It is the old grandfather who, lifting the little one, says to Golaud, "It is the child's turn now."

In the early morning of the day of the last re-. hearsal, Sir Edward Burne-Jones died.   I read it first on the placards as I left the theatre.

"44, Belgrave Square.

"Dearest Beatrice,

"I must write to you although I can say nothing. Your heart is with Margaret to-day, this bitterest of days for Margaret and all his, mine is with her also. . . . And I really grieve for you to have to act to-morrow with this on your heart, but so life goes on.

"He was to have dined (they were all coming to-night) with me for my birthday, but now he dines in the Courts of Heaven.   The King of Kings needed him.

"Ever yours affectionately,

"MADELINE WYNDHAM."

The play had an overwhelming success, M. Maeterlinck being still more warmly hailed as the Belgian Shakespeare.   Mr. Robertson was lauded for his discovery and his discernment.

I have often wondered why Mr. Robertson, who had been so loth a convert, did not disclaim the honour of the enterprise.

But the main triumph was that a thing of beauty had been given to the theatre forever.

There were many hundreds of criticisms. The critics were on their nettle. At the moment I can only find one, the rest must have gone to the American manager, when I produced the play in the States.

"The Guardian.

" . . . One love scene challenges comparison with the most beautiful in the world, where Mélisande leans out of the window and Pelléas tries to kiss her hand. She lets her long black hair fall down until it touches his shoulders. He knots it to the branches and makes her a willing prisoner. Whether as a piece of literature it will bear comparison with the balcony scene of *Romeo and Juliet* I cannot say, for nobody who saw it could judge it merely as literature. It is not given to many women in a generation to be so beautiful as was Mrs. Campbell, when she leant out from the window, her whole body yearning towards her boy lover, yet with unconscious innocence suggested in some indescribable way: playing it was, play you felt it to be, yet behind every word and gesture of the girl at play, there was the woman latent. . . ."

"Golaud: 'Vous êtes des enfants. . . . Mélisande, ne te penche pas ainsi à la fenêtre, tu vas tomber. Vous ne savez pas qu'il est tard. Il est près de minuit. Ne jouez pas ainsi dans l'obscurité. Vous êtes des enfants . . . (Riant nerveusement) Quels enfants! . . . Quels enfants!' "

I give letters from M. Maeterlinck and others:

"Dear Madam,
    "I need not tell you with what joy I read of your great

triumph in the papers of yesterday and of the day before. Nearly all have endeavoured to say how supremely perfect and wonderful you were. Yet the most enthusiastic did not throw into their expressions of admiration half that ardour which I could have wished they had done. Maybe that only he whose imagination produced Mélisande can appreciate how perfect was your presentment of her, in reality more lovely and more lifelike than in his most vivid and beautiful imaginings she had ever been. Before I saw you I did not know that a creature of one's dreams could come to be purer, more harmonious, and more adorable even, in real life. You have taught me that one need never be afraid of dreaming dreams of too great beauty, since it is our good fortune now and then to meet a privileged being who can render them visible and real.

"When you see Mr. Forbes Robertson please convey to him my sentiments of admiration and my thanks. He too was perfect; he was in a word, worthy to stand at your side; and he too redeemed the piece more than once, even as you redeemed it from first to last.

"In a few words, you, and the delightful, the ideal Pelléas, filled me with an emotion of beauty the most complete, the most harmonious, the sweetest that I have ever felt to this day.

"Thank you once more. It will give me infinite pleasure to see you again on Thursday.

"M. MAETERLINCK."

STUDLAND,

WAREHAM.

Chère Madame:

Je n'ai pas besoin de vous dire avec quelle joie j'ai vu votre beau triomphe dans les journaux d'hier et d'avant-hier. Puis-que vous avez essayé de dire à quel point vous avez été parfaite et merveilleuse. Pour

-t ous, le plus enthousiast
n'a pas mis dans son
admiration la
moitié de l'ardeur
que j'eusse voulu
qu'il y mît. C'est
peut-être que celui là
seul qui un jour
imagina Mélisande
peut savoir à quel
point vous avez su
la réaliser plus belle
et plus vivante qu'elle
ne fut jamais o!
ses désirs les plus
vivants en les plus
beaux. avant de

171

vous avoir vue. Je ne
savais pas qu'un person-
-nage de rêve, pût deve-
nir ~~mademoiselle~~, plus
pur, plus harmonieux,
plus adorable encore
dans la réalité. Vous m'
avez appris qu'on ne doit
jamais avoir peur de
faire de trop beaux
songes, puisqu'on a
parfois le bonheur de
rencontrer un être privi-
légié qui sait les rendre
visibles en réels.
Quand vous verrez
Mlle Forbes-Roberts

Veuillez lui rappeler
mon admiration et
ma reconnaissance.
Lui aussi a été parfait,
il était digne d'être à
vos côtés, et c'en tout
dire, et lui aussi, plus
d'une fois a sauvé
la pièce, que vous
sauviez toujours.
Pour tout dire en un
mot, vous, lui et la
délicieuse, l'idéale
Pelléas, vous m'avez
donné l'émotion de
beauté la plus complète,
la plus douce et la plus
harmonieuse, que j'ai
jamais été exposé [...]
Merci encore, [...]
vous revoir jeudi. M. Maeterlinck

"23, Young Street,

"7th November, 1898.

"Dearest Stella,

". . . James Barrie writes to me 'I don't think I was ever so entranced by a play; I came out of the theatre quite light-hearted with delight. Mrs. Campbell is beyond comparison; better than she has ever been in anything else. . . .'

"J. M."*

"Dearest Stella,

"This performance is what I have been waiting and longing for, for three years; and you may judge what I would have given to see it, but I could not. . . .

"But I must tell you that one of our people here, an unimpressionable highly educated man of fifty or so has just come back from seeing the last performance to which he went merely from curiosity, and because of my name, fully expecting to be bored.

"He was carried away with the beauty of it from beginning to end, and said he had never believed in you before, but did now, that such a play could not die. . . .

"Your affectionate,

"J. M."

"Limnerslease,

"Guildford,

"Thursday, 24th November.

"My dearest Lady Mélisande,

"I must write to tell you what a wonderful pleasure yesterday afternoon was to me. I have come back with a strange feeling of having been rested and smoothed out, and somehow to-day I have been running up little hills in my day's work, that for weeks seemed to me quite

* J. W. Mackail.

impossibly high and steep. That is the effect Mélisande, Pelléas and Golaud had upon me, and I thank them from my heart.

"The whole thing lifted one into a new mysterious world, in a way not easy to understand, except that one knows one has been drawn out on a wave of beautiful things, colour, sound, movement, charm, and that one has been passing over the boundaries of reality into a place as living and real, but which one can never touch or reach.

"I suppose only genius can take one there, and it seemed to me that your acting, and Mr. Forbes Robertson's was *full* of it, and indeed every part went without a jarring sound.

"You have got the spirit of a beautiful Burne-Jones picture into it all; how wonderful it is to have done that for us.

"I should have liked to come and thank you on the spot, but I felt that no one ought to ask for a minute more of you, you had given so much, and I hear that there is an evening's work to drain you still more. I have told Signor G. F. Watts about it as well as I could, it made him talk again and again of it to-day.

"Good-bye, dear beautiful Mélisande, may all good and blessed things be about you, and may they repay you in your own heart's desires for all you gave to me yester-day.

"Yours affectionately,
"MARY WATTS."*

"133, Gloucester Road, S. W.,
"6th November, 1898.

"Dear Mrs. Campbell,

"I saw your Mélisande yesterday, and it gave me ex-

* Mrs. Watts, wife of the great artist G. F. Watts.

quisite delight. It seemed to me that what you have been trying to do with your art for this last year or two rather hazily, you had suddenly accomplished so triumphantly that the result is sheer beauty. The whole thing is a joy to look at, and listen to, and think about, and I can't resist the desire to tell you how it inspired me.

"Yours sincerely,

"J. M. BARRIE."

Madame Sarah Bernhardt was brought to see the play by Mr. W. Clarkson, the popular wigmaker. She was very much moved by its beauty, expressing a warm wish to play Pelléas with me. I thought it only a pretty compliment she was paying me.

Six years afterwards on one of her visits to London for a short season at His Majesty's Theatre, Stella and I went to meet her at the Carlton Hotel. Sarah took me up to her bedroom and pointed to a little cot where a child was asleep, with a roll of parchment tied up with ribbon, at her feet. "Voila 'Yniold,'" Sarah said: she had taught the little thing her *rôle* in *Pelléas and Mélisande,* and Sarah herself was ready to play Pelléas with me. My dear Sarah. At first I was very nervous at the thought of acting in French. Sarah only laughed at me, saying Mélisande would speak French just as I did, and that she could play Pelléas with no one else.

Lady Eden * lent me her children's French governess, Mademoiselle Drouin, to live in my house for

* The beautiful wife of Sir William Eden.

two weeks. She talked her perfect French with me
practically all day and half the night, besides coach-
ing me in the pronunciation of the actual words of
Mélisande.

So I ventured—how dared I?

I took the rehearsals, and the company never
smiled as I "directed"! Sarah altered nothing, but
asked my permission to turn her back to the wall
of the tower that my hair might fall over her face!
Her Pelléas was a wonder. She carried her body
with such ecstasy and breeding: her voice was the
voice of a youthful melancholy spirit, gradually
melting into a tenderness, that more than once almost
rendered me speechless for fear of breaking the spell.

Mr. W. L. Courtney, in *The Daily Telegraph,*
wrote:—

"When criticism has nothing to say one may be sure
something has been seen rare, and strange and beautiful:
Madame Bernhardt, in the very beginning, found her
note and kept it, low in tone, and rich in music.   Mrs.
Campbell's Mélisande is known to us from one or two
previous representations.   We venture to say that in its
French form it is more gracious and childlike and poetic
than we have ever seen it before.   Scene after scene
passed with short intervals, and the air of mystery and
unreality was never broken.   We watched the first meeting at the Fountain, we heard the quiet fatalism of old
age uttered by the lips of Arkel.   We saw the slow
development of the unescapable tragedy enveloping all
the characters as it were with vague and shadowy nets,
and the light was one which never was on sea or land,

and we were—spectators and actors alike—such stuff as dreams are made of. Once, and once only, did we seem to touch earth. It was in the fine scene where Golaud, in a mad access of jealousy, holds up the little Yniold to the window to watch the two lovers within.

"We have never seen a better Golaud than that of M. Decoeur. . . . As one watches this Mélisande the words rise to one's lips: 'Will no one tell me what she sings?' For she too has caught the secret of 'old unhappy far off things and battles long ago.' "

During a previous season of Sarah's in London the play she produced had not been a success financially (a Napoleonic play, I forget the name), and at the moment Sarah was hard pressed for money: to my delight she sent M. Pitou* to ask if I could help her. Wonderful to relate, I had a hundred pounds in the bank, and I thanked heaven that I was able to do her a service.

During one of these performances of *Pelléas and Mélisande*, Sarah Bernhardt returned to me the hundred pounds, in five pound notes, in a little silver casket, before the many people who were in my dressing-room. She said how grateful she was to me—the simple graciousness of her act! Did she ever know, I wonder, how my heart almost choked me?

Sarah is the most generous of women. I think she feels, as I have often felt, that money belongs to those who need it most. Unfortunately, as this feel-

* M. Pitou had been Madame Sarah Bernhardt's secretary for something over twenty years.

ing slowly beggars us, it changes, alas! or it should!

A story of a really generous man, told me by Sir Edward Burne-Jones, comes to my mind.

A friend came to a generous man to borrow twenty-four pounds. The generous man had only twelve pounds in the world. These he gladly gave to his friend; but afterwards, whenever they met, the generous man hung his head: he felt he owed his friend twelve pounds.

In July, 1905, a year later, on Madame Bernhardt's next visit to London, she and I went to the provinces meaning to give only a few performances of the play. But we met with such a brilliant success that we played it every day for three weeks.* Only in Dublin did one critic demur. He wrote:

"Mrs. Campbell played Mélisande, Madame Bernhardt Pelléas; they are both old enough to know better."

There are delicious memories of this three weeks' tour. A little story Madame Bernhardt told me of her first arrival in America touched me very much. She carried a rather large handbag of some soft velvet stuff. On landing, the official insisted on looking inside. They found a small bundle tied carefully with ribbon. Sarah implored them not to open it, "je vous en prie, Messieurs, je vous en prie" They insisted. It contained her son's first baby shoes of white patent leather, and his first little baby shirt.

* Sarah paid me £240 a week, and £35 for each additional performance, and paid all travelling expenses. I provided the scenery and dresses.

I remember one night a discussion we had on "flirting." Sarah took this word very seriously; she said that flirting stirred and excited animal passion. That flirting was a peculiarity of English men and women. A French woman loves and gives herself; but to excite passion, "pour passer le temps"— "never," she declared. I said she was wrong, that "flirting" and "coquetry" were one and the same thing: the effect it produced depended entirely on the man and woman's moral character. She laughed and shrugged her shoulders unconvinced. She told me that on her first visit to England a supper was given in her honour; she was treated like a queen, and felt a queen. Her host, when seeing her to her carriage "stole a kiss." She did not speak to him again for years. It was *abominable,* she said, *abominable.* It showed he had no respect for her. I tried vainly to explain that flirting did not necessarily mean kissing, she only repeated *abominable.*

Sarah's love of animals is very remarkable, and she was always buying a new pet. One morning at the hotel, when we were playing together at Liverpool, I heard strange and terrible growls, and coarse men's voices coming from her room. I went in and found two low-looking ruffians. They had inside a large iron cage a wild tiger-cat. Sarah was saying, "Il sera plus heureux si vous ouvrez la porte," pointing to the not very secure iron door of the cage. The men were suggesting that the door could be opened later, and that they wanted £30.

WITH MADAME SARAH BERNHARDT IN "PELLÉAS AND MÉLISANDE"

It was not till I persuaded Sarah that such animals cannot be tamed, and that it would break out of the cage in an hour or so and probably eat her up, that she said it might be a trouble on tour and she would not keep it. The men were furious, and I had great difficulty in getting rid of them.

On one occasion I remember Sarah was charged in her hotel bill for thirty or forty bottles of beer for her servants. We had stayed there only one day and night.

Sarah was tired, and did not stop to think that her servants might have treated friends; she only knew they could not have drunk so many bottles of beer. The manager was sent for, and she argued with him until she raged. Hearing the raised voices I went into the room. The man was white and trembling; and I saw Sarah was almost ill with anger. When I had grasped her argument, I turned to the manager, saying: "What matter how many bottles of beer have been drunk, how dare you contradict Madame?" My voice was the loudest, and the man rushed distracted from the room.

Her company indiscreetly told me that Madame Sarah had never been known to make fun, or to laugh on the stage. In a tobacconist's shop I saw a tobacco pouch made in the shape of a fish, and painted to represent one. I bought it, took it to the theatre, and tied it down to a bit of canvas at the bottom of the well at the Fountain.

At the performance, when Sarah came to the second act and stood by the *fontaine des aveugles,* she spied the fish and began improvising about *les poissons là.* . . . She stooped gracefully over the edge to take the fish out; as it was tied, she nearly lost her balance. Without concern she went on calmly with her part. I laughed, spoiling my lovely little scene.

When the curtain fell Sarah did not allude to what had happened, neither did I. The next day when we lunched together she had a strange, preoccupied expression on her face. Later, at the matinée, when we came to the Cave scene, at the point where she tenderly takes my hand and helps me over the rocks, she took hold of my hand, hard—squash—she held a raw egg in hers.

I did not smile, but with calm dignity I went on with my part. I can see now the tears of laughter trickling down her cheeks, and her dear body shaking with merriment as I grew more and more dignified to the end of the scene.

Her company told me afterwards almost with awe, that Madame must love me very, very much.

The most beautiful performance I have ever seen was a performance Sarah gave of *Phédre*—she held a crowded house spellbound for over two hours, with scarcely a movement or gesture to detract from the lovely Alexandrines—the great pulsating passion seemed to wind about the audience like a web—it was magic.

They tell me Sarah had seen the great Rachel's

performance—what 1 saw was her own: I knew it by the sequence of its beauty.

The world knows her genius and her colossal courage; but not everyone knows the thought and affection she has always ready in her heart for her friends.

At a most tragic moment for her, she remembered my anxiety and sent me this cable to America:

"Doctor will cut off my leg next Monday. Am very happy. Kisses all my heart.
"SARAH BERNHARDT, Bordeaux."

To go back to 1898, *Pelléas and Mélisande* at the Lyceum was followed in September by Mr. Robertson's production of *Macbeth*. We had already played it in the English provinces and in Germany.

I have since learned that it was easier to act Lady Macbeth with Mr. Robertson than with Mr. James Hackett, with whom I played the part afterwards in 1920.

Perhaps Mr. Robertson was inclined to look upon Lady Macbeth as the "star" part, to use the word of the theatre. Mr. Hackett surely looked upon Macbeth as the solar system. It seemed to me, he realised my presence only at his "cues," and more than once seized the opportunity during a strong speech of mine to turn his back to the audience and clear a troublesome catarrh.

We were all proud of Mr. Hackett's success. It was undeniable: his splendid Salvini-like voice—no perceptible American accent—made a great impression. But he had a strange effect upon me; I could not for one moment forget I was on the stage. On his first night I was suffering from an influenza cold; an apology to the audience would have depressed the occasion; there was nothing to do but get through.

I wore Mélisande's dresses (twelve years old and made of gossamer). The dresses for Lady Macbeth in Mr. Hackett's wardrobe did not fit me, so that in no way was I in tune with Mr. Hackett's overwhelming Macbeth.

Mr. Bernard Shaw wrote to me at the time as follows:

Macbeth as a production was an ancient Victorian absurdity. Hackett is still in the eighteenth century. He would have done just as well with Miss R— S—, as you could have done just as well with Mr. A— S—; the intervals with the entr'acte music played sixteen times over killed the play. People know that it is not Shakespeare who is the bore, and that B—— or B—— A—— could have made a success of it with principals at £15 a week.

"As it happened, when I saw it, you made only a few blunders:

"1. You should not have played the dagger scene in that best evening dress of Lady M., but in a black wrap, like a thunder cloud, with a white face.

"2. You should not have repeated the exit business by

which Macbeth conveyed that he was going to see a ghost on every step of the stairs up to Duncan. You should have gone straight off like a woman of iron.

"3. You should not have forgotten that there was blood on your hand and on his, and that you dared not touch one another for fear of messing your clothes with gore.

"4. In the sleep-walking scene, you should not have rubbed your hands realistically (drat the blood, it won't come off), nor worn an idiotic confection that wound your feet up more and more at every step and finally pitched you—off the stage—on your head. That scene needs the whole cavernous depth of the stage and the draperies of a ghost. It was maddening to hear you deliver the lines splendidly and be in a different class to all the others and then throw it all away by half a dozen stupidities that the call boy could have corrected. . . .

"G. B. S."

As a matter of fact, I was out of gear with Mr. Hackett's method, and by his side my performance was very ineffective.

But I must not jump the years like this.

Of the Lyceum performance, I quote Mr. A. B. Walkley's criticism: "Mrs. Campbell's Lady Macbeth is also novel and interesting, but it is also something more, and something very important—it is a perfectly possible and plausible interpretation of the character. . . . There are reasons à priori why Mrs. Campbell should find no particular difficulty, 'modern' though she be, with the part of Lady Macbeth. Where her modernity comes in is in the substitution of a mysterious sensuous charm for the conventional domineering of a virago. I have tried to sum up this type in the words of 'Baudelairean.' I see that my friend, the theatrical critic of *The Leader,* calls it an Aubrey Beardsley type, which is another way of putting exactly the same thing. The woman clings and kisses and casts a spell, she magnetises her Thane. When words fail she rests her two hands on his shoulders, almost winds herself round him, looks him straight in the eyes with a strange smile, and the poor man melts like wax. It is the 'Baudelaire' enchantress, the 'femme serpent,' and, as I have already said, it delights me—partly because, like every other man in the audience, I cannot but feel something of the fascination that overcomes Macbeth, partly because it appeals to me as true, for Macbeth was moulded by his wife, not merely by the influence of a strong will over a faltering will, but by the witchery of woman over man."

CHAPTER X.

IN June, 1899, I produced *Carlyon Sahib,* by Professor Gilbert Murray, at the Kennington Theatre. It met with little success, though it seemed to me a very good play.

At this time some friends of mine, including, among others, Lord Grey,* Dr. Jameson,† and the late Lady Meux, offered to put, under the control of Mr. Bouchier F. Hawksley, £12,000 (at some arranged interest and return of their money) to "back" me in management.

The enterprise filled me with enthusiasm, but I felt ungrateful at the idea of exploiting myself independently of Mr. Forbes Robertson, after the fine parts I had played under his management, and I begged that he should be included in the venture.

This at first met with some objection, but finally I won my way.

Mr. Robertson was under contract to produce a Japanese play, *The Moonlight Blossom,* by Mr. C. B. Fernald (author of the *Cat and the Cherub*). As I remember, he agreed to join me if this play was our first production. Though I did not particularly care for Mr. Fernald's play, I accepted the con-

* Late Governor-General of Canada.
† Sir Starr Jameson.

dition, and we started management at the Prince of
Wales Theatre in September, 1899, with *The Moonlight Blossom.*

The production was a most expensive one; the
piece a disastrous failure. The papers said Mr.
Robertson looked like "Widow Twankey," Mr.
Bernard Shaw wrote that I was "a child playing a
tune with one finger"; our attempt at impersonating
Japanese met with no success.

To try and save the situation we added to the
programme, after about three weeks, a one-act play,
The Sacrament of Judas; translated from the French
of M. Louis Tiercelin by Mr. Louis N. Parker for
Mr. Robertson. This one-act play, though successful, unfortunately did not help matters financially.

The next production was *The Canary,* by George
Fleming, (Miss Constance Fletcher), on November
15th. Mr. Robertson's personality was not suited
to any character in this comedy, and he decided to
break our partnership. This seemed to me unfair
to the enterprise; so much money having been
dropped on *The Moonlight Blossom,* and the expense of launching the dual management. However,
I returned him his plays, and Mr. Gerald du Maurier ·acted the leading part in *The Canary.*

My losses, I was told, were over £5,000. There
was nothing to do but to get into a smaller theatre
and try and pull things through. This I did, taking
the Royalty at a rental of £90 a week. I opened

there on the 28th of January, continuing the run of *The Canary;* and retaining the business staff of the Prince of Wales—including Mr. Ian Robertson (Mr. Forbes Robertson's brother) as stage manager.

On February 19th I revived *Magda,* and played with it *Mrs. Jordan,* a charming one-act play by Miss Constance Smedley. The work was hard and my responsibilities great, but I was supported by an excellent company.

The following letter shows my effort was sometimes obvious to the audience:

> "3, Whitehall Gardens, S. W.,
> "February 28th, 1900.
>
> "Madam,
>
> "It appears from the papers that you propose playing *Magda* and *Mrs. Jordon* at two matinées weekly, in addition to nightly performances.
>
> "I was fortunate enough to see your impersonation of both characters last night, and the absolute pathos of your appearence at the close of the second act, utterly tired out—'done,' as you seemed—haunts me still, and led many of those round me to express their fears that the task you had set yourself would prove too heavy. May I, if I may do so without offence, voice what, I am sure, must have been the feeling of the whole house last night, and ask, for the sake of the public, who cannot afford to run any risk of losing you—apart from any consideration of yourself—that you spare yourself, if possible, the terrible strain of at least one of the two weekly matinées?

"Could you have seen yourself as we saw you last night, you would understand how the house felt about you, and would pardon, as I trust you will, the expression of that feeling.

"PITTITE."

Magda ran five months. An incident of some interest occurred during this revival.

Mr. Albert Gran gave a very remarkable performance in the insignificant part of the young lieutenant, Max von Wendelowski—the late Lord Wemyss told me this clever young actor appeared to bring the German army on to the stage with him.

Mr. Gran had to leave me in a few weeks to keep a contract he had with another management, but he promised to give in his fortnight's notice after the first week, wishing to return and continue in his success with me.

I asked Mr. Ian Robertson to engage Mr. Granville Barker for the period of Mr. Gran's absence, and this he did.

After Mr. Gran returned to the Royalty, Mr. Granville Barker wrote to me saying he was entitled to his salary for the run of *Magda*. I discussed the matter with Mr. Bouchier Hawksley, who, after, I believe, some correspondence with Mr. Barker, advised me to take the matter into court, as there was neither letter nor contract to support Mr. Barker's claim.

I was interested in the idea of being in a court,

and dressed myself in my best. Mr. Barker, on the other hand, seemed to me to appear in very shabby clothes and a much worn straw hat.

Mr. Fred Kerr—that delightful actor—stated that, unless specially stipulated by letter or contract, the precedent was a fortnight's notice.

I went into the witness-box and explained that I had made it clear to my stage manager, that Mr. Granville Barker's services were required only during Mr. Gran's absence.

Mr. Barker, in the witness-box, whilst admitting there was no letter or contract said the verbal understanding between him and Mr. Ian Robertson was "for the run of the play," otherwise he would not have accepted the engagement.

Mr. Ian Robertson, on being called, remarked that he did not remember what he had said in the interview with Mr. Barker. He was chided by the judge, who asked him if it was not his business to remember, or words to that effect.

The Jury left the court and returned, giving the verdict to the plaintiff—£60 was, I think, the sum claimed.

I turned to Mr. Hawksley and said: "What do I do now?"

"Go and shake hands and congratulate him," he replied with a smile.

Mr. Granville Barker did not look as triumphant as I thought he ought to, and I will go to my grave believing that he owes me £60.

My management at the Royalty was a success, both with the critics and the public. My work had become more free, and more assured; but nothing could be done financially, against most disastrous difficulties.

The Boer War was breaking people's hearts, and then—later—Queen Victoria's death, which emptied the theatres for many weeks.

At home we were all anxious. Pat had decided to join Lord Chesham's Yeomanry, and he left for Africa towards the middle of March, 1900.

On April the 5th poor Pat was killed.

I remember how I heard the news. My uncle met me at the theatre. It was Saturday; there had been two performances. He said: "Let us drive to the War Office and see if there is any news." He told me to wait in the hansom. He returned in a few moments, saying: "There is no news." For the rest of the drive he was silent.

When we arrived at my house in Kensington Square we went in and sat in the dining room. I noticed how white and drawn his face was and how questioningly he looked at me. I spoke of my plans at the theatre. Suddenly there was a knock at the front door. I opened it. Mr. Shackle—Pat's friend and my acting manager—stood there. He said: "It's true." I asked: "What is true?" He answered: "Pat is killed." I realized that uncle had known all the time.

We three sat without speaking; at last uncle said:
"I don't like leaving you alone, dear." I answered:
"Stella is sleeping with me to-night."

Then they left—letting themselves out.

A strange thing happened. I found I could not
move from my chair. How long it was before I
pulled myself up and was able to get to the foot of
the stairs I do not know, but I remember well the
climb up the staircase, both hands on the one banis-
ter. . . .

I took Stella in my arms. . . .

I whispered very gently to her what had happened—"Poor Daddy has been killed"—I felt her
little body tremble; she held me tightly. "Oh,
mother," she said. . . .

I kept quite quiet and she fell asleep again. . . .

I thought of my boy studying for his entrance examination into the Navy—it might put him off his
work—

Gradually I fell into a very deep sleep—

Sunday, the front door bell rang and rang; letters
and cards were dropped into the letter-box. Monday brought many hundreds more. I saw one or two
friends; they seemed strangers to me. The theatre
was closed; it was Holy Week. I went away with
Stella into the country. My boy wrote:—

"H. M. S. Britannia,
"Dartmouth.
"My darling Mother,
"Thank you so much for your letter. I am so mis-

erable about poor, dear daddy. The chaplain has just told me about him. I want to be at home so much now to be able to comfort you. I was confirmed to-day by the Bishop of Exeter. Only one week and four days now to the holidays. All next week is exams. Poor, dear daddy! It was rather hard the news coming on my confirmation day. Don't worry, mummy, dear. I wish I was home to comfort you.

"With all the world and the stars and seas and sun full of love and kisses and comfort from.

"Your Loving Son.
"Beo."

And again he wrote:—

"Darling Mother,

"Thank you so much for the telegram. I had a talk with the chaplain, and decided to wait till the end of the term, as two of the exams count in the final examination: but I wish I could come home a day earlier—that is, on the Wednesday, as there will be such a bustle on the last day, and the chaps who are in the carriage I am in will want to fool about, and they might not just because I was there. On Wednesday I could travel down with a very nice boy called FitzGibbon. He was one of the first to hear about poor daddy, and he sent me a letter, which he put in my locker. I enclose it. This boy has to go to France, and, therefore, goes a day earlier. Tell me what you think.

"Give my lovingest love to Stella.

"I am glad daddy died fighting and doing his duty, for you have to die some time, and it's much better to die gloriously than at home in bed.

"All the world and stars and suns and moons full of love.

"Your loving son,
"Beo."

"Dear Mrs. Campbell,

"Your son was confirmed by the Bishop of Exeter yesterday, and I was so sorry to have to tell him afterwards of his loss.   He is in grief, but, as he says, he cannot realise it fully; it will come with memory later.   I have had further talk with him to-day, and he thinks perhaps he had better face his sorrow and just go on with his work and the coming examination, especially as the end of the term is near, when he can join you.   Captain O'Callaghan left him free to do what he thought best about coming home, and he has decided in this way.   I think that under the circumstances your son has taken a right view of what is best to be done.   He is not a boy who loses his balance easily, and, though he is in grief, I think he will acquit himself creditably in his examination.*

"A. W. Plant (Chaplain)."

Lord Chesham cabled:—

"Patrick Campbell was killed instantaneously in final attack, and was buried with military honours in Boshof cemetery.   I have written you full details."

* Beo passed, at his first trial, fifth on the list in his first competitive examination in life, out of two hundred competitors of the same age.

"Camp Moliens Farm,
"Orange Free State,
"10th Imperial Yeomanry.
"My dear Mrs. Campbell,

"I write to you in great grief to tell you how sincerely we of the 10th Imperial Yeomanry sympathise with you in the terrible affliction which has come to you. We feel with you and for you. We have lost a fine soldier and a good friend, and honour him for himself; at the same time he has ended his short career with the greatest honour that can come to a man.

"We attacked the enemy. Patrick Campbell was among the first (we were within fifty yards of the Boers with fixed bayonets and charging) when he fell, death being instantaneous. We, his comrades, honour him as a brave soldier, and the ten prisoners (chiefly Frenchmen) also said to me how gallantly our men had fought. No one was doing better in the regiment than your husband, and his loss will be much felt. We lost two officers besides, and our three brave comrades now lie in the cemetery at Boshof, with the French general (who was killed in the action), Villebois de Mareuil, near to their graves.

"We buried them by moonlight on April 6th with many a sore heart as the bugles sounded 'The Last Post' over the graves of three as brave Englishmen as had fallen in the war.

"I hope you will forgive me writing to you as I do. I have had much trouble myself, and so write, knowing how powerless attempts at any comfort are and how little good writing can do, but to assure you of the very deep sympathy all ranks of the regiment offer to you and of the high respect they feel for your gallant husband.

"Believe me,
"Yours sincerely
"CHESHAM."

Courtesy Sun and New York Herald Syndicate

IN "MRS. JORDAN"

I find my letter to my uncle written during Holy Week:—

"Sevenoaks.

"My darling Uncle,

"We are quite safe and it's beautiful here, and now I am going to try and write some letters. Don't you, dear uncle, feel torn and worried? Remember all you have done for him and for his children and for me . . . and if you didn't discourage him from going remember his going has brought him glory and peace and the everlasting respect and honour of those he loved. . . .

"Don't worry about me, dear uncle. When I see you again I shall be quite brave and strong and ready for work. You have helped me bear so much. . . .

"Your loving
"BEATRICE."

These letters brought their comfort:—

"Saighton Grange,
"Chester,
"May 17th.

"Dearest,

"I think of you so, and the last letters must be reaching you now. I have copied an account of that day from a letter of my brother * to his wife, which I enclose. I daresay you would rather not read it now, dear little one, but I thought you might like to put it by with others for your boy.

"Do not answer this; it must be such a hard time for

* Lord Scarborough.

you now, but your work will help you.   I hope you have seen angel Mrs. Wyndham and George.†

"Yours Affectionately,

‡ "SYBIL GROSVENOR."

These two letters from Lord Wemyss were written within a few hours:

"23, St. James, Place,

"Saturday night.

" . . .

"You will have heard, why we did not come behind the scenes to see you, and surely no greater compliment could be paid to a great artist, than the tears, the soul-shaken state of my daughter Hilda.*   She says she could come every night, and I feel as she does—only, alas! I hear now almost nothing; and thus lose so much that if it were not for your unequalled expressive gestures, I had best stay at home.

"How delighted your audience is with you.   The wonder is your being able to stand a matinée as well; you looked so beautiful throughout.

"Hope you have good accounts of 'My Pat,' and that your child's knee is well.

"All good with Stella.

"Yours,

"W."

† The Right Hon. George Wyndham, M. P.

‡ The Countess Grosvenor, wife of Mr. George Wyndham and mother of the present Duke of Westminster.

* The late Lady Hilda Brodrick.

"Sunday morning.

"Oh my poor friend,

"Is there anything it is possible for me to do? You know how gladly would I help you, body, soul, and spirit, if I could. Send for me if you would like to see me, or if I can be of any use to you or your child.

"And to think of you *last night* and *this morning!*

"The enclosed I had written last night to send this morning.

"I may well say, 'Good with Stella.'

"Yours,
"W."

"Her Majesty's Theatre.

"My dear Mrs. Campbell,

"I saw the report of your husband's death, and am writing to you to express my sincere condolence. You will, I know, be very sad at his loss, but he could not have wished for a better death. I always found him good and kind and full of charm and love of you.

". . . .

"HERBERT TREE."

"Fountain Court,
"The Temple.

"Dear Mrs. Campbell,

"I cannot help (though at the risk of seeming intrusive) writing to say how deeply sorry I am at the news I have just heard, coming at the very moment when you have proved to the whole world that you are the only actress on the English stage worth listening to. It is as though you have thus to suffer to counterbalance that triumph of your art, but do remember, even while you suffer, that only suffering greatens one when one is an artist, and that you will be a greater artist in the future for every bit of suffering that you go through now. There is no other consolation for unhappiness, but may one not accept so much consolation? It is what I wish for you with all my heart.

"Believe me, dear Mrs. Campbell,

"Always your most sincere,

"ARTHUR SYMONS."

"Strode,

"Ivybridge,

"S. Devon.

"My dearest Mrs. Campbell,

". . . I am so glad to feel that he was so happy the last few months, and I like to think of how well and happy he looked that last Sunday, when he said 'Goodbye' and he was so full of hope. . . .

"I will, if you like, talk to you more of the days at Enfield when he used to talk to me of you. He always said, 'if you knew her you would love her.' I do love you, and I would give anything to be able to help you bear this pain.

"Yours always,

"FLO SHACKLE."†

After joining Lord Chesham, Pat had written to me:—

"White Hart Hotel,

"Dearest Stella,

"I am hard at work down here and everything looks very bright to me. I messed up with Lard Chesham

† Mrs. Frank Shackle.

and all his officers last night; they were all very nice to me, and I think I shall be of great service to him. I easily passed my riding and shooting test, and see the doctor to-morrow. I understand I shall have no difficulty in passing my medical.

"Chesham has asked me to stay down to-morrow and help inspect some recruits and horses. They have a splendid lot of men here, and he hopes to get us off by the 20th at latest.

"I am so glad the recitation goes so well. I knew it would.

"With love to you and the children.

"PAT."

"I really think I'll have a good chance."

Seven days' quiet and then I returned to play *Magda* again at the Royalty Theatre. The house was crowded. I was bound to struggle desperately against the sympathetic applause of the audience, or I could not have gone on. Some of them wept, and so did the actors. At the end I was exhausted.

In my dressing-room I quickly slipped into my black dress—someone had persuaded me to buy heavy mourning; the skirt had a deep hem of crêpe —I did not think of changing my stockings, which were pale pink.

At the stage door, the little dark passage leading to the pavement was full of people, chiefly elderly women dressed in black. As I passed them they whispered, "Poor thing!" I lifted my foot to step into the hansom cab, and I heard a startled and horrified "Oh!" from those standing nearest me—my pale pink stockings had looked like bare legs. The humour of it bit into my heart—I felt a clown.

We started almost at once rehearsing—for a series of matinées—*The Fantasticks,* cleverly adapted by "George Fleming" from Edmond Rostand's *Les Romanesques,* Gerald du Maurier playing the leading part. *Magda* was still in the evening bill. Also we revived for four matinées, *Pelléas and Mèlisande,* with Mr. Martin Harvey playing his original *rôle.*

My season ended on July 14th with a matinèe of *Pelléas and Mélisande,* and an evening performance of *Magda.*

Then there was a provincial tour, returning to the Royalty with *Mr. and Mrs. Daventry*—written by Mr. Frank Harris on a synopsis by Oscar Wilde— both Mr. Frederick Kerr and Mr. du Maurier distinguished themselves in this play. Then matinées of Mr. Max Beerbohm's *The Happy Hypocrite;* a production of *Mariana,* by José Echegaray; a revival of *The Notorious Mrs. Ebbsmith;* and a revival of *The Second Mrs. Tanqueray.*

All this work was done in a little over eighteen months against tragic odds, in the vain hope of saving the remaining £6,000 of the "backers" money, but all of it and more had gone. Mr. Bouchier Hawksley explained the calamitous position, and then he and I with a dear friend of mine—Miss Melicent Stone—had a long talk.

I would not hear of bankruptcy. I felt I must be allowed to make one more effort.

In the end Mr. Hawksley agreed to my plan—to go to America, signing a document with him to give half or three-quarters of my weekly earnings towards paying back my creditors—it was about 3 A. M. when this interview was over.

I had a telegram from Lord Grey next day; "Congratulations on all night sitting."

An agreement was come to with Messrs. Liebler and Co., for a tour of twenty-two weeks in the United States, with the repertoire I had played at the Royalty Theatre on these terms—according to notes I have:

Messrs. Leibler would pay the salaries of my company and all travelling expenses, paying me £200 a week, and 15 per cent. to £1,000, 20 per cent, to £2,000, and 35 per cent. on all over; on the gross weekly takings.

It was arranged that I should do a short tour of the English provinces before sailing. This I did, returning to the Royalty Theatre to produce *Beyond Human Power* by Björnstjerne Björnson—translated into English by Miss Jessie Muir for nine matinées.

The play tells the story of the bedridden wife of a Faith-Healer. She cannot move, and for weeks she has not slept.

The play opens with the visit of an American

sister-in-law to the sick woman; who describes her husband's divine "healing" gift. She tells how he goes for miles and miles across the fjords to heal the sick, believing that he "walks with God."

"Why does he not heal *you* then?" the visitor asks. The woman answers, "Because I do not *believe.*" Her husband has told her that if she will only have 'faith' she will be cured.

He arranges to have a service in the church, where he will pray until she sleeps. The church bell will continue ringing to let her know that he is praying. He says their two children must also kneel by her bed and pray, until she falls asleep.

. . . The children come in and kneel by her bed. The church bell rings. Suddenly there is a tremendous unearthly noise; a great avalanche falls down the mountain side, destroying everything in its way, but leaving the church untouched.

The noise is heard of people screaming and shouting and running about in fear—the children rush to the window crying out what they see, then back to the bed to comfort the poor bedridden woman, who, they think, is dumb with terror. The noise subsides, and as they lean over the bed looking into her face the curtain comes down on the words, "Mother's asleep!"

It is a miracle—God has answered the prayers.

In the next act there is a great discussion between various pastors as to the meaning of what has happened. The husband is still praying in the church and the bell is still ringing—he has been praying two days and two nights.

The neighbours want to see the sleeping woman. The pastor returns, the choir singing follow him into the room.

The bedroom door opens, his wife enters and walks across the room with her arms stretched out towards him. He comes forward to embrace her, his face radiant with joy, as she drops down dead at his feet. The pastor gives an agonised cry as he says, "This is not what I meant, not this!"

I quote a few interesting letters:—

"10 Adelphi Terrace, W.C.

"My dear Mrs. Patrick Campbell,

"That was a really great managerial achievement. In future, when people ask me whether I go to the theatre I shall say, 'To the Royalty, not to any other.'

"I think the 'Hallelujah Chorus' might be improved by steeping in boiling water for ten minutes or so before the next matinée. And if *Rachel* must have a scream at the end, it might be well to give her, at rehearsal, something to scream for. Titheradge was so remarkable a parson that you really ought to play *Candida* (*Candida* is an old play of my own, with a most parsonic parson in it), for his benefit; he would cover himself with glory as *Candida's* husband; but he is wrong to gurgle like *Othello* cutting his throat. That scene gets far beyond the screaming and gurgling kind of realism. These physical obstructions and inconveniences have no business among the spiritual agonies. May I suggest, too, that Titheradge's determination to die parallel to the "floats" with his heels O.P.* and his head P., whilst you occupy the corresponding position P. and O.P., rather spoils the picture? After all, it is not natural that he should die unassisted, especially after gurgling; and it would be a great improvement if he would breath his last in the arms of Horatio—say the sceptical parson who wants the miracle. That would compose the picture much better. It is one of the drawbacks to your power of rousing people's sense of beauty that even trifles jar on it if they are unbecoming.

"However, all that is nothing. The impression was overwhelming.

"Yours enthusiastically,
"G. BERNARD SHAW.

". . . . I was greatly touched when Mrs. Theodore Wright, who was a friend of Karl Marx, and has been in all sorts of revolutionary circles got so indignant at the conduct of Pastor Lang that she clenched her fists and glared at the wickedness of religion, instead of giving you your cue—the 'My dear' cue. Forgive her—it was a generous slip."

And in another letter from him:—

"Thank you for the beautiful photograph; but I should have photographed you in bed, saying, 'It's tempting Providence.' That was the finest passage in the play. After all, there are lots of beautiful people about; and some of them can, perhaps, even thread needles with their toes; but they can't take a filament of grey matter from their brains and thread it through that most elusive of

* Opposite Prompter.

eyelet holes in the top of a dramatist's needle. Besides, that produces a new sort of beauty, compared to which natural beauty is a mere reach-me-down from Nature's patterns. Long ago, when everybody was maudlin about your loveliness, I snapped my fingers—admired nothing but your deft fingers and toes. Now I admire you *enormously*. You have picked the work of Nature to pieces and remade it whole heavens finer. It is the power to do that that is the real gift. . . ."

"I wish you had a theatre of your own; for if the Lord Chamberlain suspended you, I could make a revolution within half-an hour of the announcement.

"The enclosed letter is from one of my Reverend Nonconformist constituents. He wrote to me in great excite-about *Beyond Human Power*. I wrote back urging him to write to the *Times* and to get a lot of other Divines to sign with him.

"Unluckily, Massingham took the words of the Lord out of the Minister's mouth.

"Yours sincerely,
"G. Bernard Shaw."

"National Liberal Club.
"Dear Mrs. Campbell,
"That was simply glorious this afternoon. It has left me exulting. I go home on Saturday morning, but will write again about this. . . .
"Gilbert Murray."

". . . I knew nothing whatever of the play before I went, and was taken by storm. . . . I thought your acting, if I may say so, even better than I have seen it before—so firm and full of nobility as well as very subtle. . . . You must have studied church congresses with a minute care which I should not have expected in you, to arrange those clergymen so beautifully. I though that scene most excellent comedy of a very delicate kind. . . .

"But the whole conception was so fine. I had been three times to the Théâtre Français the week before, and I enjoyed your Björnstjerne Björnson quite infinitely more. . . .

"GILBERT MURRAY."

"17, Hanover Terrace,
"N.W.

"Dear Mrs. Patrick Campbell,
"Permit me to congratulate you very warmly on your wonderfully delicate and spiritual performance this afternoon. We have come back dazed like people who have seen a vision. . . .

"Quite apart from the transcendent beauty of your personal part in the piece, you claim the highest applause from every serious-minded person for your courage in presenting a poem, the interest of which is so unusual and so intellectual. Just behind where we sat the critic of one of the biggest newspapers sat snuffling and wriggling, and I heard him mutter (just at the most exquisite point of your third scene), 'Fancy coming to a thing like this! It is about as amusing as a funeral!'

"Thank you again for an immense pleasure, in which and with kindest remembrances my wife joins me.
"Yours very sincerely,
"EDMUND GOSSE."

The following letters from my friend, Mr. W. B. Yeats are particularly interesting:—

"18 Woburn Buildings.

"Dear Mrs. Patrick Campbell,

". . . Will you permit me to thank you by letter for the performance? Your acting seemed to me to have the perfect precision and delicacy and simplicity of every art at its best. It made me feel the unity of the arts in a new way. I said to myself, that is exactly what I am trying to do in writing, to express myself without waste, without emphasis. To be impassioned and yet to have a perfect self-possession, to have a precision so absolute that the slightest inflection of voice, the slightest rhythm of sound or emotion plucks the heart-strings. But do you know that you acted too well; you made me understand a defect in Björnson's play which I had felt but had not understood when I read it. Björnson's hero could only have done those seen or real miracles by having a religious genius. Now the very essence of genius, of whatever kind, is precision, and that hero of his has no precision. He is a mere zealous man with a vague sentimental mind—the kind of man who is anxious about the Housing of the Working Classes, but not the kind of man who sees what Blake called 'The Divine Vision and Fruition.' I happen to have in my pocket 'The Revelation of Divine Love,' by the Lady Julian, an old mystical book; my hand strayed to it all unconsciously. There was no essential difference between that work and your acting; both were full of fine distinction, of delicate logic, of that life where passion and thought are one. Both were utterly unlike Björnson's hero.

"The actor played him to the life; but I was miserable until he was off the stage. He was an unbeliever's dream of a believer, an atheist's Christian. . . .

". . . . .

"W. B. Yeats."

"18, Woburn Buildings.

". . . . Yes, I agree with you that Björnson's play is a fine thing—living, passionate, touching issues of life and death. In London the subjects which people think suitable for drama get fewer every day. Shelley said that when a social order was in decay, the arts attached themselves to the last things people were interested in— imaginatively interested in. Here people look on the world with more and more prosaic eyes, as Shelley said they did in dying Greece. There, as here, nothing kept its beauty but irregular love-making. He called the poetry that had irregular love for subject and was called immoral, 'The Footsteps of Astrea departing from the world.'

". . . . .

"W. B. YEATS."

". . . I have no right to criticise the play, but I must say I think the solemnity of it is marred in the second act by a stupid introduction of the comic element when those parsons are met together, and I would give much for that controversy or symposium upon the question of miracles to be re-written up to the present standard of thought. The remarks on both sides are a hundred years behind the age, but the play as a whole will do good, and the first act is one of the most impressive scenes I have ever witnessed on the stage. The dual problem proposed is the most momentous that can occupy the mind of man:—

"(1) What think ye of Christ?

"(2) What *is* answer to prayer?

" 'Oh, I didn't mean *that*.' The pathos, the disappointment of it! And yet thus it must be if we believe that it is an all-loving and all-knowing Father to whom we pray.

"Some day I should so like to talk over this play with you.

"With renewed thanks for giving me this treat.

" . . . .

"BASIL WILBERFORCE
"(Archdeacon of Westminster)."

CHAPTER XI.

I OPENED in Chicago at the Opera House on the 7th of January, 1902.

Again, as on my "first appearance on any stage" so many years before, the audience seemed a hundred miles away. The enormous proscenium opening—the scene on the stage only the few chairs, the table, the bowl of goldfish, the writing-desk, the couch, and the antimacassars of *Magda.*—

I could not go out to that huge audience, and so again I "gathered" them up to myself. "How did you do that?" the reader will say; it is very difficult to answer.

I have heard it called "hypnotic" power, as when an Indian throw a rope up into the air and climbs it before your eyes.

A certain hesitancy, shaping of pauses, tentativeness, sudden precision, instinctive rhythmical movement, calling with my heart—"Love, and listen, to what I believe true and beautiful"—how much personality helps, I do not pretend to know; but I am sure my gift is no more than that of a robin redbreast when he sings. . . .

I remember the applause at the end of the first act had an extraordinary quality: it was a roar that seemed to say: "Ah! this is true, we are not going to be bluffed"—and I felt I had won.

Nowhere in the world are artists received with more warmth and enthusiasm than in Chicago—that city where men fight against heat that stifles, and snows that kill: the miles of great, bare, flat front between you and beautiful Lake Michigan: not sand or stone, but black mud. . . .Further along are the great palaces, the "homes" of the millionaires, looking on to that gorgeous lake that seems to reach to the end of the world—sometimes calm, sometimes with gigantic opalesque waves. . . .

Before the curtain was down on the last act, I knew I was wonderfully rich in *friends*. All that applause could not be for my talent: I felt they had taken a fancy to me!

And then the good time they gave me—

The balls, the dinners, the suppers, the luncheons, the musical parties—on the same evening Paderewski and Kreisler!—the flowers—roses as tall as girls—the sweets—the books.

Mrs Arthur Caton, Mrs. Spencer Eddie, Mrs. Franklyn Macveagh; and many, many others. Their gaiety, their broad, liberal spirit, their unstinted hospitality, and their loyalty and frankness—it was intoxicating.

How long ago! I have made six visits since, and incidents of this first visit may get mixed up in my mind with incidents of other visits—but one stands distinct.

I remember Mrs. Macveagh saying at a luncheon party—where only ladies were present—that the most immoral woman is no worse than the most moral man. I wanted dreadfully to get up and make a speech, but I was young and very uncertain upon questions of life and morals.

I had been brought up to believe that woman is the Mother of Goodness, so that immorality in a woman is the worst that could happen.

But I said nothing of this at that luncheon party. I enjoyed the novelty, the fun, and the amusing talk, and the pretty clothes.

The following letter from Mr. Bertram, my business man (whom I had taken on from the Prince of Wales Theatre to the Royalty Theatre, and had now brought to America), to my uncle, gives an idea of the financial success of this American tour:

"C|o Lieblers and Co., Knickerbocker Theatre Buildings,
"New York City,
"21st Jan., 1902.

"Dear Mr. Tanner,

"In reply to your letter of the 10th inst., I am delighted to say that Mrs. Campbell is both an artistic and financial success; if I tried to explain how great her success was, I am afraid you would think I was exaggerating. We are playing in a small theatre to the same prices as charged only by Sir Henry Irving and Sarah Bernhardt, and you know the amount of scenery and the large company they travel; in our case there is only Mrs. Campbell. Why, in Chicago all records were beaten. Mrs. Campbell holds the record house, the record matinée, the record week, and the record for the city, for no star has played to so much money in two weeks as she did; the gross receipts for the two weeks were nearly £7,000.

"I am so pleased she is playing her repertoire, for one critic may like her Paula and Magda and run down her Clara Sang, and another critic praise her Clara Sang and not like her Paula and Magda. Another thing that has to be considered is, we are not playing with the Syndicate, and they try to influence the press against her, but it does not matter, the public buy up the seats, and at every performance the house is sold out and the spectators obtain advanced prices on the side walk. Only last night I saw people buying single seats at $5 (£1) that we had charged $3 (12s.) for.

"We play *Pelléas and Mélisande* Tuesday and Thursday next week at a larger theatre for two matinées only, and the advance sale is enormous. In three weeks Mrs. Campbell has sent over £2,000 to Mr. Hawksley. At this rate we shall very soon have cleared off all the debts of her syndicate, and she will have money of her own to commence work again.

"I have sent you to-day some more cuttings, both good and bad, but the press here is so different to England, no one takes any notice of it.

"Yours faithfully,
"A. BERTRAM."

On our arrival in New York—I took to America my faithful Julia,* my little griffon, and a maid—

---

* Dear Julia was my dresser for twenty years. She came to me first as maid to my children.

two or three hotels refused to take my dog. At last we settled at the Park Avenue Hotel.

When I arrived I found twelve men with notebooks waiting for me in the reception-room—"Interviewers."

The fool I felt was beyond words to describe—and I am afraid I said something like this: "How perfectly dreadful, why do you do it? Is it for your living? It seems to me so insulting."

But they wrote kindly of me, and I grew to like their sharp-cut features and intelligent faces and their eager outlook for something to write about—in their parlance, "a new viewpoint"—"an original stunt."

As everyone knows, New York is built upon a rock. During this visit of mine they were constructing the subway, and every inch of the tunnel had to be blasted with dynamite.

I was playing eight and nine performances a week of a repertory of six plays, all tragic, emotional parts.

The din of New York—the rush, the tall buildings, and the strange coloured people; Italians, Russians, Chinese—all sorts everywhere—the noise of the elevators, the nasal twang—black boys, bell boys, and the noise of the street cars—I do not want to be unkind, but to me it was demoniacal.

Then there were all my trunks—those that couldn't fit in the room were in the passage outside—and never a "cup of English tea" for my maids—all this, to

ON HER FIRST AMERICAN TOUR

the accompaniment of underground explosions. . . .

I tried to bear it, but some unknown voice whispered in my ear "get out of this hotel." After a week I said to Julia: "Pack up, I must go." She looked more than miserable—demented—she thought of the three hotels that had refused to take me because of "Pinkie."

She packed up and we went—twenty-four hours afterwards the hotel was blown to smithereens—comic pictures in the papers of headless bodies running searching for their heads, and heads with eyes searching for the rest of their bodies; noses and ears and fingers scattered about . . . to help cheer the public up, I suppose, who had shares in the enterprise.

In the next hotel—the Majestic, I believe—there was sometimes a shuffling outside my bedroom door.

My only companion was my little griffon, and to her I would talk my special dog language. The following is what appeared in the newspapers:

"Those who have listened outside the great actress's bedroom door will have heard the words spoken to her by her deceased husband on the phonograph she carries with her always. She turns on the phonograph every night before she goes to sleep."

"New York.

"Darling Uncle,

" . . . I work, work, work, all the time—you get the papers, and from them you will know what it is like.

Mr. Hawksley makes out my debts at nearly £12,000; this includes all the money I want to repay.

"Expenses are so heavy here it means my coming home without a farthing, however hard I work. . . .

"The audiences are not so large now; it is so warm and I believe I am in the wrong theatre.

"I have to play *Pelléas and Mélisande* in the theatre next door, as the orchestra in our theatre only holds seven performers and is above the proscenium.

"Chicago was like a wonderful nightmare. Five plays in a fortnight, and nine performances a week, and speeches, and all the parties—but, however great the success, the money *must* go back to my creditors, which is, to say the least of it, depressing. £500 is added for A. G.

"Perhaps you will see Mr. Hawksley and suggest that if I pay £8,000 now it will be sufficient, and others must wait.

"I am afraid I won't get a new play on, if the ones I am doing continue to draw good audiences.

"My maid W. has had a bilious attack ever since she left England. She wears a long train! . . .

"The noise in front of my hotel, in fact all round, is awful. They are building an underground railway. There are the noises of the explosions, and the noises of iron girders being lowered all night long. I'm afraid I will have to move.

"The two nights in the train from Chicago upset me. I was very sick and jumpy. . . .

"I am writing in the night, after two performances and a rehearsal.

"Dear letters from Stella—short ones from Beo— he's young to be away so long. . . .

"Nine performances last week. I send you my

speech, which was a great success, given in my night-gown, after *Beyond Human Power*. I have been ill, my voice and appetite and my sleep went for days, and have left me rather weak.

"Mrs. Clarence Mackay sent round all sorts of nice things; I am better, really quite well, only rather hoarse. I have played every performance; I was so afraid I would have to give up.

"Isn't the enclosed cutting lovely? . . .

"BEATRICE."

The New York *Evening Journal*,
February 4th, 1902.

"THE LADY AND THE PUP.

"Here to the left is a very interesting photograph. The writer does not know the lady of the fine, calm, powerful face. He does not even know the dog, the strange, inbred wild little creature.

"This picture is printed to call attention to the folly which women show in regard to dogs.

"The picture represents a feature of dog life of an ethical rather than a practical kind.

"If the lady in the picture—the famous and able actress, Mrs. Patrick Campbell—had this picture taken with a scientific view, it was all right. If she meant to illustrate the marvels of evolution and natural selection by contrasting the wild, crazy, big-eyed snub-nosed face of the little dog with her own high development, morally and mentally, her idea was a good one.

"But if she meant to indicate in this photograph, affection for the animal, and her opinion of his right place in the universe, we are obliged to disagree with and to criticise her.

"It is all very well to repeat what one woman said: 'The more I see of men, the more I think of dogs.'

"The dog's place is on the floor, and not in a photograph next to a woman's cheek.

"There are in man and woman whatever qualities we seek for, and the human being that cannot find in one of his own kind the highest companionship, the fullest friendship, and affection, is curiously lacking.

"There may be exceptions. This picture doubtless portrays one of them. But in general we venture to say that the woman who likes a dog better than a child or a man, ought not to have a child or a husband.

"If the lady of this picture will pick up in the streets the poorest little child, and have her photograph taken with that child's face in the place of the dog's face, we think that she will be delighted with the result. We shall be very glad to print such a picture in this same place, and along side of it Mrs. Campbell's views on the relative satisfactoriness of pups and human children."

There is a peculiar gaiety about American women, not usual in Englishwomen. It may be explained by the electricity in the air, or the difference in the clock—it is day here when it is night there—

At a party everyone is buoyant. It would be infinitely ill-mannered to be morose, critical, silent, self-absorbed, or to appear "out of it." You are there to be happy, and to make others happy.

It seems noisy and fatiguing at first, but it has its magnetic warmth and charm. There is nothing of that funny cliquishness you find so often in English Society.

And then how they dance—and how well they dress!

Mrs. Dana Gibson's silver legs and her little feet—this lady always wore silver stockings—how they twinkled as she tangoed or cake-walked—whatever the fashionable dance was then. Her irresistible fun too; the gaiety of her passion when she sang French love songs; her gravity when she imitated an Englishwoman and the "British accent."

And the kindness of American men!—people would have me think American women have taught them that; I do not believe it.

The care and the cherishing of the white woman belongs to early days, and the instinct has lasted through.

I must not write all the admiration I have for the American Poppa; it might be thought I was hard on the American mother and daughter. . . .

I remember at a luncheon party a distinguished American, sitting next to me, suddenly looked me straight in the eye and said: "Some man has made you unhappy; it is an insult to your sex to allow it, and it shows a lack of sense of humour." I answered: "Do you know why God withheld the sense of humour from women?" He said he could not imagine. I replied winningly: "That we may love you, instead of laughing at you." I made the remark—it was not original, but I have the credit for it—because I disliked what I thought his impertinent curiosity; he pretended to think I was flirting with him, and shouted "Fire! Fire! Fire!" and turned the laugh against me.

*   *   *   *   *

To-day a lady who has been in America three or four months announces that the American man makes the "best lover." It is a comic remark.

Someone has said: "As a man *is,* so he loves." The dishonourable man dishonourably; the coarse man coarsely; and so on. . . .

A friend of mine thinks: "The secret of married happiness lies in politeness"; if so, I suppose in Europe the palm should be given to the Frenchman; in Asia to the Chinaman. . . .

I insist that I have found the manners of American men more kindly; of Frenchmen more courteous; of Englishmen more sincere; of Irishmen—God defend us! . . .

By February 5th I find in another letter to my uncle that I had sent £3,442 towards my liabilities.

By the end of the tour, owing to the great heat, the business was not so good, but I paid back in all, just on £7,000 at the end of the twenty-two weeks.

My next tour in America was in September of the same year, and I continued paying up; so that people who say I have never saved money—it is true I have not the accepted "right sense" of the value of money —must remember this effort of mine.

In those days in New York Mr. Norman Hapgood was the dramatic critic upon whom the actors'

minds centered; and his flattering notice of my work
is interesting.*

There is a very fearsome person in America called
the "Press agent." It is his business to see that the
newspapers talk about the "star." His power of in-

---

* DRAMA OF THE MONTH.

"For a long time nothing in the theatrical world has done so much
good in New York as the visit of Mrs. Patrick Campbell. . . .

"She was in the city three weeks, her plays received almost the united
censure of a Press that thinks Björnson and Maeterlinck ridiculous,
Sudermann dull and *The Notorious Mrs. Ebbsmith,* immoral.

"Nevertheless, it took but a few days for the idea to spread among
people who care, that Mrs. Campbell was something that must not be
missed, and there were many who were turned away from the theatre
every night. . . .

"Some of them liked Björnson best, some Maeterlinck, some Pinero,
but all cared. They were in the presence of an art which would make
a difference in their feelings and in their ideas. Speaking to them
publicly after their enthusiastic reception of Björnson's intense spiritual
drama, *Beyond Human Power,* on her last night, Mrs. Campbell said:
'I see no reason why the drama should not be selected for its beauty
and truth, its possession of those qualities which give worth to other
aspects of life.' It is not only for excitement that we all go to the
theatre, not to be carried off our feet by sheer power. It is to have
three hours in which the mind and taste are encouraged, pleased, and
corrected.

"Mrs. Campbell prefers omission to fabrication. Such simplification
might lead to barrenness, but the more I see it in this actress, the more
it appears in the light of harmony and purity, for the methods which
she does use are sufficient to paint widely different women with lasting
solidity. America has not seen Mrs. Campbell try *rôles* in which much
power is needed, or unclouded joy. Her most distinguished work
has been deep, clear, pure and in the minor key, yet the future may
shows other truths, for nothing in *Mariana, Magda, The Second Mrs.
Tanqueray,* or *The Notorious Mrs. Ebbsmith* could prepare one
for the fairy innocence of "Mélisande, or the profound devotion of the
pastor's wife in *Beyond Human Power.* ....

"My own opinions have been changed in several ways and always in
favour of the author, a characteristic result of Mrs. Campbell's
thoroughness of interpretation......................................."

vention, contrivance, and ingenuity is beyond conception to the normal mind.

One night at the theatre, just before I was going on the stage in *Beyond Human Power,* the press agent (this particular man was a German and his name was "Worms!") put his head in my dressing-room door and said: "If anyone says 'tanbark,' you know nothing." I called him back and asked him what "tanbark" was. He looked delighted and answered: "I guess you'd better not know."

That night the noise outside the theatre ceased. The street cars have one kind of bell that jangles when they start, and another when they stop; and I think there were three sets of tram rails outside this theatre, but on this particular evening all was silent.

The next morning the mystery of "tanbark" was explained in the following article in the newspaper:

"TANBARK

"Three car loads of Tanbark were dumped in front of the Theatre Republic on West Forty-second Street, just off Broadway, this morning.

"An army of 'White Wings'* were soon busy spreading it in even layers over the granite-blocked pavement.

* The name of street cleaner and sweeper, who wear white linen coats.

"As the street cars approached, the motor men jammed down the brakes and slowed up, and refrained from ringing the gongs.

"The ill-mannered little boys who eke out an existence crying 'Wuxtra!' 'Wuxtra!' were gagged.

"The Italian organ-grinders were warned not to go further north than 'West Twenty-ninth Street.' The cries of babies on the block were stifled with paregoric.

"Even the detectives from the Tenderloin Police Station wore gum shoes.

"The patrol men conversed in whispers.

"The bar-keepers over at the Metropole and Rossmore Café's shook up the cocktails and gin fizzes with muffled ice.

"All was still. All was silent.

"The man from Sullivan County, who came down to town in a straw hat and a fur-trimmed duster, asked if the Mayor was dead.

"The peanut vendor at the corner, who had been cautioned to plug up the whistle of his roaster, or suffer banishment to 'Little Italy,' leaned over the kerbstone and whispered gently in the off ear of the man from Sullivan County, that Mrs. Patrick Campbell, the famous English actress, was going to play *Beyond Human Power* to-night at the Theatre Republic, and it was necessary that she had absolute quiet.

"So it was that the streets were tanbarked, and various warnings were issued to various employees of the city and corporation, that quiet must be the order of day and night.

"And, 'Pinkey Pankey Poo' was as happy as ever a genteel doggy could be.

"It all began from a request from Mrs. Campbell's manager to President Cantor, of the Borough of Man-

hattan, that the city spread tanbark in front of the theatre. The manager explained there was so much noise
because of the rumbling of wagon wheels and other
vehicles that the beauties of the actress's acting were
partly lost upon the audience.

"The manager was referred to Doctor John McGaw
Woodbury, Superintendent of Street Cleaning. Doctor Woodbury was out, and the plan unfolded to his
assistant, Captain Gibson. It sounded real reasonable
to the Captain and he said: 'All right, the tanbark goes
down.'

"Doctor Woodbury was back in his office this morning.

" 'How about that tanbark?' asked an *Evening
World* reporter.

" 'What tanbark?' asked the doctor.

" 'In front of the Theatre Republic.'

" 'I don't know what you're talking about,' said the
doctor.

"Then the secretary explained matters. 'Did Gibson give permission to the theatre to spread the tanbark?' the doctor queried.

" 'He did,' said the secretary.

" 'Ah!' said the doctor, 'I pass the whole matter up
to the Commissioner of Public Works. There is where
it should have gone first. My business is to clean the
streets, not litter them.'

"George Livingstone, Commissioner of Public Works,
listened patiently.

" 'If the Street Department has littered up the streets,
why, it will have to clean them up again,' said the Commissioner.

" 'I have nothing to do with it. I don't just see why
the whole town should sleep while Mrs. Campbell acts.

We might just as well put tanbark in front of the other theatres. If Mrs. Campbell is looking for quiet, why doesn't she wait until she gets to Philadelphia?'

" 'If I find the tanbark around the theatre an obstruction in the street, I shall order the Superintendent of Encumbrances to remove it,' said President Cantor.

"Mr. Cantor does not actually say he will order the tanbark to be removed, but he intimates that such a step may be taken.

" 'Captain Gibson had the right to grant such a request, but I do not propose to get into any fight over the matter, but the tanbark may be scattered all over the adjacent blocks and become a nuisance.'

"But Mrs. Campbell's manager did not rest content with getting the tanbark. He made a request to the Metropolitan Street Car Company, to instruct their motor men to abstain from jangling the gongs, and to slow up when the cars on the cross town lines pass the theatre. This was granted.

"Then the manager requested that Fire Chief Croker order his firemen to muffle the bells of the fire engine if they should be called upon to run by the theatre. The chief said he would have to refer the matter to the Fire Commissioners, and would get a decision from them.

"Noting the success of Mrs. Campbell to obtain quiet, the other actresses in the city began to flood the street-cleaning department with letters asking for similar favors. These letters just began to come in at noon.

"Among them were these epistles:

" 'Dear Doctor,
" 'I know you are a real nice man, and are always willing to help on a poor girl. The push-cart man makes so much noise in front of the Bijou Theatre that I can-

not hear my own jokes, and am apt to spring a chestnut on the public. Please send seven cars of tanbark to me by return mail.

" 'Yours for health,

" 'MAY IRVINE.'

" 'Doctor Woodbury,

" 'I think it awful mean that Mrs. Campbell is getting all the tanbark. Won't you please send me 10 or 15 cents worth? I am very fond of rest myself.

" 'Yours truly,

" 'ANNA HELD.'

" 'Dear, dear Doctor Woodbury,

" 'Oh! I should so love to have some genuine tanbark. I haven't seen any since I played in the back counties of Michigan, when they used to put it on the floor of the Town Hall, so that you couldn't hear the lumber men when they came in.

" 'Yours hopefully,

" 'VIRGINIA HARNED.'

" 'Dear Doctor,

" 'I always did like tanbark, except I hear it makes the skin tough. If you can send me four or five carloads c.o.d. I shall be so grateful.

" 'Yours respectfully,

" 'LILLIAN RUSSELL.'

" 'Dear Doctor,

" 'We do want a lot of tanbark so that we cannot hear the loud suits of clothes of the wicked bald-headed men who sit in the front row at the "New York."

" Yours,

" 'A BUNCH OF FLORIDA GIRLS.' "

There are some actors and actresses in America

who say that my success was entirely due to "tan-bark."

At one of the performances of *Beyond Human Power* a man asked for his dollar back, saying it was a "bum show."*

When we were playing in St. Louis—it was over 100 in the shade, and not a breath of air—I arrived at my hotel exhausted. I lay down and shut my eyes. Something made me open them. On the wall to my right was this:—

to my left, two of these, on my bed three, and on the ceiling six—at least, so it seemed to me. I jumped up, rang the telephone, and called down: "Send some people to room 174 immediately." A bell boy came.

I was standing in the middle of the room trembling, with Pinkie in my arms. I said "Look!" pointing wildly about me. He grinned, as only a coloured bell boy can, and said: "Why dat's a 'stink bug.'" "Stink bug!" I shouted. "There are hundreds all over the room." He continued smiling,

---

* "Bum" is the American for "dud."

and said: "I guess der are." I screamed "Kill them!" He answered: "Oh, no, Ma'am! dem smell bad if dem killed."

I do not remember what happened next.

In September, 1902, I was again in America, and opened at the Garden Theatre under the management of the late Charles Frohman in *Aunt Jeannie,* by E. F. Benson ("Dodo"). It was a play full of charm and elegance, and received some splendid reviews, but I fancy it was a little trifling, after my serious repertory, in the early part of the year. Mr. Frohman kept this play on only a few weeks, and I started almost immediately rehearsing Sudermann's *Es Lebe Des Leben,* translated by Miss Edith Wharton—*The Joy of Living.*

This play was a great success, and, with the exception of a few special performances of *The Second Mrs. Tanqueray* and *Magda,* ran to the end of my engagement.

When I produced it on my return to England at the New Theatre, it was a complete failure. It had already been played excellently in London by a German Company, but had been condemned by the English critics. I had hoped for the impossible.

Charles Frohman and I shared the expense of the production in America, which was in every way splendid. I am ashamed to say I remember candlesticks costing £12!

Mr. Frohman quarrelled with me over rehearsals.

TOURING THE UNITED STATES UNDER THE DIRECTION OF
LIEBLER AND COMPANY

It was an intensely difficult play to rehearse. Beata was the emotional woman who does not weep: and I fancy he thought my reserve, and constraint, would be dull and ineffective. I remember he wanted to drop the curtain at the end of the scene—when with great dignity, she walks out of the room without noticing a small gilt chair in front of her, almost falling—as the chair topples over—cutting out the scene which followed. I would not hear of it; so Frohman would have nothing more to do with the production, and I became solely responsible.

But for the aid of Prince Hugo von Hohenlohe, who happened to be in New York at the time and gave me some help in the details of German Court etiquette—and the late Mr. Conried,* who attended three rehearsals, giving me the most brilliant assistance; I could never have got through the production of this five-act play in two weeks—Sudermann, too, sent me a very complete prompt book.

These rehearsals, with eight performances a week of *Aunt Jeannie* were a tremendous work. In the end the production had to be put off for two days— I was suddenly taken ill and had to lie in bed in the

---

* The late Heinrich Conried was at that time manager of the Irving Theatre in New York. He enjoyed the reputation of being the most accomplished stage manager and director of modern plays in the world. Mr. Conried gave as a compliment to me, a professional matinée at the Irving Theatre, of acts from four different plays, including *Beyond Human Power*. All the actors appeared to me to play equally brilliantly. He sent me a gold and silver laurel wreath and said: "If you ever act with a leading man who is a genius, you will reach the heavens."

dark for forty-eight hours. The first night went brilliantly, and the papers thought it the best work I had done.

The action of this play takes place among the higher classes in'Germany, and the theme of the play is that social sin reveals itself, and cannot go unpunished. Fifteen years before the play begins "Countess Beata" has been in love with Richard, her husband's friend, but out of consideration for family ties their *liaison* has been at an end for twelve years. The spirit of love still exists between them, most deeply upon Beata's side, upon whom the long strain of suppressed emotion has developed heart disease.

In a most touching scene, Beata says, speaking to Richard: "We've grown old, you and I, there is a layer of ashes on our hearts, a layer of conventionality and good behaviour, and weariness, and disappointment,—who knows what we were like before the fire went out? Not a trace is left to tell— not so much as a riband, or a flower. The words are forgotten, the letters are destroyed, the emotions have faded. Here we sit, like two ghosts on our own graves."

Through Beata's influence and her husband's; Richard's political advancement is secured, and Michael (her husband) resigns his seat in the Reichstag in favour of Richard.

But old love-letters have fallen into the hands of

a former secretary—a Socialistic agitator—and he uses them as a weapon of political attack.

Michael hears of the scandal. To preserve the happiness of his daughter—who is in love and engaged to Richard's son—and to preserve the honour of the family, a council is held.

BEATA: You have questioned me, Michael, let me question you. Must every natural instinct end in remorse and repentance? Sin? I am not conscious of sinning. I did the best that it was in me to do. I simply refused to be crushed by your social laws. I asserted my right to live, my right to self-preservation, perhaps it was another way of suicide—that's no matter. You know what my life has been since—how I've had to buy it, hour by hour, and drop by drop at the nearest chemist's. Well, wretched as it is, I've loved it too dearly to disown it now! yes, I've loved everything—everything around me—you too, Michael; ah, don't laugh, yes, you too, even if I've—ah (*her breath comes in long gasps and she reels and clutches a chair*). Which one of you will help me to the door?

MICHAEL: Beata, from now on there will be no one to help you.

BEATA: Thank you (*with an intense effort she walks out of the room, nearly falling over the chair which she does not notice*).

MICHAEL (*to Richard*): And now——?

RICHARD: Do what you like. Say what you like. Curse me—shoot me—I shall not defend myself.

MICHAEL: You admit that one of us must die?

RICHARD: No, I don't admit it, but I am at your service.

MICHAEL: A duel between us is impossible.

RICHARD: Impossible——

MICHAEL: I have pledged my word not to bring any scandal on the Party. You are under the same obligation.

RICHARD: I know a way—but (*his son's voice is heard outside*)——

MICHAEL (*with sudden decision*): Norbert!

RICHARD: For God's sake, Michael, do you want to disgrace my whole house?

MICHAEL: You shall see—Norbert. Come in, my boy, come!

NORBERT: Uncle Michael, what is the matter with Aunt Beata? The doctor is with her and Ellen has been called.

MICHAEL: Nothing serious. Don't be alarmed. Norbert, your father and I were just talking of last evening. You remember that stupid business interrupted our talk, and we never heard the end of your argument. Let us have it now. Sit down,—sit down, Richard. There was one phrase of yours that struck me. You said— you said—that if——

RICHARD: You said that if a man of honour has injured another and is called on to atone for it, he is the best judge of his own punishment.

NORBERT (*laughing*): Did I? Very likely but my head is so full of other things just now that I couldn't swear to it.

MICHAEL: That was not quite what I meant, but no matter. Suppose we take such a case. If the injured person says "one of us two must die," what ought the other to answer?

NORBERT: Why, Uncle Michael, I should say that depended on the nature of the injury—doesn't it?

RICHARD: Let us say, for the sake of argument, that the wrong is the gravest that one man can do another; let us say he has seduced his friend's wife. Has the husband a right to the other man's life?

NORBERT: Why, father, there can be but one answer to that. And if the other man is a man of honour—though I don't see how he could be, do you?—he would be more eager to give his life, than the husband could possibly be to take it.

RICHARD: H'm, perhaps you're right. Thank you, my boy.

NORBERT: Uncle Michael, at what time to-morrow may I see you?

MICHAEL: I'll send you word, Norbert.

NORBERT: Thanks. Don't make it too late, will you? Don't keep me waiting too long. Good-bye. Good-bye, father. (*Goes out.*)

RICHARD: Well, are you satisfied?

MICHAEL: You put the question in a way that suggests suicide. That was not . . .

RICHARD: It is your own choice. All I ask is two days' respite. You won't refuse it? (*Michael shrugs his shoulder.*) Good-bye. (*Goes out.*)

Hearing of Richard's decision, Beata gives an official luncheon, and at this gathering of the notabilities she triumphantly drinks to "The Joy of Living." . . .

Beata, rising from her seat at the luncheon party, speaks:—

"My dear friends, you all go on wishing each other a

long life, but which of us is really alive? Which of us really dares to live? Somewhere, far off in the distance, we catch a glimpse of life—but we hide our eyes and shrink away from it like transgressors. And that's our nearest approach to living. Do you really think you're alive—any of you—or do you think I am? (*She springs up with an inspired look.*) But I, at least—I—whose life is one long struggle against death—I who never sleep, who hardly breathe, who barely stand—I at least know how to laugh—how to love life, and be thankful for it. (*She raises her glass, her voice no more than a hoarse whisper.*) And as the only living soul among you, I drink to 'The Joy of Living.' " (*Her eyes rest on Richard, and then turning to Michael*), "I think I will take your advice and go into the other room for a little while" (*She rises with an effort and with a last look at Richard, says*), "I shall be back in a few minutes." (*A heavy fall is heard in the next room.*)

She had put an overdose of her heart medicine in her glass.

Everybody but Richard and her husband, thinks she has died from heart disease.

Richard's last words at the end of the play are:—

You see, Michael, that I live because I must—that I live because I am dead——

The play is full of the finest stage craft, its simplest scenes leading to situations of the most intense interest.

In San Francisco its reception was extraordinary.

CHAPTER XII.

MY next engagement in London, after the production of *The Joy of Living* at the New Theatre, was with the late Mr. Lewis Waller at the Imperial Theatre—February, 1904—in *A Queen's Romance*—a fine translation of Victor Hugo's *Ruy Blas,* by John Davidson. A generous production, that, unfortunately, ran only a fortnight.

The critics found it tedious. They called it a piece of literature, rather than a stage play. This was tragic for John Davidson, who had put some of his best work into the play.

The public, unfortunately, do not think it is their duty—though the play be the work of a distinguished author, produced by a recognised management, and played by artists of quality—to come and see it, and judge for themselves.

It was the first time I had played with Mr. Lewis Waller and in one review of the play, the criticism of our different method was interesting: ". . . If we are to take Mr. Lewis Waller's fine presentment of the hero by itself, or Mrs. Campbell's gracious and beautiful embodiment of the Queen by itself, there would be nothing but praise to give to each; but the play requires that the two should be combined in one harmony, and harmony is precisely what we do not find. The histrionic method of the two lovers is absolutely distinct. . . ."

The reason I would give, is that Mr. Waller addressed his blank verse to the universe; I spoke my blank verse to him.

Mounet-Sully was a superb exponent of this "speaking to the universe" method. I saw him play only once—in *Antigone*—at the time I remember I thought "he is mounted on a horse, and rides most gloriously."

It was during this fortnight's run of *A Queen's Romance,* that a great sorrow fell upon me. My uncle was very ill—dying. I told Mr. Waller all it meant to me, and many times during that fortnight he drove me from the theatre to Chelsea, that I might get back to the care of my uncle more quickly.

This uncle of mine, of whom the world has never heard, was the most unselfish of men.

Looking back now, I feel my youth was spent at court in the presence of a king.

His life taught that a fine sense of rightful responsibility is the soul's best armour.

He took the sting from poverty, the burden from obligation.

My people said he spoiled me. I alone know the courage he gave me—he showed me the right door—and I always felt sure of his trust.

These few letters show a little, his love and sympathy, and that to him my heart was bare:

"Chelsea,
"June, 1898.

". . . Will Maeterlinck come to London? Do you think the play will appeal to the general public? Will not its wonderful symbolism be lost upon them? I believe you are the only one who has the power to make it understood and appreciated on the stage. . . .

"It will be a memorable production if rehearsed with true heart and understanding. I am feeling many shades better, though by no means what you would call fit. I don't know that I ever do.

"It is so distressing, dear, to hear of your deep unrest and depression. Would God would put things right for you; but you must do your part, too, and that bravely and loyally.

"Try to look at life squarely in the face. There is error in Ideals. As we build, so we inhabit. . . .

"A thousand blessings
"From your affectionate
"Uncle Harry."

Writing to Berlin:—

"This should reach you a few hours before the curtain rises. How I would love to be there! I do hope you will be in perfect form—and that the round of receptions, at homes, and suppers will not have taxed your strength and nerves overmuch. Mind you act the mad scene just as you did on the last night at the Lyceum.

"The Berliners cannot help but love you.

"There are long paragraphs in the London newspapers about the handsome way in which you are all being treated in Berlin, and the great excitement there.

"I hope everyone you meet is sympathetic and kind.

"Bless you, dear, and may you win all hearts.

"Your affectionate
"Uncle Harry."

"P. S.—I hope they will see that you have a thoroughly good piano for *Mrs. Tanqueray*. Try it beforehand if you can."

" . . .

"I hope you are feeling better; you wear yourself out too much. There won't be a rag left of you soon. Take rest. I saw *Sibyl** yesterday afternoon at the New Gallery.—and I loved her, and you for reading so much into her and telling me. It is the jewel of the gallery.

"Bless you. . . .

"Do be firm and give your throat every moment of rest possible. Guard against chills, wrap up warmly—you cannot be too careful. . . ."

This letter shows how he indulged my vanity—a tender habit of his to shield me from my savage self-criticism.

---

* "J'ai voulu réprésenter la Sibelle dans le douloureux devoir; c'est de prédire l'avenir—Elle va prophétiser—elle enlève lentement les voiles qui l'entourent, et les malheurs qu'elle ne peut qu'entrevoir la fait souffrir.

FERNAND KHNOPFF.
This beautiful marble was bought by Mr. Agnew.

"Dear . . .

"I have been thinking about your idea of my writing your life; there is one petition I would place on the knees of the gods, that they would give me the ability to do that in a manner something worthy of your dear, precious self. Oh, if they would grant it! But my life, my daily occupation is so out of harmony with such a sweet, heavenly work. How is it possible? Only a poet could do such a thing full justice. Can you imagine a miserable sign-painter producing a Botticelli? . . .

"Your affectionate

"UNCLE HARRY."

" . . . Am I really philosophical and unselfish? I am very unsociable, and have absolutely lost all taste for mixing with people. I never did learn the art of making friends—you know that you've often told me as much. In one sense I am not philosophical, I am only just dull, and I plod away at my work. . . .

"What are my attainments in languages and literature, art—echo answers 'What?' My education has just been sufficient for me to secure a clerkship in the city! Such is your uncle, dear, with all his philosophy. Well, but he loves you and your dear Beo and Stella, and longs for your happiness, and would count it a blessing beyond compare if he were able to contribute to it really, and could stay those many things which disquiet the nerves so mercilessly. . . .

"Your affectionate

"UNCLE HARRY."

"How mysterious, how strange and unfathomable all is! You said how majestic is death— and he is a king-maker, if only we understood it—and it is only those that are left that are the uncrowned—he plucks out the thorn, and the bitterness passes for ever. It is all too deep and beyond—I am so glad I was at the theatre, and I am happy to think too, that you were glad I was there. . . .*

"God bless and bless you.

". . .

"UNCLE."

"Chelsea,
"21st March, 1903.

". . . From your tour card I see you were this week in Kansas City, and that next week you will give performances in *five* different cities. How strange, and to you who detest travelling, how abominable it must be to have to scour the country, and to bounce into and out of new places day after day in this fashion, like a pea in a frying pan! However, you will be in California on the 6th of next month, and there you will enjoy the climate like anything. When you are in San Francisco you will be nearer to Beo than you have been for over two years. . . .

"Your mother is well and sends fond love. . . .

"I haven't heard from Stella lately. Expect she's studying hard. She is going to be very clever, I'm sure.

"Much love.

". . .

"UNCLE HARRY."

This letter telling me I could bring my little dog home without putting her in quarantine, was a great relief.

* This letter refers to poor Pat's death.

Uncle and my sister Nina understood the comfort the little creature was to me in the long hours in the railway train and in the hotels.

"Chelsea.

"Dear Beatrice,

"Welcome, and thrice welcome! I hope you have had a pleasant and enjoyable crossing so far. Nina and I will meet you at Liverpool. We go up by the midnight train. Now as to Pinkie, we sent you a cable which you should have received a few hours before sailing from New York, that a concession had been granted, relieving you from the obligations of the new quarantine law. The new Licence is enclosed herein. So you are now entitled to bring Pinkie home and keep her with you, instead of packing her off to Sewell's quarantine quarters. You have to thank Nina for having worked the oracle so successfully. She and I called on Mr.—— at the Board of Agriculture, and she made an eloquent appeal to him for Pinkie, her main argument being that when you left England in December last you didn't know that such severe regulations would be made in place of the then existing ones; that Pinkie cost between £40 and £50 and would certainly die if separated from you for any length of time. Many other things she also said in a very sweet way, which we will tell you when we meet; but the end of it was that Mr.—— very kindly granted the concession; and no words can describe the difference in our feeling when we knew that Pinkie was free; such a burden seemed to roll off our spirits that Nina said she felt as if she could fly in the air like Ariel. . . .

"Your affectionate uncle
"HARRY."

To quote the words of another:—

Uncle never "exalted material over immaterial things, or claimed any foundation for the Arts but in moral and in spiritual truths." He knew "compromise is as impossible in literature and the Arts, as in matters of faith; and that the general public shrinks from the laborious and exhaustive ecstasy, in which literature and the Arts are understood."

———

Hundreds of my children's school letters lie before me—no different, I suppose, from hundreds of other children's school letters.

How often the thought was with me—"can it be that they are happy, quite well, and I am not there—the daily, hourly outpourings of love—hushed—and yet the child is well and happy—better perhaps—happier?"

My art, as it were, became my *gift* to my children, as well as their daily bread.

Who will destroy these letters—this heap of early treasures? Not I—they carry the joyous echo of youth and hope—the root and fibre of my endeavour. . . .

My boy wanted to be a sailor—the Royal Navy—that meant money, success, social influence—I must work hard—I did—he had his wish.

How happy he was at school, and on the *Britannia!*

"Darling mother,

". . . I am glad the plays were a success. I also had a little success this week, for I got my 'colours' for Rugby football. . . .

"We had a test exam. in Algebra yesterday, and I got 148 out of 150, and two other boys got 150. I hope I do as well in the real exam. . . .

"With all my heart full of love and kisses,

"BEO."

On the *Glory* in China years afterwards he wrote:

"H. M. S. *Glory*,
"China Station,
"At Wei-Hai-Wei.
"Sept. 2nd, 1902.

"Darling Uncle Harry,

" . . . I have been everywhere, and seen everything since I last wrote: Japan, Manchuria, Wei-Hai-Wei, Malay Peninsular, Corea, practically everywhere on the China Station. The people are absolutely different in each place; up North the Chinese are magnificent specimens, all about 6 ft., with tremendous arms and legs and broad, open faces, the remnant of the old fighting race of thousands of years ago. Down South they are small, wizened, and half of them deformed from opium smoking, and dissipation in all forms.

"Before we went our summer cruise with the Fleet we went to Taku, which is the port of Pekin where all the fighting took place. They are still very turbulent there.

"Then we went to Shang-hai-kwan and Ching Wang Tao. We saw the great wall of China at Shang-hai-kwan; it is wonderful. Thousands of years old, and over a thousand miles long, extending from the Eastern Coast of China to the boundary of Thibet. It has Pagodas or forts about every mile, all communicating with one another by underground passages. It was built to keep the northern 'barbarians' from invading China, in her prime.

"We are at present at Wei-Hai-Wei; we have been here since the Coronation.

"Shooting is going strong; snipe simply abound on the mainland.

"Some adventurous mad French millionaire built a magnificent hotel on the mainland at Mahto (or rather Port Edward now), the village opposite Len Kung Tao, the island of Wei-Hai-Wei; thus attracting some few people who come for their health, for Wei-Hai-Wei is a very healthy place.

"I am enclosing a copy of the *Wei-Hai-Wei Gazette,* which is our only paper here. We pay 10 cents, or 2½d., for it. It is the Coronation Number, so extra grand and flashy.

"I pass for Sub-Lieut. in April, 1904, so don't expect me home till about June, 1904. I then have six weeks' leave and go to Greenwich College for six months, and then to Portsmouth College for six months; I then go to sea again. . . .

"I am sending this letter by the Siberian Railway, which has just opened, so yours will be one of the first English letters to go by it. It takes exactly three weeks for a letter to go from Wei-Hai-Wei to London. By P. & O. steamer it takes six weeks or more. All we do is to send our letters to the Russian Consul at Chefoo and ask him to post them with Russian stamps and send them in his mail. It is very convenient and more novel.

Fancy going home by it! Three weeks in a train with only a Russian Boor as a companion. Ugh! . . . I will write again and send you some photographs.

"We go to Japan soon. Hurrah! Lovely Japan. It instils new life into one to breathe the air and see the scenery there. This Admiral keeps midshipmen well employed. Every month he gives us all a job to do in our 'spare time.' This last month we had to illustrate the fighting power of every nation on the China Station, all of it intelligence work. Mine filled a foolscap-sized book about one inch thick. . . .

"I have been getting on pretty well with my cricket and games. Ours is a very sporty ship, from Admiral downwards. The Admiral goes bathing every morning and is a keen golfer. Every officer in the ship plays golf. . . .

"Must end now, and will write longer next time. We are going through our yearly firing at the Range.

"Give my love to *everybody* and tell them to write to me.

"Tons of love,
"From your loving nephew,
"Alan U. Campbell."

H. M. S. *Glory,*
"China Station,
"August 18th, 1903.

"Darling Mother,

"Thank you so much for your last letter. I have plenty of news to tell you this time. To begin with, *I shall probably be home by Xmas or soon after.* Isn't it lovely? We have been at Wei-Hai-Wei for about three months and leave it for the last time on the 26th of this month. We have been very gay. I have been playing two cricket matches a week. I always play for the 'Navy' in large matches. My batting average is 60 now. About two weeks ago I made the record score out on this ground *213* not out.

"I and a few other mids have been creating quite a 'furore' by giving magnificent society picnics. Of course, they are very easy to give from a ship, because you can always get a large boat.

"I am glad the clothes and make-up gear are coming out. We have quite a lot of talent amongst our midshipmen, who are a very sporty lot in every way.

"We sail on the 26th for Vladivostok. Ugh! The average temperature in the year is 36 degrees, I believe. Then we are going to Hakodate in Japan; lovely riding on beautiful ponies. . . . After Hakodate we go to Hong Kong for four days to coal, and then to Singapore to meet Rear-Admiral Curzon Howe. Then we come up to Hong Kong about 1st November, and after that *we may go home at once,* or we may refit out here and *go home about February*—it is the cause of great argument amongst the officers.

"I shall have a six week's leave when I go home, and then go to the Channel Squadron for about two months, and then pass and go to Greenwich College, where I shall be near you for about three months at least. . . .

"I will write again and tell you some more news.

"Give my love to Stella and tell her to write at once.

"With all the world, sun, moon, and stars full of love and kisses,

"From your loving son,
"BEO CAMPBELL."

Then came a change in his letters.

"H. M. S. *King Alfred,*
"Posted at Port Said,
"March 8th, 1904.

"Darling Mother,

"Our mails have gone astray for the last three months, so I have not received a letter from you for a long time. Mind you and Stella are on the Portsmouth Jetty to welcome me home.

"Fancy, three years and three months.   I don't expect you will recognise me.

"Darling mother, you must withdraw me from the service: bodily, nobody could be better suited to it than myself, but in mind I am miles from it.

"I expect you will laugh at me . . . it sounds rot, I know, but I have that feeling. . . .

"I have become sick of foreign countries; they all copy, and not one is as good as England.   Besides, I feel as if I want to be near you and Stella. . . .

"Dear mother, do write and let me know what you think.   Write to:—

"H. M. S. *King Edward,*
"On Homeward Passage.

"I just missed making 1,000 runs last season at cricket. My average was about fifty, and top score 213 not out. I have left my two golf cups to be inscribed, but they will come afterwards.

"We have a concert on board every Friday night, which helps to pass the time away. . . .

"Please do write and let me know what you think as soon as you get this, and I shall receive it before I leave Malta. . . .

"Don't think this letter is written on the impulse of the moment; I have been wanting to write it for a year and a half, but I have waited to see if I changed, but I did not.

"Mind you see about it.

"With all the world, sun, moon and stars full of love and kisses,

"From your loving son,
"BEO CAMPBELL."

"P. S.—The Diplomatic Service is the one I should like most of any *service*. . . .

"So do, do, do take me out now, at once. . . ."

I realised he wanted a different life—Oxford—the Diplomatic Service—to write plays.

When he came home, his old schoolmaster had a long talk with him, and, in the end, on his advice, I withdrew Beo. His schoolmaster said, "the boy has character and determination and has made up his mind; better withdraw him."

And so we plot and plan for our children's success and happiness, but they take their lives into their own hands, with all the courage and faith and trust in this world's goodness, and its fine chances, with which we have imbued them; and on our side we must have the greater courage and faith to "let go," and the day came when I was glad I did as he wished.

And here before me are three big bundles of my Stella's letters:

"Darling, darling Mother,
"Good night, good morning, and good-bye until next

Saturday. I feel a tiny bit sad, but I will cheer up, for next Saturday will come soon again and then I will stay with you until Monday.

"You do not know how much I love you, my darling mother. I will try my hardest to be good.

"Your own loving little girl,

"STELLA."

My lovely daughter—she must be well educated—she must be presented at Court—she must have every chance to make a happy marriage, and be able to bring up her children in comfort, without this dreadful, nerve-shattering toil of mine; and so her letters, like my son's, urged me onwards, and bound "ardent hope upon my feet like shoes."

I sent Stella to four different schools, but she grew restless at them all. And then on the advice of friends, I sent her to Germany, where I felt she would study restfully—and have the fun of the Opera and plays—away from the excitement of my work.

I went to stay with her in Dresden, and saw how well she was taken care of; but, at the same time, I thought the Fräuleins took a little of the "home" love away from the girls—I wonder?

"Wederstrasse, 16,

"Dresden, A.

"February 16th, 1902.

"I am so glad you are having such a success, darling. You can't think how I love being here, and I love my lessons, too; somehow the Dresden air seems to make one want to work. I am trying so hard to get on with my music, but I am afraid I shall never be able to play well. I am also drawing hard. Fancy, to think I have been here nearly four months. It feels like four weeks. Only I don't feel a bit strange; but I wish I could just run over to America and give you a hug and then come back again; wouldn't it be just lovely to spend a few hours with you? Are you coming home in the Autumn, or when? Don't tire yourself too much, darling. Eight and nine performances a week and all the parties and things are *far* too much for you.

"I want to go to *Beyond Human Power* (*Uber unsere Kraft*). It would be very interesting to see how they do it, wouldn't it? I believe the Pastor Sang is dreadful—always wears a beautiful smile all through the piece, like the cat in 'Alice in Wonderland.'

"From your own loving daughter,
"STELLA."

"Dresden.
"Thank you a million times for your dear letter. I was wild with joy when I got it. I hadn't heard for so long—but I was ever so much wilder when I heard the news. Darling, I daren't believe it *too* much in case something happens to prevent your coming. Oh! it would be lovely. You must come to the Albertshof so that you can get me if you want anything. Then at first you must be regularly lazy and thoroughly rest yourself and lie down a lot, and go for long drives to the woods—they look so lovely just now, all shades of brown and green. And then, when you are quite rested, I must take you to the beautiful statues and pictures and old jewelry and to see Weicke act. Oh, darling, it will

AGAIN IN "THE SECOND MRS. TANQUERAY"

be glorious, and you really will learn German won't you? You learn so quickly. And if you learn with Fräulein Nachtigal she'll teach it you very soon. Oh! it will be nice, and I've such a heap of lovely books for you to read when you know German. Oh, mind you come, darling. . . .

"Best and best love to you, darling, and mind you do come, my darling Mother.

"Your own STELLA."

"Dresden.

"Darling Mother,

". . . Lady Elcho took me to see *Tristan and Isolde* the other night. It was *lovely*. I do so want you to hear the music. And this week I went to hear Weicke recite—how I wished you had been there. It was wonderful. You know he interests himself greatly in literature of every nation—and he occasionally gives a sort of lecture; that is, he takes some unknown, or not very well-known, poet and tells you a little about him, and then recites different examples of his poetry. I knew the poetry fairly, and had read everything he recited, so I enjoyed it immensely. He read so well that one kept thinking he was speaking his own thoughts. Fräulein Nachtigal was with me, and the whole time we said to one another—if only you had been there! . . .

"From your own loving
"STELLA."

Then she grew restless in Germany and begged to come home. She wrote to me, saying:—

"Darling Mother,

". . . I'm not despondent, but the only thing I really

would care to do, is—act. But, of course, if you think
I have no talent, I shouldn't want to—but *do* give me
a chance. . . ."

When she came, she had a season in London and
dances, and much gaiety. D. D. Lyttleton presented
her at Court: but social life did not interest her; it
was the life of the stage she wanted.

So again, as with my son, I had to "let go." Was
there ever a mother worthy of the name, or a wife
either, for the matter of that, who did not feel that if
things went wrong in her ambition for those she
loves, that she was in some way to blame—such a
juggernaut is conscience—if we keep it alive.

When my boy left the Navy, and when my girl
wanted to act—I was *quite sure* that I had failed in
my duty to them in some way. The thought seems
foolish enough to me now.

This letter from the late Lord Charles Beresford,
who saw Stella when I was acting at Blackpool,
speaks of her beauty:

> "H. M. S. *King Edward VII*
> "Channel Fleet.

"You delightful woman,
    "I am so disappointed and cross that the weather
prevented my coming to see you play to-night. I did so
want to see you, and that girl. . . . I never saw such a
beautiful darling in my life as she looked last night.
What was the matter with the people; they were as
enthusiastic and delighted in their welcome to me as if

I had been the King of Ireland. I am sorry the weather prevented either the officers or the men landing, or the people coming to the ship, sea and beach.

"Bless you, my dear, give my love to that infinitely attractive and charming girl.

"Yours ever sincerely,
"CHARLES BERESFORD."

* * * * *

I was very much of a child with my children: feeling, I suppose, that they must be helped by simple standards, until old enough to form their own opinions: so that when the "pull" came it was particularly hard for me. . . .

The awful problem facing us to-day—how far the parents' happiness should be sacrificed to the child's faith in life—is not one to go into here . . . to-day, when we have to repay, rebuild, make our *amende honorable,* for the faith in the *cause,* that drove our young to make the greatest sacrifice of all. . . .

EVEN AS AN ANT-HILL.

In a garden near to a yard was an ant-hill. How long it had been there I do not know; it was a very large ant-hill. There were palaces, store houses, prison houses: there were theatres, too, where ants used to perform—one ant had a trick of impersonating any other ant he chose—they were paid in honey.

Another ant was able to put the emotions of his

heart and head into his little feet, and he could dance as no human being ever danced. There were wonderful buildings, walls, roads, and halting places, little air holes for invalids to breathe in the strengthening air, and shafts for sunlight, canals for the dew. And there were schools with teachers of morals, teachers of philosophy. And there were many prayer houses, where they prayed in silence, and the prayer in their hearts was always against Destruction.

And this is what happened.

An enterprising and ambitious ant went on a long expedition of discovery. He climbed many stones, bricks, large pieces of wood—smiling at difficulties that only made him climb higher.

One day he came to a smooth place, very white; he smelt delicious scents, and there was a warmth beyond his dreams, and all round him was sugar: when he had eaten his fill he went further, and found the other nice things that are kept in a larder. After surfeit and rest, back he went with his little pouch full, over the great distances, up and down bricks, the stones and wood, back to the beautiful ant-hill, and told the emperors and empresses, the kings and the queens, and the councillors all about the good things he had found. There was much debate and grave discussion; he was made a great general and given an army of many millions, and slaves went before him to make the road easier. Yellow sand was found—wonderful sand, which before, only with the greatest labour, could they get, and they needed this sand to make their ant-hill secure.

And the food and the sand were brought back, and the ants grew lazy; there was no need to work so hard, to store and fetch sweet honey. They spent their time dancing and singing, and dancing developed so, that they could dance any way—on their heads, upside down——

To wander and to get, was the ambition of their hearts, and less and less they prayed their silent prayer.

One day a lady said to her maid: "Twice, Mary, I have found a horrid ant in the bread. You are not clean; you do not clean your larder carefully." Mary was offended, and she said to her fellow servants: "I know where those beastly little ants come from; it is that horrid ant-hill outside the yard by the garden gate."

With great determination Mary went into the kitchen, and took the kettle of boiling water off the hob, walked deliberately into the yard and poured and poured the boiling water on to the beautiful ant-hill. She passed many ants on her way—a billion ants would not have covered her foot, and two billion ants would not have covered the kettle. Ants *could not see things so much larger than themselves.*

They perished and were scattered. Some were filled with the madness of horror that stole their wits away—some were filled only with evil excite-

ment—some just ran on, crowding stupidly together
—some became inert with grief and died. But the
cunning ones quickly began to build another ant-hill.
They called their work "progressive"; they had run
such a long way. They gave freedom to others, and
these thought themselves fine, original fellows.

And a new religion cropped up that each and every
ant was free to live as he chose—to work as he
would—for in the scattering and the rush, all selfishness came to the surface, and sin and discontent were
everywhere, and Destruction was *within* themselves.

In time evil became exhausted, as it always does,
and what evil bred, perished. The old eternal wisdom of simple, selfless faith in right-doing, slowly
got the upper hand, and the honest workers trium-
phed over the lawless ones.

Another beautiful ant-hill grew. And in the
prayer houses silent prayer was again in the hearts
of all, against Destruction, but these words were
added aloud: "If it come, let it not scatter our wits—
blinding our vision."

CHAPTER XIII.

IN June 1904, at the Camden Theatre, I produced *Warp and Woof,* by Edith Lyttelton.* What ·a first night it was! The mounted police had to be called to keep the curious crowd from the door. They came to see all the "fine ladies and gentlemen," for it had leaked out that the play was by the wife of a distinguished Member of Parliament, and that all the smart world would be present.

It was an excellent little play.

A dreadful thing to contemplate, but a very true thing, is that to produce an intelligent play of a friend, is far more exciting than to produce a play by William Shakespeare, and for many reasons. To begin with, Mr. Shakespeare is not present to blame, to praise, or to please. If his play is a failure it is your fault, if it is a success, you do not really share in it. Every word, every scene is known beforehand; there is never the thrill of surprise; he is covered from his crown to his toes with tradition; it is all a "fly on the wheel" business. And if you want to do things your own way, in Mr. Shakespeare's play, you are called "difficult"—until you almost burst with indignation.

* The Hon. Mrs. Alfred Lyttelton.

But in the case of a friend's play, what a difference! There is the happiness of helping a friend to success, and it is all such fun. . . .

Warp and Woof was full of simple, straightforward sincerity; many characters were well drawn. The papers called it a "tract," a "sermon"; it showed up the thoughtlessness and selfishness of one class, the wicked "sweating system" of another, and the suffering of the helpless. To those who were not aware of it already, there was the discovery that the authoress was a woman of much more than ordinary intelligence.

My next venture was a third visit to America, and this time Stella accompanied me, though not to act.

The fatigue of constant travelling told upon her, and after some weeks she went to stay with friends of mine in Canada.

On 11th October, 1904, I opened in New York, under Charles Frohman's management, in *The Sorceress,* translated by Louis N. Parker, from the French play of Sardou, *La Sorcière.* The play was a great success in New York, and later on in all the big cities.

I played nothing else that season from October to April.

Everywhere the showy, splendid production, and the brilliantly theatrical *rôle* of "Zoraya" delighted the audience. This *rôle* was entirely different from anything I had played in America before. The statement that had often been made—that most of the women I played were alike—subsided.

I fancy the human mind naturally notices most actively what is strange to it, and this, perhaps, explains the fact that on my first visit, there were those who found my acting monotonous.

To an eye unfamiliar with a certain style of painting, an artist's pictures, whether reproducing a haystack or a Cathedral, look alike; it sees in all, that style which is novel to it, but when the work is more familiar, it is different.   Then the imagination of the artist, and the many different aspects of his mind—his points of feeling and "attack"—are gradually recognised.   Perhaps it was a little like this with my work.

In Philadelphia, after I had been on tour for about five weeks, I slipped on the step of the brougham, which had come to take me to the theatre.

I had Pinkie under one arm, and some books under the other.   The books I dropped, but I did not drop Pinkie—and I broke my knee-cap in two.

What a happening it was!   I remember being carried out of the brougham—in some peculiar way in slipping I had fallen into it.   They lifted me out on to a chair with my knee somewhere near my chin, and the broken part of my leg dangling.   Doctor Martin was sent for.   When he came he broke up a wooden hat box to make a splint, and then pulled down my leg and placed it straight. I had noticed in the mirror when I was being carried up in the chair in the lift, that my face was blue. I asked the doctor why that was, and he said, breaking the knee-cap was the most painful thing in the world.

I insisted at once on sending a cable to my mother, and as the doctor was getting the splint ready, I dictated it to my dear friend Miss Waldron. She was sitting on my bed as she wrote it down, with her face turned away from me. I asked her why she would not look at me; she would not answer. She told me afterwards that my face was distorted with pain.

I remember my one dread was, that my mother might be terrified by some awful accounting in the papers. She was very ill at the time. I cabled

"DO NOT BELIEVE EXAGGERATED ACCOUNTS IN PAPERS. NOT ANYTHING SERIOUS."

Then there was a long drive to the Pennsylvania University Hospital. I was told that fifteen doctors were in the room when Doctor Martin set and wired my knee. They knew the accident meant the loss of a small fortune for me, and perhaps of my career—and somebody stole my black silk stocking as a memento!

I remember that kind and most gifted actor, the

late Richard Mansfield, telegraphed, asking whether he could take on my company, that he would be delighted to do so, if it would help me.

"Ouida" sent me the following letter:

Lucca,
"10th January, 1905.

"Dear Madam,

"I am unknown to you, but I venture to thank you for the admirable example you give of affection for your dogs.

"It is most valuable in a world which is so cruelly indifferent to the canine race.

"I was grieved to read of your accident, and hope your captivity will be sooner over than the doctors think.   It is a very great misfortune to befall one so gifted and admired.

"With my sincere sympathy,
"I remain,
"Faithfully yours,
"OUIDA."

Dr. Martin told me that if I could bring myself to realise that I was quite well, and that only my knee was sick, and if I absolutely controlled my nerves, no crutches would be needed, and I would be able to act again in less than five weeks.

Stella, who was still in Canada with my friends, was sent for.

Beo wrote from England:

"4th January, 1905.

"Darling Mother,

"Poor you! How it must have hurt. I can't bear being so far away from you, and you ill. Is Stella with you? . . .

"Do write please.

"I wish, oh I wish I could come out to you. I am sure if you don't let me come out to you, I shall come as an emigrant for £2. . . .

"Have you really to abandon the tour? They have huge placards up, bigger than when Port Arthur fell.

"I wish I was with you to comfort you. . . .

"Tons and tons of love,

"BEO."

"5th January, 1905.

"Darling Mother,

"Do write and let me know everything I am so anxious. The *Daily Telegraph* says, 'internal injuries are bad,' and that you may be permanently lame. Do tell me all, it is so awful being so far away; I hope Stella is a comfort to you. . . .

"Tons of love, darling,

"BEO."

And how we were spoilt!

Friends called in battalions, and flowers and sweets and cakes poured in upon us.

In that Quaker City, the people seemed to me more simple, more home-loving than in other cities in America. They speak differently; they look at you with a deeper glance; they quickly get a little hold of the real feeling in you. . . .

But to go on with my story. I was allowed no crutches. The third week two young doctors were allowed to walk each side of me; I hobbled up and down the corridors with them, and we used to sing glees.

One dying man asked to see Pinkie—my little dog had been allowed in the hospital—and she went in to visit him. He was very ill, and in his delirium he used to say again and again: "Oh, the little dog, the little dog."

The matron, Miss Marion Smith—never was there such a comforting woman—mothered Stella and me: how did she find time with all her responsibilities? I was in my own home in that hospital.

After two weeks I became depressed. My leg was out of the plaster cast, but I could not move it. I realised all the money I had lost, and would lose, and that perhaps I would never be able to walk properly again. Doctor Martin was sent for. It was about nine o'clock in the evening. He did not listen to more than three words, and then said: "Oh, well, if you are feeling like that, you must come to the ball to-night. It is *the* ball in America; the 'Philadelphia Ball' "; and he turned to the nurses and said: "Dress her, make her look beautiful, and I will come back for her in an hour." And they dressed me in a lovely black velvet gown, embroidered with gold thread that Mrs. Osborne had made me—that wonderful dressmaker who died long ago—and they carried me downstairs and laid me in a carriage.

Doctor Martin, and a nurse drove with me, and they carried me into the ballroom and put me on a couch, and there I remained until five o'clock in the morning. Needless to say, I forgot all about my broken knee and my worries.

Doctor Martin pointed out to me a man who was dancing in a most high-spirited but odd fashion, and said: "That is one of my patients." I asked what was the matter with him, and he answered: "He was too eager to catch the train to get to his business— he fell, and the train went over his two feet." I said: "But he has two feet." "Oh, yes! They are wooden feet, but, as you see, he dances all right."

How many friends I have in Philadelphia, and how often I wish they were not so far away!

I think it was in less than five weeks I was acting *The Sorceress* again, but for over two years I sometimes suffered severe pain in my knee.

A certain Doctor Chamberlain was in the wings watching me on the night of my return, and when I came off the stage after the big act—in which I had a very difficult fall, and had to remember my knee—he felt my pulse and said "Normal; few artists come off the stage with a normal pulse; you are all right, my dear, knee and head."

One amusing incident on this tour I remember.

We had arrived at some town after a long, dreary, and airless journey, and, though it was freezing hard, Stella and I felt we must have a drive before we went to the hotel.

We sent the maid on with the boxes, and drove in a large open brougham and pair, that had come to meet us at the station—to see the sights and the park. I may mention that, so far as my memory goes, every town in America has a park.

As we were driving across a bridge, we saw, in the very centre of the frozen river, a spotted brown and white dog, standing shivering on a piece of loose ice—the most forlorn, miserable object. We stopped, and got out of the carriage, and leant over the bridge gazing at the poor animal, wondering what on earth we could do.

Some rough-looking boys came up; I said: "I will give you three dollars if you will go and fetch that dog." They grinned, saying: "Not much," or "Nothing doing"—"Not if I knows it, not for Joseph," in the American language. "Five dollars," they turned their backs on me. "Ten dollars," they stood still. I turned to Stella, remarking in a voice they could hear: "An English boy would go in for nothing." To them I said: "I wish my son were here; he would go in fast enough." Stella whispered: "I'm glad he isn't, mother; I know he would not." In despair—"Twelve dollars." One of the boys slowly turned, went round the bridge and down the bank into the river, cracking through the ice, and fetched the dog—to our great relief.

A few days afterwards Stella and I were in a street car, and the conductor came up to me and said: "Well, you saved Mrs. ——'s life." I stared, not knowing what he meant. "Why, that money you gave for that Spot dog got her the doctor, and the medicine she wanted, and she'll be all right now." I am sure I blushed, as the other passengers smiled at us; both Stella and I felt a little uncomfortable, but were glad to hear "Spot" was all right.

And this reminds me of a "brain wave" that saved Pinkie from being turned out into the cold.

A fussy official came up to me in a car, and said: "No dogs allowed on this car." Only the tip of Pinkie's nose was showing out of the fur of my coat. With a Sidonian sneer, I said: "DOG? It's a 'Verberduna.' " He paused, looked at her, and then at me, and said: "Better keep it in a cage," and walked on.

And I remember finding a bird shop kept by some cruel man. Many of the birds were dead, with their heads through the bars of their cages, in their little water troughs. Never was there such a sight, or such a filthy shop. I spoke to the man. I wonder now what it was I said. He did not answer, and as I turned to go, I saw a bowl of water quite frozen with some goldfish wriggling at the bottom. I lifted it up without a word and walked back to the hotel with it. I then sent for the manager, and told him of the hideous sights I had seen.

As I placed the bowl of fish on the mantel-piece, he asked me if I had bought it. I said: "No, I took it out of the shop and brought it here, so that the ice might thaw. Look at the poor fish." He said: "They won't hurt, but the man will have you up for theft." I rang the bell for the lift and went up to my room. When I came down the bowl of fish had gone and there was a smile on the manager's face.

Another incident happened during this tour which was, to say the least of it, startling.

Returning to my hotel late one afternoon, the elevator boy refused to take me up to my floor "because there was a fire on the floor below it." I explained that my daughter was in my room. He said that he could not help that; it was the rule of the hotel. Some expression came into my face, and some sound into my voice as I exclaimed: "Good God! Is my child to be roasted alive for the rules of this hotel? Take me up at once!"—the boy obeyed me like a lamb!

It was nothing serious; someone had fallen asleep smoking a cigar.

At Pittsburgh there is a long walk, stretching for I do not know how many miles; and straight down from the pavement are the thousands of steel industries, a boiling hell, a hundred and two hundred feet below you. There is no handrail, or any fence between you and the drop, and often there is a dense, black fog from the fumes and the smoke. I asked an American what happened when people fell over. He said: "I guess they don't do it a second time."

At the end of the tour I had to smuggle Pinkie

home to England. How I did it I suppose I ought not to tell.

There was no possibility of getting another permit, and so I bought a Mexican parakeet and took it into my cabin with me. I thought if the sailors heard Pinkie bark I could say it was the parakeet. Unfortunately I told this to Lord Charles Beresford, who was on board, and he amused himself by asking passengers if they had heard Mrs. Campbell's remarkable parakeet "bark."

People began to suspect.

I was still lame—not noticeable on the stage—and my knee was very painful going up or down steps. But when the "Donkey" came up to the side of the ship there was a lady who wanted to go to Holyhead, and down the ladder she went; nobody noticed that under her coat was a small black silk bag. Many anxious faces were watching her from the deck above, amongst them her daughter.

At Holyhead the lady went to an hotel, and in the morning she caught an early train to London, and——

Pinkie was very old, and nearly blind, and I must be forgiven.

But there was trouble, although I had avoided the quarantine.

Mr. Bouchier Hawksley appeared in court for me, and he said, I believe, that the little dog was blind and had no teeth, and that I had broken my leg rather than drop her.

AS ELIZA DOOLITTLE IN GEORGE BERNARD SHAW'S "PYGMALION"

The judge asked Mr. Hawksley what he thought would be the right fine to impose. Mr. Hawksley said gravely. "In view of all the circumstances, thirty shillings."

I had understood the fine was one hundred pounds, and the captain of the ship also would be fined one hundred pounds. I was much relieved.

On my return to England I played the tour I have already spoken of with Madame Sarah Bernhardt in *Pelléas and Mélisande,* reappearing with her in London at the Coronet Theatre.

In May, 1906, I produced at the Criterion Theatre *The Whirlwind,* translated by Mr. Melville from the French play of Mr. Bernstein, *La Rafale;* also *Undine,* a poetic one act play by Mr. W. L. Courtney. Neither of these plays met with much success.

I also produced *The Macleans of Bairness,* a romantic play by Edith Lyttelton. This play had some charm and imagination, but did not appeal to the public.

Then came what to me was a nightmare—*The Bondman* at Drury Lane, by Mr. Hall Caine.

I remember one or two things about this play— the blowing up of a sulphur mine to "Rachmaninoff's Prelude," Miss Henrietta Watson and I squashed up against the wall in the dark, like flies, quite certain that the next moment we would be killed by the most awful "business," "properties," sulphur fumes, rushing and screaming "supers," "property" walls, earth and stones hurled about. Also there were real cows that I had to lead across the stage. I had a short-sighted dresser of the "hook-scratching-down-the-back-for-eye" kind. My own dresser, Julia, was engaged elsewhere, and was unable to come to me. I remembered saying I could not act, I could not live, I could not breathe in the din and the misery; and dear Miss Henrietta Watson came into my dressing-room, and helped me to dress for the rest of the run of *The Bondman*. Bless her kindly heart!

And so it will be seen that some spoiled me utterly, others condemned me eternally.

I can still hear "Rachmaninoff's Prelude" that I had once thought beautiful.

POM!

POM!

POM!

I remember, too, at the rehearsals of this play getting into great trouble because I suddenly asked, "Whose are these children? Are they mine?" Lots of children were about me, catching hold of my hand and my skirts. I had not read the book, and I could not grasp the plot of the play. I believe now they were my brothers and sisters, but I do not remember.

On the first night I found Mr. Hall Caine white

and trembling behind the scenes. I felt dreadfully sorry for him, and thoughtlessly said, "Is this your first play?" I have been wickedly accused of saying it on purpose, and of being heartless, which was just what I was not. Ignorant, impulsive, yes; for, had I stopped to think, I should have remembered his many successes.

These plays were followed by an interesting engagement at the Court Theatre in Ibsen's *Hedda Gabler,* under the management of Messrs. Vedrenne and Barker. I think, perhaps, too, in the background somewhere, Mr. Bernard Shaw.

Mr. Barker attended the rehearsals, and sometimes Mr. Bernard Shaw; their "basso-relievo" method fidgeted me. However, so far as I remember, they left me alone.

My Latin "genre" was the very antithesis of "Hedda"; that I knew beforehand, but I hoped I could overcome this.

The translation used was, I fancy, by Mr. William Archer, but I think it had been tampered with. To me it was unsatisfactory; words here and there, I thought badly chosen, and I regretted more than once that I could not read the play in the original.

The following are some of the thoughts that came to me as I, for a fortnight, studied "Hedda" into the early hours of the morning.

Hedda's physical condition should never quite be out of the mind of the audience—she is in the first months of pregnancy, and the child she carries is of a husband who is a figure of ridicule to her, and a man whose voice, whose love, whose presence, tear her nerves to ribands—that "immortal ass Tesman," but "a respectable man," and a man who was "eager to provide for her"—she thought it safe to marry him. . . .

Eilert Lövborg's nature she scorns—a licentious dreamer, a drinker—such a man she could not marry. She knew him too well through his "confidences"— they had been together mentally in deep dangerous waters—to believe that anything or anyone could save him.

Hedda was not jealous—in the accepted meaning of that word—of the fluffy, golden-haired Thea; neither was she spiteful nor malicious. The destruction of Eilert's manuscript was a *psychological* and *physiological* action—Thea and Eilert's "child."

So dangerously near melodrama, that situation on the stage! . . .

Hedda hands Lövborg a pistol—she is a "General's daughter." "Do it 'beautifully,' Lövborg." . . .

"Shoot yourself through the temple like a man; a man who knows the beast in him is his master. . . ."

A "beautiful" deed—yes, Hedda could respect *that*—she could respect him then. . . .

Hedda is essentially a good woman, a proud, intelligent woman, a well-bred woman in the highest sense. A vital creature, suffocated by the commonplace.

People have told me Ibsen " hated " Hedda—that she was a " great snob," a " cruel woman."

Hedda's absurd feeling for " beauty," her warped " sense of honour " defies the word " snob " and the cunning vulgarity the word suggests.

She is acutely and tragically unhappy—her pride in the dust—this, in her physical condition, explains her neurotic savagery.

And then the end.

Morbidly she foresees her child another Tesman —and Tesman closer to that silly, foolish Thea than he could ever be to her. . . .

Lövborg, the man who has enchained her spirit— dead—and she herself in the power of Judge Brack, a cunning animal, of yet lower strata. . . .

Again she is the "General's daughter." Better dead.

She shoots herself through the temple. . . .

Someone has said Ibsen is never "unjust," always "intolerably, fatefully true."

And this means his actors and his audience must *think,* and think *straight.*

My engagement was for seven matinées, to be played within three weeks. I was delighted. I felt sure if I could play "Hedda" with success the play would run for months. I spent on Hedda's wardrobe well over the salary I would receive.

The Court Theatre was packed at all the matinées, to its capacity.

Mr. Barker came to my dressing-room and told me I could have the translation to take to America and to the English provinces, but that the Court Theatre was not for "stars," and the play would not be continued after the seven performances agreed upon, and then he remarked, "What beautiful hair you have!"

I went in misery to Mr. Hawksley, asking if anything could be done. He pointed out that my contract was for seven matinées only.

Mr. Heinemann, who held the acting rights, made every effort, but Messrs. Vedrenne and Barker were adamant.

Hedda Gabler was taken off. If my memory does not fail me, *The Silver Box* was put on.

So this play by a giant genius; a play perfectly constructed—no empty contrivance, no set speeches, every thought, every word, magnificently significant; demanding the best an artist can give—this play on the eternal tragedy of *im*personal love *un*-awakened—ceased, because the management took exception to the "star system"—at least, such was the reason given to me.

Why I was looked upon as a "star" I do not know.

The picture in my mind of a "star" is a lady who walks on red carpets between ferns and palm trees, people behind her carrying her bouquets, and elderly, devoted admirers standing each side of her, hat in hand. These good things have never happened to me.

An affectionate letter from that clever artist, Miss Henrietta Watson, shows that some members of my profession were pleased with my performance.

"Wednesday night.

"My dear friend,

"I wish I could but half tell you the extraordinary impression you made on me yesterday and all of us with your 'Hedda.' I wouldn't have missed it for anything. You stood so utterly alone; you looked and felt the part most wonderfully. I followed your every thought and expression, I believe. You seemed so marvellously real, I quite forgot the dear woman I love and admire, and found myself looking at this curious, fascinating, and unsatisfied creature. Oh, I can't tell you how I have talked about you. I should have liked to have sat with you for a whole hour and talked of nothing but you in your 'Hedda.'

"I loved your level, still voice, but what meaning and what repression!

"My dear, you were wonderful, and I kiss your feet.

"You must be very tired.

"My thanks and love *always, always*.

"HENRIETTA WATSON."

One London critic of repute said: "Mrs. Patrick Campbell's 'Hedda Gambler' was not one hairsbreadth out." On the provincial tour the *Manchester Guardian* said: ". . . By virtue of a perfect sensitiveness, Mrs. Patrick Campbell marked the quality of each separate personal relation. . . ."

This is just what Ibsen enables one to do.

After my losses at the Criterion Theatre and these few matinées at the Court Theatre, there was nothing for it but America again, but this time Stella was to come with me to act, for at last I had given in. She had done good work with Miss Rosina Fillipi, the teacher she herself had chosen.

I find in a letter written by me to my mother at this time:—

"Darling Mother,

". . . . If Stella can do well, life will be much more interesting for me, for I am very tired of being alone in my work. . . ."

In another letter I say:—

" . . . Beo may go as secretary with Mr. Hawksley to Africa. Mr. Hawksley is doing his best to arrange it. If this falls through there is an idea of his doing some work with a man who is making torpedo boats, and to-day I hear from D. D. Lyttelton that both Alfred Lyttelton and she have heard of two things that might suit him . . . and yet D. D. has found time to worry about me and my affairs. She is such a darling . . . .

"Catherine Horner's wedding to young Raymond Asquith was very pretty. Stella wore the dress she is wearing in the third act of *Tanqueray* when 'Ellean' returns from Paris. We went to the wedding and to the reception at Mrs. Gladstone's.* Then I had a rehearsal from 8 p. m. to 11.30 p. m. in the large room at the Café Monico. After this I came home, dressed, and

* Viscountess Gladstone.

went to the Asquith's ball.   We stayed there until 3 a. m.
I found Beo and Stella dancing reels, and everyone so
gay and happy.

"Stella has been rehearsing beautifully.   Beo came
and was delighted with her and very surprised.   I am
grateful that I can help her.   She is wonderfully obedient
and quick, and sees in a moment when she is stiff or ineffective. . . .

Another letter in which I say:

". . . . Mr. Hawksley is doing his best, but it is
very difficult.   So many want the post—young Englishmen out there, with plenty of experience. . . ."

In the end the appointment for Beo fell through,
so it was decided that he, too, should come with me
to America.

Stella and I had started the tour in the English
provinces to get ready for America, before he joined
us.

From Edinburgh I wrote to my mother:

"My darling Mother,

"Beo has joined us as happy as a lark.   I will take
him with me to America; there are so many opportunities
there.   He will meet interesting and influential people,
and it will be good for him to see the country and look
after us.   He is at this moment playing bridge with
Stella, and I have some young people to be with them
this evening while I do some study.   I am sure you will
think it better for Beo to come with me than to go into
an office in London and live in lodgings.

"The Wemyss's are within motoring distance from here, and D. D. We will see them all this week.

"Let me know if there is anything you particularly want, dearest.

"My love to you. . . .

"Your loving
"BEATRICE."

"Cardiff.

"Darling Mother,

"Stella got on splendidly as 'Mrs. Elvsted.' I wish you had been there. She was as plucky as could be. We are rehearsing all day.

"And now for the great news!

"Beo is gradually making up his mind to be an actor. What do you think?

"So there will be him for me to teach, too, and if I haven't learned enough patience by the end of the American tour it will be a strange thing.

"Beo cannot quite make up his mind, because he first wanted to be an 'Admiral' and then a 'Prime Minister,' and just an actor seems a 'come down' to him.

"I am so grateful to the stage, I cannot feel as he does; we talk together about it at night. I think Stella's success has encouraged him. . . .

"Your loving
"BEATRICE."

I remember an early rehearsal on this short tour.

Our hotel was next to the theatre. Beo arrived in his mackintosh over his pyjamas. The members of the company endeavoured to appear unconcerned, and I tried to keep my dignity. Beo saw my serious face, and said "Well, mother, I overslept, and I thought it would worry you more if I was late"; but he had that look in his eye, so sure that his naughtiness would amuse me.

As far back as 1902 I had arranged for my mother to live at "Gensing Lodge," St. Leonards. I found her on my first return from America in apartments alone, circumstances having led my unmarried sister to live with a girl friend in the country.

"Gensing Lodge" is a delightfully peaceful convent and pension, kept by Augustinian Nuns— French ladies who had come over from Paris some years before.

My mother lived there until she died at the age of 73 in 1908.

The Convent and its little chapel and the gentle Nuns pleased my mother, who could never have found peace or happiness in "apartments."

She was strangely sensitive to her surroundings, and the religious atmosphere, the gardens, and the view of the sea over the trees from her window, brought her the beauty she needed always.

Stella and I used to stay with her, and there was something extraordinarily restful, after the life of the theatre, in the simple religious life—hearing the voices of the Nuns singing at early Mass, and the scent of the incense.

Some of the ladies who lived in the Convent were interesting and amusing, and my mother had many friends.

The Nuns, too, were fond of me. I remember the Rev. Mother saying: "It would be wonderful if you would devote your great energy and gifts to the service of God."

Very many years afterwards in America, Mrs. Edgar Kent, who had just left "Gensing Lodge" to join her husband—a clever member of my company —told me the Nuns often spoke of me and remembered me in their prayers.

This letter I wrote to mother a few days before sailing to America with Beo and Stella:—

"33, Kensington Square,
"28th, October, 1907.

"Darling Mother,

"I cannot tell you how much there is to do here, but I must come to you on Wednesday. If it is late, I will go to the Hotel first, and come to you in the morning. I shall have to be back in town again on Thursday for an afternoon rehearsal. I hope I shall find you looking well.

"Remember all you want to ask me, darling, for it will be many months before we meet, and I would not like to forget anything.

"Beo has absolutely gone mad at the idea of America, it is impossible to manage him. I think he is wild with joy at the thought of being on the *Lusitania*.

"We have a suite of rooms on the sunny side of the upper deck, quite regal; and all through the tour in America I am to have a private train, brass bedsteads, dressing room, observatory room—so you can see miles down the railway line. Imagine it! Stella and Beo and Pinkie, our man servant as well as a maid, all the company; and we carry a coloured cook, four other coloured servants, and four English 'stage staff.'

"And now they cable me from New York that they want me to produce there Hoffmannsthal's *Electra*, together with a little one-act Japanese play called *The Moon of Yamato*.

"Good-bye darling, all news when we meet.

"Your own loving
"BEATRICE."

My mother answered:

"My darling Beatrice,

"I can imagine how alarmingly busy you must be. I am not surprised at Beo going mad at the idea of America. When he smells the sea again he will wish he was an Admiral. I hope you will keep well, it is rather a great deal for you to think and plan. . . .

"The train sounds so pleasant and jolly, with sitting room and observatory car, but I am wondering if you will get any sleep.

"I cannot tell you how delighted I am at Stella's success. Father O'—— was also pleased, and gave me the enclosed cutting of Stella from the *Graphic*.

"I cannot think of anything I want, the jacket only, perhaps one or two cushions would look well in my sitting room. . . .

"My love to Stella, to you darling, and Beo.

"I am better, so don't worry about me.

"Your loving
MOTHER."

In a letter to her I say:

"It is your beautiful nature that keeps you well and young and lovely."

My mother was suffering from a fatal illness; my anxiety for her was a vital moment to me, and yet another incentive to hard work.

She wrote to me more than once:

"A thousand thanks for all your goodness to me darling, do take care of yourself also."

Again I find myself writing to Mother:

". . . We have begun 'one-night stands,' and the work is rather dreadful, but the thought that I have a little money to spare in case those I love want it, is a great comfort, and you, darling, have first claim always. . . ."

It must not be thought that I am peculiarly generous; it is in our blood. Every member of the family, if they had it, would give away at once what they thought, at the moment, was needed more by another.

People will say this leads to the workhouse. I can only speak for myself and say it has found for me very many generous friends.*

I remember a certain aged Peer telling me in great distress that his son had gambled away all the money he himself had saved, over and above his inheritance,

---

* Many years ago Bernard Shaw said to D. D. Lyttelton, "We had better dress up as beggars and go to Stella's door, and what we collect may keep her until she gets another engagement."

during his long life. I said, "Why take it so seriously? To me that large sum of money only represents the money you have not given to those who
may have needed it." He never mentioned the subject to me again.

The life of the stage is a hard one; the sacrifices
it demands are enormous. Peaceful normal life is
made almost impossible by the ever over-strained and
necessarily over-sensitive nerves—caused by late
hours, emotional stress, swift thinking, swift feeling,
and that odd *reculer pour mieux sauter* which comes
upon all public performers: but the reward is no
mean one, and my gratitude to my profession is unbounded.

To go back to the *Lusitania*. Every delight and
amusement young people could wish for surrounded
Beo and Stella, and I was happy, too. They were
safe, beautiful, full of eager life, and my heart was
full of pride and hope, and above all, they were *with*
me.

On our arrival we went to the Plaza Hotel and
then came the "Interviewers!"

Beo coming into the room, and seeing the Interviewers—with me sitting in the centre, Pinkie on
my lap—according to a newspaper, said with a
"British drawl: 'I say, it looks like a game—I
haven't had my dinner.'—and the young Englishman
strolled out." I do not remember this, but on
another occasion, when I was vainly trying to say the
right thing to them, Beo strolled into the room and

said, "I say Mother, I can't find my boots. For some extraordinary reason this remark thrilled the Interviewers. I suppose no American boy would have said this to his mother at such a moment.

Hedda Gabler was received with much praise in New York.*

I remember a performance of *Hedda Gabler* in Kalamazoo—practically the city had turned out to see it. Ibsen had never been played there before. I wanted to send a cable, but was assured there was no one in the post office.

In another town I was told by my business manager that this serious play, and my quiet method, had filled many of the audience with deep sympathy; they made sure I was an invalid.

New York Evening World.— . . . It was a merciless, cold performance. The smouldering fire in the gloomy eyes flamed brightly only once, when, with figure drawn up and head thrown back, in a pose of magnificent challenge, Mrs. Campbell held out the pistol that was to make an end of the disgraced and drunken Lövborg. Mrs. Campbell's personality seemed to exhale suggestions of some vague, mysterious evil in Hedda's relations with Lövborg. Mrs. Campbell's Hedda seemed to have nothing in common with the stage.

CHAPTER XIV.

IN the middle of this tour I was hurried back to New York to produce Arthur Symons' translation of Hugon von Hoffmannsthal's *Electra,* and *The Moon of Yamato,* an original Japanese play of the sixteenth century translated by Comte Robert d'Humière.

"Chicago,
"February, 1908.

"Darling Mother,

"Just a line to send you my love and to tell you that I am quite well again, but Stella has been ill.

"I am not taking her on with me for the next seven days of 'one-night stands.' I am leaving her with a dear old lady, Mrs. Franklyn Macveagh, who has a gorgeous house and loves Stella, so she will be happy, eat well, and rest, and have no end of fun.

"Our tour has been altered, I am glad to say, after these 'one night stands.' I believe we have three days in St. Paul and Minneapolis, and then a season in New York, opening about 7th February. I am to play both the Japanese and Greek heroines. I am very nervous of the work. I wanted Stella to play the Japanese, but the managers want me to do both. Stella will play the sister in the Greek play. I am afraid it will be a strain, for her voice is not matured enough, and the verse is difficult.

"We gave a dinner party, or, rather, a supper, on Beo's 'coming of age' birthday to twenty-five people here, and many of them brought their friends to the dance afterwards, and every one was very happy. Beo and Stella's power of enjoyment is extraordinary.

"Beo made a speech and drank to his mother of twenty-one! Every one stood up and toasted him on his 'sixteenth' birthday! I wish you had been there, dearest.

"Stella looked lovely, but a little delicate, the excitement of acting and not eating regularly. I try my best, but it is hard to manage them.

"My love to you, darling. . . .

"Your own loving,
"BEATRICE."

"Canada.
"Darling Mother,

"Just one line of love. I hope it will get to you for Christmas. . . .

"We are all tired, but we are all three happy. Beo has chosen a difficult part in the Greek play. He plays the Italian manservant in *The Notorious Mrs. Ebbsmith* beautifully. Lord Grey was delighted with him and with Stella. We had a grand house in Ottawa, and Lord Grey and Hanbury Williams came round twice, they were so pleased. Lady Grey wrote asking us to luncheon the next day, but we couldn't go; we had to leave that night. We travelled from 3 a. m. until 6 p. m. and then played *The Notorious Mrs. Ebbsmith*. Think of it!

"I told you in my last letter we are no longer living in the train; it was too stuffy. Next week we have a week's rest, no salary, and I rehearse *Electra* with Beo and Stella and the new little Japanese play that I am going to play with *Electra*. . . .

AN IMPRESSIONISTIC PHOTO

"Pat's sister and her husband and her two children spent a day and night with us—these people who thought my going on the stage a dreadful thing, now envy me and the high spirits of my children!

"The Reverend Mother is right, Beo is full of talent, and I believe will make a fine actor. He looks so big and strong, and has a splendid voice.

"Write when you can and get all you want, and be comfortable in your little sitting-room.

"From your own loving
"BEATRICE."

I had asked M. Gabriel Faurè to write the music for *The Moon of Yamato*. He replied:—

"I am heartbroken over the fact that I am unable to do what you wish me to—I have absolutely no time left, and would not run the risk of delaying your performance. I am *generally* very busy, but in addition, the Ministry has ordered me to attend to a very important Government work, and this is what makes it utterly impossible for me to undertake a task as pressing as the one you did me the honour to ask me, and which I should have been only too happy to accomplish for the "never-to-be-forgotten' 'Mélisande,' had it only been possible.

"Believe me it causes me true regret. . . ."

I had seen *Electra* in Germany at the "Kleines Theater," and thought the German performance, though excellent exaggerated the horror with a crass, brutal realism.

Arthur Symons' translation, without harming the

vivid realism of the original play, put a magic mist of loveliness upon it.

I am told that Hugo von Hoffmannsthal has "preserved the dramatic dignity, the fury and passionate hatred, and the melting pathos of the original play as it has been handed down through the centuries." Though, according to a lover of Greek tragedy, *Electra* played at the Théâtre Français follows the Greek more closely, and "Orestes" plays a mighty part, which adds potently to the effectiveness of the whole.

"The scholar cries out for the Greek chorus."

I have seen the freakish effect of the Greek chorus on the English stage; the figures unimpressive, and uninspired, earnest, drab, drear: a certain music, but the imagination of the artists not awake to that keen inner worship of truth and beauty—the true Greek feeling.

I wanted very much to play Professor Gilbert Murray's beautiful *Electra of Euripides.* I do not remember quite what happened about it; there were words in the contract to the effect that I must produce it "as played at the Court Theatre." My spirit rebelled—I wanted a free hand.

Under the discouraging obstructions things really worth while are met with in the theatre, it was a difficult feat to bring frivolous New York to *Electra,* a play so far removed from themselves.

The part of "Electra" is nearly as long as "Hamlet," with no exit or "curtain" until the end. One particularly touching speech of hers to Orestes and his exclamation: "O my sister!" never failed to make my heart ache and move the audience to tears.

ELECTRA:
>   . . . Who then
> Am I that you should cast such loving looks
> Upon me? See, I am nothing. All I was
> I have had to cast away: even that shame
> Which is more sweet than all things, and like a mist
> Of milky silver round about the moon
> Is about every woman, and wards off
> Things evil from her soul and her. My shame
> I have offered up, and I am even as one
> Fallen among thieves, who rend off from my body
> Even my last garment. Not without bridal-night
> Am I, as other maidens are; I have felt
> The pangs of child-bearing; yet have brought forth
> Nothing into the world, and I am now
> Become a prophetess perpetually,
> And nothing has come forth out of my body
> But curses and despair. I have not slept
> By night, I have made my bed upon the tower,
> Cried in the court, and whined among the dogs.
> I have been abhorred, and have seen everything,
> I have seen everything as the watchman sees
> Upon the tower, and day is night and night
> Is day again, and I have had no pleasure
> In sun or stars, for all things were to me
> As nothing for his sake, for all things were
> A token to me, and every day to me
> A milestone on the road.

ORESTES:
>   O my sister!

How I worked! One week to create two *rôles*—
stage manage and produce, and rehearse Beo and
Stella.

Much sensitive anxiety is added to our labour, when
we rehearse those we love; all producers know this.

I cabled to Lady Tree, then Mrs. Tree, to play
"Clytemnestra." She came over from England and
gave a fine performance, and looked splendid.

This clever actress has an odd waggish intelligence
that does not fail her—even in tragedy.

Stella was lovely as the gentle "Chrysothemis."

An interviewer, the day after the opening performance of both plays, says, speaking of me:—

"The woman is weary, weary, weary—gesture, voice,
and soul—all overcome as by an infinite lassitude." *

I knew the work I had done was good, but my
rival was *The Merry Widow,* and in spite of the following notice in *Town Talk,* alas! *The Merry
Widow* won!

". . . If the mantle of any past-mistress of the mi-
metic art has fallen upon the graceful shoulders of Mrs.
Campbell it is one that never before did I see. Her
genius is unique; not in method, not in technique does
she excel, but in something; perhaps it is nothing more
than her individuality that stands out distinct and all-
satisfying. It would be absurd to hold that she is the
arch-priestess of that academy of acting which holds as

* I am afraid, in spite of the happiness of having my children with
me, and of our success, I was paying blood-money so far as my nervous
system was concerned.

its cardinal principle, the utter eradication of the player's personal identity. It is not to be seriously argued that the blend of Italian and English blood in her veins has given her a temperament that qualifies her beyond all her contemporaries for great artistic achievement. Perhaps there are some actresses whom she does not surpass in imagination, in ingenuity of technique, or in faculty of dramatic invention; but the fact is, she accomplishes more with her art than any woman of whom I have any knowledge. In the exuberance of my enthusiasm inspired of her 'Electra' I seriously doubt whether there is any other woman who can hold an audience from the beginning to the end of that sombre tragedy as adapted for the modern stage by Hugo von Hoffmannsthal.

"With an art that speaks with an electric shock she keeps her audience as much alive as she is herself. How she does it I do not know. . . .

". . . . She creates, one after another, illusions that suspend the power of specific criticism. You see her haunting eyes looking forward to a dreadful consummation, and the horror of the spectacle appals you. In the subtle play of her countenance is mirrored emotions that to you are real. Her very anguish is infectious. The dignity of her grief and resentment is so strong in its appeal that you find yourself in league with her in her horrible designs. Never does this wonderful woman indulge in that explosion of passion which most actors deem essential to the production of the highest dramatic effects. Never does she produce a harsh note. Smoothly, without a jar, her whole life seems to flow into one harmonious, tragic rhythm which is like the solemn beat of a dead march. . . . It is a stern picture of implacable hatred for the living and inextinguishable reverence for the dead. It is the perfection of an art that baffles criticism and analysis."

Speaking of *The Moon of Yamato,* one paper said:—

"The first hour of the evening is given to a tragedy translated literally from the Japanese and acted in imitation of the Japanese way, with Mrs. Campbell bigger than any Japanese actress, if not greater, as she is nearly six feet tall, while a Jap woman of that stature would be put in a native museum as a giantess. The usually statuesque beauty looked a curiosity, anyway, with her black hair coiffured in the mode of Tokio, her big eyes slanted, her habitually bared arms hidden in the sleeves of a kimono, and her erect poise changed to the hinge-back, toggle-knee, grovel and kow-tow manner-isms of 'Yum Yum' in *The Mikado.* Not only did she mince and toddle, she spoke in a weak falsetto and cooed softly as she trotted in and out of her bamboo and paper house. It was a more faithful portrayal of a Jap lady than Blanche Bates in *Madam Butterfly.* For a while the audience was inclined to take her in fun, and to re-gard the unwelcome wooing of a wife by a terrible bandit as comedy; but it developed a tragedy fit to win a medal of originality for its Oriental author."

Within a fortnight I was ill from fatigue and for two nights I could not play.

Then I thought I would like the theatrical pro-fession in New York to see *Electra,* so I invited them to a matinée.

A throng of at least 2,500 people appeared. The theatre was crowded to the last inch.

And so the spirit of *The Merry Widow* drove me once more "on the road," this time to California.

In San Francisco signs of the great earthquake were everywhere, fires were still smouldering–

Some stone pillars, stone steps, a bit of iron railing, a few geraniums and ferns, a great mountain of dust and débris—*that* was once a mansion with beautiful gardens; so on for miles—as far as the eye could see.

I played "Electra" in a large, low, corrugated-iron building. For the hour and three-quarters the audience sat breathless—the play appealed to their imagination—and again as so often before, I was overpraised, spoiled, petted and fêted.

Among the many stories told me about the earthquake, one carries the character of San Francisco.

Immediately New York heard of the catastrophe, she sent a long train loaded with cheap and useful necessities of life. It was sent back with its goods, to bring all the best and finest luxuries—San Francisco would accept no charity.

She started building immediately: many made large fortunes by clearing away the dust.

A drunken man slept through it all; when he awoke and saw the world flattened out and the roaring fires, he went to bed again, thinking he was still drunk. . . .

And then the story of Caruso, who lifted up his head and sang his highest note, to see if his voice was all right.

One of my dearest friends lives near San Francisco—Mrs. Harriet Carolan.

And another—Edward Sheldon*—who is loved by many of us.

He sent me cables and letters that pulled me through dark hours, and, though I do not want to anticipate what the years brought, I quote a cable that melted my heart:

"Los Angeles.
"July, 1919.
"Stella dear, I love and believe in you. Wish I was there. Sure this cannot conquer you. You are so high above their reach. Tenderest thoughts and affection.
"NED."

And a letter:

"Los Angeles.
"August 30th, 1919.
"Stella dear,
"Your letter has just come. . . . I wish courage and wisdom could keep you from suffering. I know they can't, but they will carry you *through* it, anyway. . . . Time usually brings out the truth, and I imagine that is what you want. Your bewilderment comes from not being able to see it now. . . . I know you hate to walk in darkness, but you won't for long. One thing I am

* Dramatic author: *Romance, Salvation Nell,* and other successful plays.

sure of, you have made no mistake in keeping your ideals high as the stars. Even what you are going through now wouldn't bring you as much suffering as trying to lower them. That is the sort of person you are, and you can never change, thank God!

"NED."

But to go back to *Electra.*

The great Modjeska saw *Electra* in Los Angeles. She wrote to me afterwards:

"Orange Co.
"Saturday.

"Dear Mrs. Campbell—beautiful 'Electra,'

"I saw the play this afternoon, but could not call on you after the performance, because I came to Los Angeles without my husband and had to catch the train in time for dinner. What a prosaic thing to speak about —trains and dinners, after having seen what I have seen.

"What a tremendous part, and what a wonderful achievement! I am so happy to have seen it, because that thing will live with me. I never shall forget the moments of real artistic delight that came to my share this afternoon, and I want to thank you for it. Your 'Electra' is beautiful and most impressive in all details, and I do not know any one who could play this part as you play it. Every pose, every modification of voice was perfect, but, what was most wonderful, the feeling, the passion, your own self animating that classic personage and making it a real—a living—suffering creature. But I must stop in fear of writing too much. I know how tired you must be playing every night and Saturday matinées, and travel, too.

"The Japanese play was charming, and your daughter very sweet in her part.*

"I was sorry not to be able to say 'good-bye' to you both, but I hope to meet you again some day.

"In the meantime I will say 'au revoir' and 'bon voyage.'

"With affectionate admiration,
"Yours always,
"HELEN MODJESKA."

In January, 1908, I heard from my mother that she had been very ill.

". . . . I am still in bed, but out of danger. I require to be very careful to get strong. There is very little cough left. The night before the nurse came the Reverend Mother sat up all night in my room. She is a perfect angel!" . . .

I was very anxious to get back to England.

In March, Stella was sent for by Sir George Alexander—Sir Arthur Pinero wanted her for his play, *The Thunderbolt,* at the St. James's Theatre—she had done splendidly in America, and I felt, with Sir Arthur's help, she would make a success in London.

I wrote from Chicago to Mother:

"I have just had your sad little letter, darling. I am afraid you are not nearly well yet, and I feel very anx-

* Stella had bravely taken up my part, as the work was too hard for me.

ious. . . . I will be home, I think, in about five weeks. It will break my heart if I don't find you quite strong.

"I hope Stella has seen you.

"The air in California—the flowers and the birds— and the palm trees!   How I wished all the time, dearest, you could have enjoyed them, too.   The people were wonderful to me. . . .

"And now a secret.   Beo has fallen in love with a very beautiful young girl, charming in every way.   I send you her little note to me, which will show you what a darling, happy thing she is.   She is very fair and tall.

"The question is, what is to be done?   They want to marry.   Her people haven't much money.   I say nothing; he is so proud and happy, I am afraid of interfering.   She is in Chicago, and he will see her on our way back. . . .

"I will write again.   In the meantime get well, dearest.

"Your own loving
"BEATRICE."

On my return from America I found my mother very fragile.   I had not realised how ill she had been.

In July she died . . . and the world was different—there was no one left to call me "child" any more.

In death she looked a marble figure of a lovely girl; her black hair scarcely tinged with grey, in two plaits around her head.

My beautiful Italian mother!

My children loved her tenderly, and gratefully.

My brothers and sisters loved her too, but I know I set her highest. . . .

"You are brave, darley, and you work so hard." That was always her praise of me. . . .

Once—how many years ago?—she said to me: "Some people have white blood, some people have red—yours is red!"

I remembered those words long afterwards when callousness stunned me.

I have so many very obvious faults. Why did my mother never censure me? I often ask myself that question.

CHAPTER XV.

SIR Arthur Pinero's fine play *The Thunder-bolt* had been a great success in London, and Sir George and Sir Arthur allowed me later to take it on tour for Stella, who had played her part with much charm; it was a sensitive bit of work and I was very proud of her.

In November, 1908, at the New Theatre, I gave a series of matinées of Hoffmannsthal's *Electra* and Mr. W. B. Yeats' lovely *Deirdre.*

I remember hearing that Sir Charles Wyndham and Miss Mary Moore surreptitiously watched me from a box conducting a rehearsal, and for the first time, I believe, credited me with some good sense.

The delicate beauty of *Deirdre* delighted the audience, and the wild, vivid, passionate tragedy of *Electra* also caught hold of them.

Mr. W. Archer headed his review of these plays, "A New Actress," and with some condescension, remarked:—

"Mrs. Campbell has an imagination which requires the magic spark of poetry to kindle it to a creative glow. . . . It is hard to imagine her after such performances as these, relapsing to the mannered prettinesses—the adroit evasions which have so often been her standby in the past. . . ."

The Times wrote with more sympathy:—

". . . Much playgoing, it may be, makes one callous, but it will be long before we shall think without a shudder of the 'Electra' we saw yesterday . . . a festered lily —something less than a woman, because it is the wreck of what has been more than most women. . . ."

But reviews had lost their interest for me now that my mother and my uncle were no longer in this world. . . .

After these matinées I went on a tour in the English provinces with *Deirdre* and *Electra,* and I remember at Southport there was a fearsome occurrence.

In *Electra* towards the end of the play, when, holding a lighted torch above her head, Electra is waiting for the death cry of Agamemnon—the lighted methylated spirit fell from the torch on to my hair—the scene was very dark—a member of my company, who was sitting in the front of the house, said the little flames dancing about my head made me look like a Christmas pudding!

As I endeavoured to put them out with my hands, they trickled down my face and arms, the audience stood up, and among the excited murmurs a woman shrieked: "Will no man save her!" This struck me as ludicrous, and I laughed.

The actors standing in the "wings," ready to rush on, seeing me smile, kept back: coming down to the footlights, I said: "Please sit down, this stuff does not hurt." By that time the flames were out—my hands were slightly scorched and a little of my hair was burned.

On the 19th January, 1909, I played at the Vaudeville Theatre, under Messrs. Gatti's management, *Olive Latimer's Husband,* by Mr. Rudolph Besier. Olive was a gentle, tender lady with a dying husband upstairs, who never appeared in the play——

As I recollect it, the lady is in love with the doctor, and her love is returned—the husband dies—her heart breaks, and love is over. It was treated simply, realistically, and was very moving.

I remember Lord Ribblesdale liking the play very much; and a delightful letter I had from Miss Rosina Filippi, which unhappily is lost.

At home, my son was fretting for the lovely girl he had left in Chicago, and I was troubled about him.

One night, after an especially long talk we had, I went to his room and sat on his bed—his eyes were full of affection for me, and love and yearning for beautiful Helen; it was more than I could bear. I said, "Perhaps I could furnish you a little flat with some of the things from here, and make you an allowance for a year—you would have to work hard, ever so hard—American girls only look up to men who work for them, and provide for them well; and for their children. I kissed him and went back to bed.

In the morning early he came to my room, with

a smile—"Was it really you, mother, who spoke to me last night, or was it an angel who sat on my bed?"

That day he cabled to Chicago that he would come. Before he sailed, a letter arrived from the American father, saying he could not let his girl marry on such conditions——

Beo only laughed and, full of hope, sailed away.

Within a fortnight came a cable, "Marry on the 25th, mind you don't get a stuffy flat, loving Beo."

Stella and I set to, and we worked hard. Everything that could be spared from our little house we carried into the small flat we had found for them on the other side of Kensington Square.

And they came—he, full of pride—she, all loveliness and charm. Her delightful manners, and witty way of expressing herself won the heart instantly: and then there were her pretty clothes, her freshness and gaiety, making Kensington Square a garden of flowers.

*　　*　　*　　*　　*

In July, 1909, I produced *His Borrowed Plumes,* by Mrs. George Cornwallis West.*

Jenny, at a luncheon party, told me that a London manager had said he would produce the play for her for three hundred pounds.

She read the play to me. It had certain points of cleverness, and I considered that, with ingenious

* Lady Randolph Churchill.

production and good actors, it could be pulled together, and perhaps made into a success.

Feeling it would be a friendly act and an amusing piece of work for me, I offered to produce it for her.

So it was eventually arranged.

After all, good plays only too often meet with a fortnight's run, and splendid plays, such as *Hedda Gabler, Electra, Pelléas and Mélisande, Beyond Human Power,* and *Deirdre,* with a few special matinées; perhaps *His Borrowed Plumes* might attract the public.

An exaggerated importance gradually grew around the production, owing to Royalty and many distinguished people being interested in it.

Serious work became difficult—but was most necessary to hold the play together—some of the actors started calling the play "Sorrowing Blooms"— a dangerous sign.

Jenny, I fancy, imagined producing her play would be of some social advantage to all of us: I was intolerant of what I thought nonsense, and showed it quickly.

At the first performance everybody who was anybody, and who could procure a seat, was present.

The critics enjoyed themselves, the applause was of the heartiest, the play was looked upon as clever.

Mr. Walkley, in *The Times,* was nice about me and funny about hats:—

"When mundane ladies—if the Gallicism may pass—
when mundane ladies produce original modern comedies
out of their own original modern and quite charming
heads, all the other mundane ladies who have written
original modern comedies themselves, or might have
done so if they had chosen, or are intending to do so
the very next wet afternoon, come and look on. These
are the occasions that reconcile one to the theatre. For
a sudden feminine glory invades it and transfigures it,
so that it becomes an exhibition of beauty and elegance;
the very latest dialogue on the stage is accompanied by
a *frou-frou* of the very latest Paris fashions in the
stalls. An especially pleasing detail is the air of sweet
resignation—is it the firm composure of the martyr or
the serene smile of the seraph?—with which the ladies
remove the wide-brimmed and very high-crowned hats
of the present fashion from their heads and pose them
very delicately upon their knees. It is with an effort
you divert your gaze from this fascinating spectacle to
the proceedings on the stage. But this is only to ex-
change one pleasure for another of the same sort. For
on the stage you have a bevy of ladies supporting—
beautiful caryatides that they are!—the same remarkable hats, with the privilege of not having to remove
them. In the presence of so many and so beautifully
complicated hats it is, of course, impossible to think of
them as mere coverings for the human head. They
really fulfil the important office of creating an illusion
about life, like the poetry of Shelley or the music of De-
bussey. With their exaggerated brims and monstrous
crowns they completely shut out the dull, the work-a-day,
and the disagreeable. Everything you feel is for the
best and looking its best, and wearing its best in the best
of all Directoire worlds.

ON ONE OF HER LATER TOURS TO AMERICA

"And yet, by a sort of paradox, what was perhaps the most beautiful thing, what was certainly the most suave and distinguished thing in the Hicks' Theatre yesterday afternoon—we mean, of course, Mrs. Patrick Campbell —wore no hat. . . ."

Then in the unexpected way things sometimes happen in this world, George Cornwallis West was seriously attracted by me. . . .

I believed his life was unhappy, and warmly gave him my friendship and affection. . . .

This caused gossip, misjudgment, and pain, that cannot be gone into here.

In September, 1909, I played in a sadly cut play of M. Brieux, *False Gods,* at his Majesty's Theatre.

I was curiously uncomfortable in my work in this theatre: a disturbing mixture of domesticity and art, of Society and Bohemia, of conventionality, and vagary—irritated me.

Besides, I always felt the polite thing to do would be to give up my part to Lady Tree.

Sir Herbert Tree, in my opinion, was the best character comedian of his day. His slightly foreign manner, distinction and elegance, and fantastic grace, gave an arresting charm to his work.

In *jeune premier* parts, I thought him tiresome; in tragedy insincere; and his "Hamlet" wearied me in its self-obsession; though full of picturesque grace.

He was a most lavish producer and a splendid "showman."

There was a strange want of sequential significance in his acting, and in himself, a manner of not unfascinating preoccupation.

His method on the stage was for "flashes." He loved his profession deeply, and independently of his own success: his friendliness, enthusiasm, and above all his warm hospitality are a household word; and he had culture, wit, and imagination.

His saddest mood could be charmed away in a moment by a witty or funny remark. He hated illmanners and ugliness—youth and beauty led him like a lamb.

When his feelings were hurt he blushed and looked bewildered, which was extraordinarily attractive.

The gods were good to him; he died unexpectedly in a moment, and many were left to mourn.

After *False Gods,* which was not a success, *Beethoven* was produced. With it I played *Expiation,* a play rehearsed to precede *Beethoven,* but on the opening night Sir Herbert had decided that it should come last.

Following the death of "Beethoven" and the great Symphony, a Russian spy story was impossible.

I was told that Tree not only made his speech, but that the orchestra played "God Save the King," and the critics and most of the audience left the theatre before my one-act play commenced! Let us hope this story is an exaggeration.

In 1910 I went to America again. I had no engagement; only a strong desire to get away from England—and gossip. . . .

And, as usual, money had to be made.

I was full of anxiety over my Stella, too; she had made up her mind to marry a man I scarcely knew, who had lived in Africa for many years. Stella was so sure she was doing right in giving up her profession and life and friends in England that, in my anxiety for her happiness, I appeared wanting in loving sympathy.

On a Saturday I decided to sail for America, and on the Wednesday I had left Kensington Square, with Helen, Stella, and Beo in charge.

On my arrival in New York I telephoned to Mr. Norman Hapgood, saying: "Here I am. I have quite a good one-act play and a lovely frock, and I would be glad of a vaudeville engagement. What shall I do?"

He said: "Ring up Albee, the head of the Vaudeville circuit."

I rang up Mr. Albee, who made an appointment with me.

Mr. Albee—one of those American men who make you feel "you are all right" and "he is all right"— saw me, and I told him I had an effective play, *Expiation,* and a beautiful dress, that I would play twice a day, and I wanted £500 a week—a large salary, but I knew well I would never be able to play twice a day and travel on Sundays for any length of time.

Some other men came into the room during my interview with Mr. Albee, and they consulted together. Eventually it was decided that I should play for a week outside New York, and if I proved worth it, they would engage me at the £500 a week for ten weeks.

I played, and they were satisfied.

In the meantime Stella was engaged by the late Mr. Harry Irving as his leading lady in London.

After a few weeks, first Beo and then Helen joined me in America, and we three travelled together.

Oh, those two performances of *Expiation!* I had to kill a man twice a day and shriek—and it had to be done from the heart—the Americans see through "bluff"—and I was advertised as a "Great tragic actress"!

Later on, Helen and Beo went to her people in Chicago, and I continued the tour alone.

One day—I forget in which town—it was time to get up and think about the morning performance. I found I was unable to make any effort to move. My maid rang the telephone for the Hotel doctor—I tried to speak; it was impossible, I could only cry. "No more acting; away to Canada, to St. Agathe des Montes, and stay there until your nerves are mended," said the doctor.

And I went, and there I remained alone, unutterably sad—walking about that lovely place. Canaries—sand—glorious sunsets—no paths, planks of wood—fields of large white daises with millions of fireflies—flat patches of water reflecting the sky. . . .

After ten weeks' rest I was well. I joined Helen and Beo in Chicago, and produced a little one-act play of Beo's *The Ambassador's Wife*. It was quite a success in its way, and gave them both great encouragement.

I then received a cable from Mr. Gesier asking me to act in his play *Lady Patricia*. I arrived in London the day before the first rehearsal, leaving Beo and Helen in Chicago.

Lady Patricia was produced at the Haymarket on 22nd March, 1911. Mr. E. Lyall Sweete—my old friend of Mrs. Bandmann Palmer days—was responsible for the production of this brilliant comedy. After the first night, he sent me the following letter:

"Garrick Club, W. C.,
"23rd March, 1911.

"Wonderful. There is nothing left on that score for me to say. The papers have said it all with one unanimous shout of delight. Oh, but I knew they would. But for the rest, how can I thank you enough for suffering a fool so gladly. . . .

"All my congratulations on a great achievement—not greater than I knew it would be, but greater than you would allow it might be. All my gratitude for your forbearance, your patience and help—invaluable in suggestion or personal embellishment and my devotion.
"T. S. . . ."

In the early part of this year Stella went away to

Africa to get married. I could not refuse my consent to her marriage any longer—my lovely sensitive girl. . . .

I understood at last the cry my mother gave 28 years before.

Amongst my papers I find this little letter from Beo whom I had left in America with Helen, written to Stella:—

"24th February, 1911.

"Darling Stella,

"Just a line to ask you to let me know exactly when you sail for Nairobi. I hope to goodness Helen and I can get back to England at least to say 'good-bye,' and 'good luck and happiness.'

"I'm just beginning to realise, old girl, now you're going, how much I love you, and how much I shall miss you.

"I went to the Zoo yesterday and looked up all the animals that live in Nairobi.

"Be very careful of the IHTZPMZZES, they are nasty creatures, and don't get bitten under the eyelids by the HPITTOPOTOHHOZSH.

"Write me a line.

"Love from Helen,

"Your loving brother,
"BEO."

In September I went to New York again, very thankful to be out of England. . . .

I played *La Vierge Folle,* translated by Mr. Rudolf Besier from the French of M. Henri Bataille.

At Mr. Frohman's request the play was much altered; the religious argument being entirely eradicated, thereby making it simply a story of a wife chasing a husband, who was enjoying life away from her with a "foolish virgin."

At the end of the play the poor girl, overhearing the wife's appeal to the husband, shoots herself.

In the French it is a fine play; the religious argument against the wilful destruction of the virgin soul, and the wife's belief in her duty to be of spiritual help to her husband, give dignity and some excuse to the ugliness of the story.

The Americans disliked the play intensely.

I was back in England again within four months. *Bella Donna* was sent to me from the St. James's Theatre to read. I did not care for the play, or the part, and refused it.

About this time Helen wrote to me from America, begging me to let her and Beo return to Kensington Square. I was delighted to send for them, for I was very lonely there.

Again Sir George Alexander sent me *Bella Donna*. This time I accepted the part.

On December 9th, 1911, *Bella Donna* was produced at the St. James's Theatre.

The smart world was interested, and the play made a small fortune.

One night during the run of this play, I was driving to the St. James's Theatre; a boy on a bicycle coming into the main road from Rutland Gate ran into my taxi. My taxi swerved to get out of the way and smashed into another taxi.

My head went through the window opposite me—I saw stars—my hatpin broke in two. Someone picked up the boy and took him to St. George's Hospital. I hailed another taxi and drove on to the theatre.

My faithful Julia said "What is the matter, Madam, you look so funny?" "I have been bumped about in a taxi"—but she had gone out of the room. In a few moments George Alexander came in. I told him I was all right and I was going to play. He told me to look in the glass. I looked, and the top of my head resembled Ally Sloper's!

Sir George sent for a doctor, who ordered me home at once; and said ice bags were to be put on my head all night. The skin was not broken, the hæmorrhage was internal. I was begged not to talk; but I was quite incapable of stopping.

Little tiny threads of cotton seemed to be pulling my head up into the air.

Next day and for some days afterwards my face was black and blue, and my eyes were imperceptible.

Within a fortnight, though still ill, I was persuaded by my friends, Sir Edward and Lady Stracey, to go with them by boat and motor to Aix. The doctor there said hot baths would soothe my stiff body and do me good. On the contrary, after a week they made me very ill.

A cable came from America offering me a fine tour with a one-act play of Sir James Barrie's. I hurried home. The night I arrived my son had come up from the country to see me—Beo and Helen had been living away from London; he was busy writing his play, *The Dust of Egypt*—Gerald du Maurier produced it later at Wyndham's Theatre with success—he looked into my face and said, "Mother, you are ill; I'm going to sleep here." I went to bed—he sent for his wife. How glad I was to have them with me!

I was in bed for over six months in one position. It was nearly nine months before I could walk. People said I was "blind" "paralysed by the taxi accident"; and the papers said I was "sinking fast." I believe nine doctors were consulted; I used to hear them talking in the room below me.

But my mind possessed one feeling only, that I need not trouble about anything any more—even to lift my eyelids or move my hand. I had no sense of time; only a glorious sense of peace.

There were whispers of "brain"; candles used to be held in front of me, and my eyelids lifted up. My body was the nearest thing to death that life can hold. My living mind grasped the utter futility and weariness of all this business of life, and I dwelt upon the ineffable quiet of death.

At first only when my son or his wife was in the room, or a friend with a frightened face, was I able to make an effort and pull myself together—

33, 'Kensington Square—a little Queen Anne house, white panelled within, clean, austere almost—where my children had grown up—there I lay, month after month.

Outside they placed straw halfway round the Square to drown the noise of the carriages that later brought friends, and many distinguished people anxious to see me, and help me if they could.

Some sat by my bed and told me stories to amuse me. From my sick-bed I looked upon them with despair. How could these things matter, how could people be amused by them?

I remember the day my devoted and beautiful daughter-in-law put her head round the screen of my bed, and whispered, as though she could hardly believe the good news, "You are going to live!" I had not seen her for many hours.

To her it seemed such happy news; it only made me wretched. I should have to stand up again, face that looking-glass, think what hat I should put on, worry about George's affairs—there was talk of bankruptcy and divorce—go to the theatre every night and act. I should have to pick up the senseless things of life and go on with my "career." Why? what for?—and there would be all the bills for this illness to be faced.

The old morbidity that had been my life-long enemy had got hold of me, and just to slip into my bed and out of the world seemed a splendid escape. I closed my eyes, and for some weeks made no fight of any kind—coward that I was.

The following few letters express the concern and affection my friends and others felt for me.

The late Lady Savile wrote:

"12, Charles Street.

"I did so love getting your letter. . . . It makes me so miserable to think of your being ill—I love to think of you as always well and happy and prosperous.

"I am getting on slowly. I still have terrible nights of pain, but it must take time to wear off, and one must be patient. The moment you can see me and I am allowed to go out I shall arrive with two able-bodied men to carry me up to you. At present the doctor won't let me leave my room; so tiresome.

"Dearest love.

"Your loving
"VIOLET."

The day came, when I asked why there were no flowers or letters from Violet—they did not like to answer me—she was dead.

Her daughter, Dorothy, wrote:

"My darling Stella,

"Thank you with all my heart for your dear, dear words of comfort. She loved you and I know you loved her. She was thinking of you all the time, and longing to make you well.

"Please take great care of yourself. . . . You were such a help to her and made such happy hours for her.

"Your loving
"DOROTHY."

"Aunt Madeline" was ill and could only come once to see me.

"December 7th, 1912.

"Dearest, dearest Beatrice,

"What a broken reed am I, not to be able to come to you when you are ill and call for me in your sickness. . . .

"I have had to stay in bed with a bronchial cold, and have not been out of my room. It is a real heart sorrow to me not to be able to come to you *now*, to-day.

"All this past week I have been thinking of you and wondering and wondering what you were deciding on with the doctors, and praying that all would be and go well with your decisions.

"I was so struck with your calmness and braveness when you talked with me that day I saw you, but I don't want you to have to be calm and brave. I want you to be well and strong and happy. You have been such a faithful, loving friend to me ever since we first met. You have made me feel that you have placed me, from the first, on the list of your first and greatest friends and have never changed, and I have always felt you love me, and so I feel sad in failing to be of any use to you now just when you want me. It touched me more than I can say when Helen told me that you would rather see me now than any other friend. God bless you for that—and I do love you, and my spirit, which is strong, is with you to-day, when my worn-out, useless body cannot come! I am glad that you are writing to me, and I hope it will not tire you. But when you have told me all that you are thinking about yourself, I shall be able to write to

you better. The first day I can get out I will come to
you.

> "Your loving and oldest friend,
> "MADELINE WYNDHAM.
"God bless you and make you well."

I felt, in some way, that I belonged to Aunt Madeline—and it was always easy to me to be quite frank
with her.

The closeness of our friendship began in the old
days at "Clouds."

When everyone had gone to bed, I would say:
"Let us sit up and talk a little, sleep is such a waste
of time," and she squeezed my arm and said: "Isn't
it?"

She gave more sympathy and understanding in an
hour than another would give in a lifetime—with
her knowledge of this world and of the world of
art. She seemed to be in touch, too, with the world
beyond. Most people are waiting for miracles. I
think Aunt Madeline found miracles everywhere. . . .

I have never seen in anyone the same eagerness to
bring friend and friend together, that each might
appreciate the gift or charm of the other. She was
all warmth and welcome; in her presence no one
could feel "out in the cold."

Many of her children and her children's children
are blessed with some of her radiance. . . .

And from Africa, loving, anxious "code" cables came from my Stella.

Among a multitude of letters from those in my profession and strangers, this little note from Ellen Terry:

"215, King's Road,
"Saturday morning.

"My dear,
"I'm so sorry you are ill—I knew nothing of your accident! I have been at my little cottage in the country with some of my grandchildren, and have been for the last three months so wrapped up in my own ills I had no time to read the newspapers. I, too, have had an accident; must have knocked up against something and broke my heart—at least, it is in a horrid condition and all my vitality gone. Sloth has hold on me, I fear, and I enjoy nothing but sleep! ! ! Although I get precious little of that!

"Do get well—and keep on being lovely Patricia Campbell.

"Don't dream of answering this note. I just want you to know I'm sorry you're ill. I hope you have good news of little Stella.

"Yours always,
"ELLEN TERRY."

D. D. Lyttelton sat with me almost every day!—endeavouring to inspire me with the beauty of life—the desire to live and to believe in life and happiness.

But directly I was alone there was that feeling that I could not take up life again.

One day George came to see me; I had not seen him for a very long time; he seemed deeply moved and unhappy. His words "Live, Stella; live, and help me" touched me to the roots of my being, and the belief that I *could* help him remained with me.

*   *   *   *   *

There was one who perhaps through the intelligent grasp of his genius, understood a little the nerve rack of my illness. Himself living in dreams, he made a dream-world for me. Only those who can understand this, can understand the friendship Bernard Shaw gave to me by my sick bed—the foolish, ridiculous letters he wrote me, and his pretence of being in love with me.

He revelled in the mischievous fun and in the smiles he brought to my face. He did not care a snap of the fingers at the moment what anybody else might say or think.

CHAPTER XVI.

Mr. Bernard Shaw

IN the early days of our acquaintance we had
had conversation something like this:

J: "What about God?"

He: *I* am God."

I: "Don't be silly."

He: "Where would you be without your face?"

I: "I'm not going to talk to you any more."

He: "Scorn me, scorn me; I don't mind. Two
hundred years hence, the world will say that you
were my mistress, and——was our son!"

There is a certain "maiden modesty" about Joey*
which, to my mind, is his inimitable charm; but
both his genius and his charm, are at the mercy of
his Irish mischievousness—disarming and enraging.

To be made to hold his tongue is the greatest insult you can offer him—though he might be ready
with a poker to make you hold yours.

His want of consideration for other people's feelings, is not from a lack of gentlemanliness; it is
necessary sport of his brilliant impudence.

But woe betide—should another say a word that
belittles! In a trice, the belittled one is lifted high

*I always called Mr. Bernard Shaw "Joey."

as the sky: mental catch-if-you-can and leap-frog, are the hobby of his genius.

Is it the song of life that Joey sings, with its tragedy and finality?

Or is it the song—accompanied by many delicious and sometimes glorious "tra-la-las"—of his pertinent intellectual triumph over some human weakness: the song of the would-be Superman?

I have sometimes thought that perhaps it is only his human heart he hides and fears.

With his permission, and braving his "You wanted to show the world that the scalp of a Superman decorates your wigwam—wretch that I love." I give only a few of his delightful letters; letters that helped me through some sad days.

> "10, Adelphi Terrace,
> "28th September, 1912.

"How are you? . . . .

"If I had another play ready I should read it to you just to find out whether you are really ill or not; but I have nothing but the Christian martyr play, a bellowing, roaring business, which would unroof your house and leave you naked beneath the worshipping stars.

"And, anyhow, I never encourage illness. When I saw you last you were ill in bed, but you had the energy of ten tigresses; and your remarkably fine neck would have carried the pediment of the Parthenon like a feather if you had been snatched from between the sheets and set up as a caryatid.

"It is I who need sympathy. I have just had a letter

from a suffragette, beginning, 'Poor ill-used darling.'

"Don't tell Helen to write to me: she must be perfectly sick of the subject of your ridiculous and probably imaginary illness. Get up and console ME.

"Ever,
"G. B. S."

"Midland Adelphi Hotel,
"Liverpool,
"23rd October, 1912.

"Stella,

"You must be either better or dead. Say, oh, fairest, are you up and about? If you are, it is your duty to write to me. I hope you have lost your good looks; for whilst they last any fool can adore you, and the adoration of fools is bad for the soul. No: give me a ruined complexion and a lost figure and sixteen chins and a farmyard of crows' feet and an obvious wig. Then you shall see me come out strong. . . .

"I haven't been quite the same man since our meeting. I suppose you are a devil: they all tell me so when I go on raving about you. Well, I don't care. I have always said that it is the devil that makes the hell; but here is a devil who makes heaven. Wherefore I kiss your hands and praise Creation for you, and hope you are well, as this leaves me at present, thank God for it. This is the Irish formula, which, by the way, I should have adopted earlier in this letter, as every sentence would then have begun with *Dear Stella*. I used to write letters for Irish servants when I was a child. 'Dear Mother, I hope you are well, as it leaves me at present, thank God for it. Dear Mother, I saw Bridget on Friday, and she desires to be remembered to you.

GEORGE BERNARD SHAW

Dear Mother, I hope you got the flannel petticoat safely. Dear Mother, etc., etc., etc., etc., etc., etc., etc., etc.'

"I shall be here until Sunday morning, I expect.

"I have just recovered from one of the famous headaches, and am not quite sane yet.

"G. B. S."

"10, Adelphi Terrace, W. C.
"30th October, 1912.

"O, beautiful, illustrious, I have mountains of work upon me here, and cannot return to town until Friday morning as ever will be. . . . I cannot find *Androcles* here, and am not quite sure that Gilbert Murray returned it to me when I sent it to him to Cromer; but if it be within my reach in London I will come on Friday at four and—unless you write forbidding me—bellow it in your coral ears until Kensington Square shakes down its railings.

"O, brave, high-souled lady and cleanser and inspirer of my trampled spirit, I would the post were in hell, since it will not wait another moment. . . .

"G. B. S."

He came and read me *Androcles*. I was really too ill to listen, and it nearly killed me; in the evening my temperature went up dangerously high.

We had some conversation about his childhood, and this unfinished letter came:

"Court Lodge,
"3rd November, 1912.

"O, glorious, white marble lady, what was done to

me in my childhood was just nothing at all of an intentional kind. I wasn't spoiled; and I wasn't helped. No direct ill-treatment was added by anybody to the horrors of the world. Nobody forbade me to discover what I could of its wonders. I was taken—and took myself—for what I was: a disagreeable little beast. Nobody concerned himself or herself as to what I was capable of becoming, nor did I. I did not know I was different from other people (except for the worse): far from being conceited, I hadn't even common self-respect. I have discovered all my powers from the outside, with incredulous astonishment, or, rather, I have discovered that everybody else hasn't got them. My shyness and cowardice have been beyond belief.

"G. B. S."

I found out afterwards that in the following letter, Joey was treating me to a stale bit out of one of his plays:

"10, Adelphi Terrace, W. C.,
"8th November, 1912.

"Stella, Stella,

"Shut your ears tight against this blarneying Irish liar and actor. Read no more of his letters. He will fill his fountain pen with your heart's blood, and sell your most sacred emotions on the stage. He is a mass of imagination with no heart. He is a writing and talking machine that has worked for nearly forty years until its skill is devilish. I should have warned you before; but I thought his white hairs and 56 years had made his philanderings ridiculous. He cares for nothing really but his mission, as he calls, it and his work. He is treacherous as only an Irishman can be; he adores you with one eye and sees you with the other as a calculated utility. He has been recklessly trying to please you, to delight you, to persuade you to carry him up to heaven for a moment (he is trying to do it *now*); and when you have done it, he will run away and give it all to the mob. All his goods are in the shop window; and he'll steal your goods and put them there, too.

"But don't cut him off utterly. He is really worth something, even to *you*, if you harden your heart against him. He will tell you that you are too great a woman to belong to any man, meaning, I suppose that he is too great a man to belong to any woman. He will warn you against himself with passionate regard for you— sincerely too, and yet knowing it to be one of his most dangerous tricks. He will warn you against his warning you, not meaning you to take any warning, and he will say later on, 'I told you so.' His notion of a woman in love with him is one who turns white and miserable when he comes into the room, and is all one wretched jealous reproach.* Oh don't, don't, DON'T fall in love with him; but don't grudge him the joy he finds in writing all sorts of wild but heartfelt exquisite lies— lies, lies, lies, lies.

"G. B. S."

"10, Adelphi Terrace, W. C.
"18th November, 1912.

"I am clearly in my second childhood (56 not 54); for you might be the Virgin Mary and I an Irish peas-

---

* This is a written variation on a saying of his which ran something like this: "Englishmen are terrors to young Irishmen. If you pay an Irishwoman a gallant compliment, she grins and says, 'Arra g'along with you.' An Englishwoman turns deadly pale, and says, 'in a strangled voice, 'I hope you meant what you have just said.' And it is devilish difficult to explain that you didn't.'"

ant, and my feeling for you could not be more innocent.

"Such concord will make me silly.   Let us work together and quarrel and come upon all sorts of incompatibilities.   Our music must have discords in it or you will tire of it.

"I think you are getting well.   I hear a ring.   I see a flash in your letter.   The able courageous Stella is stirring.   And perhaps she will put me away with the arrowroot.   No matter, I shall rejoice and glory in her.

"Good nightest.

"G. B. S."

"Ayot, St. Lawrence,
"27th November, 1912.

"Oh, all they say is true.   I have no heart.   Here I am with my brains grinding like millstones, writing a preface for my long belated volume of plays, and stopping only to bring my quick firers into action by hurling a devastating letter into some public controversy. Grind, grind; bang, bang; broken heads and broken wings everywhere within range; 'and this word Love, which graybeards call divine, be resident in men like one another and not in me: *I* am myself alone.' (Applause, started by the tragedian himself with his boot heels.)

"Stella!   Who is Stella?   Did I ever know anybody named Stella?   Can't remember; what does it matter? I have articles to write and the preface to finish.   I have to debate with Hilaire Belloc in the Queen's Hall on the 28th January.   Not an advertisement has appeared, and the hall is nearly sold out already.   And actresses talk to me of their popularity!   I want no Stella; I want my brains, my pen, my platform, my audience, my adversary, my mission.

"Parents and children: that is the theme of my preface. The tears of countless children have fallen unavenged. I will turn them into boiling vitriol and force it into the souls of their screaming oppressors.

"It is certain that I am a callous creature; for I have let you write to me twice—no, that can't be! I *did* answer. But would not a man with a grain of heart have written ten times? Oh, I have been as hard as nails for a fortnight past. I was when I began this letter. I shall be so again when I post it. But now, just for a moment—only a moment—before the grindstones begin again.

"Your set-back makes me desperate: I had set my heart on your getting well with a rush this time. Oh, you must, you must, you shall. You shall be torn out of bed and shaken into rude health. Oh, why can't I do anything? What use are grindstones after all? Good-night and forgive my follies.

"G. B. S."

"8th December, 1912.

"My dear Mrs. Patrick Campbell,

"It is so many years since I have heard from you that I have lost all hope of your retaining any kindly feeling for me. I am like a dentist: there is so much that is wounding about my work that I am continually afraid of your going back to hard thoughts of me in my most detestable moments. *Mésalliance* may have revived all your dislikes. I don't like myself well enough—though I admire myself enormously—to expect anyone else to like me.

"I now have a mystic theory of your illness: it is a trap of the Life Force—the Elan Vitale. I once fell into that trap. I will explain *viva voce*. I recovered. You will recover. But these traps of the Life Force sometimes set up a morbid routine out of which the victim has to be shaken. . . .

"Now I wonder what would happen if you told the doctors that you distinctly recollect that you swallowed a brooch at rehearsal in a transport of fury and that you can feel it in your appendix. Insist on being X-rayed to detect and locate the foreign body, and see what will happen. Those X-rays are rum things: they will upset the routine that the illness has started, and they won't hurt or harm you (I speak from experience: I have had my inside X-rayed as well as my foot). I am overwhelmingly convinced that you want a change of some sort, or a shake.

"I should like to see you if I may come some day next week (*this* week it will be when you get this). I have a very indelicate question to put to you on a matter of business, which I have put off and off and off; but I have been a little uneasy about it all along, and now I think I had better ask it, and have done with it. Could you spare me a moment on Tuesday afternoon? I had intended to chain myself to the gate here and have a week in the country, as my speech at the Irish Meeting on Friday—violently overacted—finished me almost; but now I am forced to produce a hasty revival of *John Bull's Other Island* for Boxing Day, and this means rehearsing every day from to-morrow on.

"If all the saints and all the angels and the Blessed Virgin were all rolled into one beautiful woman and all the prayers and adorations, and loves and worships they drew to themselves were concentrated into one holy passion, it would all be as—no room to finish. Guess the rest.

"G. B. S."

I do not remember his coming and talking to me about this "matter of business"; evidently he did, and I was offended. This letter was the outcome:

"10th December, 1912.
"Shall I tell you the calculations I have been going over in my head ever since you became ill? Listen.

"Money. She must have money to go on with. Has she any? Let me see. £116 a week all through the run of *Bella Donna.* Half to the bankers to pay off debts. That leaves £58 a week going to her credit. But it also proves that the bankers must have allowed her to overdraw recklessly. For that, the bank manager ought to be sacked; for there are no securities: she told me she had saved nothing. Unless the bank has insured her life, the manager's conduct in permitting the overdraft is unbusinesslike to the verge of malversation. Therefore, either the manager or the firm (or more probably all of them) is in love with her. That being so, they may say: 'Perish the bank; let her have the last sovereign in the safe rather than she should have a moment's anxiety.' In their place I should have that impulse.

"But business is business: in practice there is a limit to all overdrafts. That limit may be approaching—may be already reached—must be near enough to cause some anxiety. Are there friends?—for pride is no use: when you *must* have money, you must take it or raise it—must, must, must, must, MUST. If friends didn't offer and insist, she might go to a moneylender. She would. Delicacy. That's the difficulty. A woman is visibly spending money like water and earning nothing; and people talk of delicacy! Thank God, *I* have no delicacy, no good taste: she said so. Oh, sweet revenge, to turn

myself, like Jupiter with Danæ, into a shower of gold!
Only I haven't gold enough. . . . No: it doesn't run to
a shower.

"How much will she need? No, I must be prudent:
how little can she scrape through with? There's the
rent, the Xmas quarter. The Xmas boxes, bills, nurses,
doctors. Of course she is saving a lot by being in bed:
no dressing, no taxis. The thought that there might be
a bill of sale on that piano is like a dagger. Insistent
problem: how much will make her quite free from anxiety until she is up again? And how much can I afford?
No use pretending to be opulent; I'm not. The Xmas
fortnight: would £250 get her over it?

"Oh, God! To offer Stella a filthy little £250. I
spit on myself; but she says she can't keep money; gives
it to whoever asks her; despicable weakness. Better,
perhaps, dole out a little at a time: other fortnights will
follow Xmas. How much can I afford? Ass. Why
ask that question over and over again? You know perfectly well that you want to give her a thousand pounds.
Very well, put your cheque book in your pocket and go to
her and ask her. If she does not want it there is no
harm done? You are no use: that is all. If she does
want it, and will not take it, there are ways—artful ways
—guileful ways—but the simple way is sincere and will
do. True, she will suddenly realize that I am, after all,
a stranger to her; but what of that! She is not a
stranger to me, and she has forfeited the right to refuse
because she has given me money, and would give it to me
if I wanted it. Can I seriously believe she will say, 'In-
solent stranger: you have violated my pride, my privacy,
my feeling that I must be a star and not a candle lighted
by a man with a match. Ring the bell, and have yourself
turned out'?

"I wasn't a bit afraid of that. And that is the whole argument that ended yesterday.

"My grandfather used to say that no living man, prince or pauper, could refuse a five pound note if you crackled it under his nose? Say what you will, there's something dignified about a thousand pound note. Wouldn't you like to take it and burn it before my face? *Quel geste?* I could take the number, swear to the burning, get another one, crackle that, too.

"Stella, if those bankers—no, don't be angry, I only say IF, IF, IF, IF, IF. And so enough of that. Only, if ever you want anything ever so little, remember— crackle, crackle, crackle crackle.

"   .   .   .   .   .

"G. B. S."

I am ashamed to say that for a moment this offer made me indignant; later I realised it was a glimpse of Joey's heart, and I was very touched; but whether he was hurt or relieved by my refusal of the thousand pounds he has never told me.

After about eight months it was finally decided that I should go into a Nursing Home.

He wrote:—

"This is the day of battle; and when the trumpet sounds, good-bye to dread and terrors; they are for cowards like me (I am your knight of the White Feather, brave Stella); you must march with colours flying and the music in D major. And you shall leave me the address of that home* which will be the home of my heart

* Nursing Home.

while you are there. And I agree that when you are well we shall be Mr. Bernard Shaw and Mrs. Patrick Campbell; for Stella means only Stella, but Mrs. Patrick Campbell will mean my adored, ensainted friend.

"A thousand successes, a thousand healings, a thousand braveries, a thousand prayers, a thousand beauties, a thousand hopes and faiths and loves and adorations watch over you and rain upon you. Good night, good night, good night, good night.

"G. B. S."

He was firmly convinced that he had been the kindest of critics during his old exploits as a Saturday Reviewer of the theatre. "If people had only known the things I *didn't* say," was one of his excuses.

I reminded him of his callous attitude towards my work, and this letter came.

"4th January, 1913.

"Dearest Liar, I have found you out. You have been tormenting me for weeks because I wrote odious things about you in the past. Well yesterday C—— wanted a copy of that American reprint of my *Saturday Review* articles which I so dread, and I got it for him. And before I sent it away I screwed my courage up and forced myself to read the articles about you. And what a revelation! What a relief! What a triumph! Never did a man paint his infatuation across the heavens as I painted mine for you, rapturously and shamelessly. Not a line would have jarred with my wildest letters to you. First *Tanqueray*. Sweep this silly piece away and let us hear this glorious woman play; it is only an unbearable interruption to her. Then *Ebbsmith* smashed, pulverized, flung into the dustbin: it proves nothing but that Mrs. Campbell is a wonderful woman. Then *Romeo and Juliet*. Mrs. Campbell danced like 'the daughter of Herodias.' Away with the play, away with Shakespeare, away with 'Juliet': nothing of it remains except her dance, and that shall endure for ever. Then I came to *Michael and His Lost Angel*, and I trembled, for I well remember how Jones read that play to me, and what he had done for you (by this I mean, how much pains he had taken to write the part for you), and what he hoped from you, and how he was at the height of his achievement then, and how heartlessly you flung him aside and trampled on him. And he had been entirely kind and helpful to me. I said to myself, 'I cannot have forgiven her for this: I dare not read the next notice.' But I nerved myself, and did: the notice of *For the Crown*. Criticism? Just Gods! a mad rapture of adoration. Not even silence about Jones, but an open declaration that the sacrifice was worth it if only it pleased you. Ten thousand Joneses and Pineros and Shakespeares were nothing in comparison. I would not hear even of your acting. 'On the highest plane one does not act, one *is*.' I would not have even 'Juliet': Stella, Stella, nothing but Stella. Nothing that you could do was wrong: everything was a glory. And you, wretch, dare reproach me for this because I did not say, 'Mrs. Campbell's rendition of the potion scene was sound and scholarly, and her readings of the text were original and profound.' *That* was what you wanted, Mrs. Crummles. And I rolled Pinero in the dust beneath your feet (the feet I kissed with my pen), and told Jones publicly that he was fortunate to be insulted by you; and these two men are my friends and have never breathed a reproach, whilst you say that I treated you shamefully and did not appreciate you. Are you not afraid of drawing down lightning on yourself? I! I, who burnt up Shakespeare so that his sparks might whirl about you in a halo of glory. I challenge you passionately to produce one word that has ever been written of you by anybody that is more abandoned in its confession, that shouts more recklessly to all the world that the writer is your utter captive.

"And so good-night, with unfathomable blessings.

"G. B. S."

Friends used to come and play chess with me at the Nursing Home. I remember Mr. Max Beerbohm playing so brilliantly that I made up my mind never to touch a chessman again!

However, one day I persuaded Joey—in spite of his hatred of all games—to have a game with me: the following letter was the result:

"10, Adelphi Terrace, W. C.
"29th January, 1913.

"It has come back to me that my mother used to say, 'Prise to your queen' when she wanted to warn me that my queen was in danger. I suppose it was prise; but it may have been preeze, or preys (or the analogy of keys), or anything. I can't imagine that I have been playing chess, or that I remembered so much about it.

"I enjoyed myself enormously. You are such a jolly playfellow. And such a child! An old-fashioned child! I should like to spend an hour every day with you in the nursery. I no longer want you to act for me: I can't bear the idea of your having to work—you are not

grown up enough. And you don't want me to be busy,
but to come and play. I am so tempted that I must set
up a barrier of engagements between us.

"There are such wonderful sorts of relations, and
close togethernesses, and babes-in-the-woodinesses, besides being in love, which, as you point out, my diet and
feeble nature forbid. I may have moments of being in
love, but you must overlook them.

"And now, having expressed myself with carefully
punctuated moderation, I shall go to bed quite calmly,
and sign myself, oh, loveliest, doveliest, babiest,

"Your gabiest,

"G. B. S."

"7th February, 1913.

"Now a last line. I wish I could write verses. Why
do not rhymes come tumbling into my head naturally, as
they did into Morris's? I have to play things, sing things,
repeat things, that you set jingling in my head. It seems
to me that all the poets have been in love with you; for
they seem to have said everything; and my words that
would praise thee are impotent things; and I was a child
and she (you) was (were) a child in a kingdom by the
sea; and it is undeniable that the moon never beams without bringing me dreams, and the stars never rise but I see
the bright eyes, and so on and so forth; but if I try to
make verses for myself I can think of no rhyme to Stella
but umbrella, and only too damn well I love Mrs. Campbell, and horrors of that sort. The thing should rush
into my head or come to my hand as prose does—ready
made. I never have to think of how to say anything in
prose: the words come with the thought. I often have
to argue a thing carefully to get it right; but when I
have found the right thing to say it says itself instantly;

and matters of feeling don't even have to be argued. Yet when I want frightfully to ringle-jingle with words they don't come that way. I suppose it's want of practice: if I had always written in verse I probably couldn't write in anything else, which would be a nuisance. When Morris talked prose in criticism of things he didn't much like, he was often at a loss for a word, and used me as a dictionary. I used to hand him the word he was looking for; and he would snatch it up with relief, though he could sling rhymes without having to think about them, and used to look at me with incredulous disgust when I told him that when I wanted a rhyme I had to try down the alphabet: Stella, bella, sella, della, fellah, hella, hell a, quell a, sell a, tell a, well a, yell a, Campbell, bramble, gamble, ramble, etc., etc. He did not consider poetry worth all that trouble—and I agree: I always tell people that if they can't do three-quarters of any art by nature they'd better sweep a crossing.

"My mother cut a wisdom tooth when she was eighty. I ask myself sometimes, am I cutting a folly tooth at fifty-six? Still, one has to become as a little child again —in that kingdom by the sea.

"I have been reading John Palmer's book on the censorship (he is my successor on the *Saturday Review* now, and much the cleverest of the lot), and he says: 'Mr. Shaw is a militant Puritan, to whom the West End theatre is definitely the gate of hell.' Am I really a Puritan? 'The beautiful Puritan pansies'—yes, I think I am. Good-night. The birds will cover us up with leaves.

"G. B. S."

Though he wrote and talked as if no other consideration existed in the world except his regard for

me, his work, his endless political lectures and com-
mittees, and his very well regulated house came before everything. Whatever might betide, Charlotte
(Mrs. Shaw) must not be kept waiting ten minutes.
To me, accustomed to the irregularities and emergen-
cies of the theatre, which make all meals movable
feasts to be put off or hurried on at a moment's notice, Joey's inflexible domesticy seemed absurd; especially as he would have me believe he only ate
apples, carrots and potatoes.

This letter is an example of his busy life, beginning as it does with an explanation that he has something better to do than to see me, and ending with
a rhapsody.

"26th February, 1913.
"Next week will be a week of oratory—two orations,
Monday and Thursday.

"On Friday and Saturday the afternoons are filled to
the last moment. On Sunday I shall be at Ayot. On
Monday, committee and oratory as aforesaid will occupy
me wholly. On Tuesday you may have fled to Brighton.
This seems to justify me in coming to-morrow, if I may?
As you must take a drive if you can, I will not come until
five. If that is too early, or if you are tired, send me a
wire before two.

"Remember that I am always your saint, and that my
ecstasy will survive disembodiment. You must always
sit enthroned in heaven for me. If you stopped doing
that, my unbreakable (or perhaps broken) heart would
harden.

"It is an enormously unreasonable demand to make on

a mortal woman; but I make it, man-like, because I do not believe in mortality.

"G. B. S.

"Keep in the clouds with her! You will never educate her on earth, and never tire of her in heaven."

"28th February, 1913.

"Who mashed Stella?
I, that rejoice
In a nice Irish voice,
I mashed Stella.

"Who made her smile?
Dis very chile,
With my winks and my wile,
I made her smile.

"Who'll be her man?
Why, he that can,
Apollo or Pan,
I'll be her man.

"Who is a fool?
I, as a rule,
(The happiest fool),
I am a fool.

"Who is her friend?
Stella's true friend,
World without end,
I am her friend."

When my recovery was complete and I was at work again, I learnt that his sister Lucy was an invalid. I said I would like to go and see her: his comment was "Go; she will tell you lies about my childhood; the relatives of great men always do." I became very attached to Lucy; he was pleased, but insisted that I must not on any account kiss her, for fear of infection.

This struck me as fantastic—an incurable invalid to be made to feel she was too infectious to kiss! Had I murmured "noblesse oblige," he would have grunted "theatrical effect at any price." I always kissed Lucy.

"17th June, 1913.

". . . .

The enclosed letter from Lucy may please you a little. This marble heart was most affectionately grateful to you for that visit. You are my friend and my darling, and I forgive you for not coming down to-day. The country was disappointed. The rabbits and field mice were waiting in the lanes for you; and when they saw it was only me on my reeking, snorting bike, they scuttled away in disgust. The heavens were furious; they thundered and hurled such mouthfuls of rain at me that the lanes became torrents in five minutes.

"You can't come to-morrow, because you have a matinée.

"If you will come on Thursday, I will not come up until Friday, though I ought to.

"If you had come to-day you would have got damp;

but we should have had tea here, perhaps. There is a little rift in the clouds at last.

"G. B. S."

Joey and I had some "words" at the theatre—probably over negotiations about *Pygmalion*—and I spent nearly an hour telling him nothing would ever make a gentleman of him; the next day he wrote as follows:

"25th June, 1913.
". . . I was in heaven yesterday. Spoke to the Queen. A dear woman and frightfully beautiful.
"She just slanged me in the most shocking way for a full hour: and I adored her and burnt endless candles to her all the time. In the end my prayers touched her. And now I have a halo inside like this.

"G. B. S."

At rehearsal, in pressing my hand on a rough wooden table, I had managed to get a splinter under my thumbnail. The next day I went to see Lucy: Joey and her doctor were there: they took me to a chemist, where a surgical instrument was found to remove the splinter.

Joey exclaimed with enthusiasm—as my nail was being slowly lifted and the splinter withdrawn, the veins in my neck swelling in my efforts to resist the pain—"By jove! what a throat, 'Michael Angelo'!"

This time I felt Joey's admiration was sincere.

His letter shows he was full of sympathy.

"6th August, 1913.

". . . I think all that was good for my soul because it tore everything that was selfish and imaginary right out of me, and made you a real fellow creature in real pain. (O Lord, my fibres all twist and my heart and bowels torment me when I think of it) : and the more real you become the more I discover that I have a real, real, real kindness for you, and that I am not a mere connoisseur in beauty or a sensualist or a philanderer, but a—but a—a—I don't know what; but something that has deep roots in it that you pluck at. Only why should you have to be hurt to cure me of selfishness and of little fits of acting? Why should it not be an ecstasy of happiness for you, that would move me too, perhaps still more deeply?

"Are you very tired and low in the counter-reaction? For in the reaction after the pain I am sure you were wonderful. If I were with you, I would cheat that counter-reaction somehow—say all sorts of things (all true) to make you forget it.

"G. B. S."

His wildest letters I do not give.

Had I asked him why he expressed himself with such frantic intensity, he would most probably have answered, "You may notice the same thing in Shakespeare."

Strong feeling exalted him—but the slightest contretemps would turn his fantastic adoration into almost alarming abuse.

When my illness was over, the real friendship which exists to-day was between us.

This funny incident happened when I was nearly well again, but not yet able to walk.

Joey insisted that he could make me walk in five minutes and jump in ten. We went for a drive to Richmond Park, and on the way he told me about physical exercises, and the force of will on the play of human muscles. We drew up before a low bench, he got out, helped me out, and said, "Watch me." With this he doubled himself up, his Aquascutum playing in the wind, and said "You jump like this" as he leapt on to the seat. I bent and tried to spring, but it was no use; I could not move. Again gesticulating and explaining, he leaped a second time triumphantly on to the seat! Mr. John Burns, M. P., passed by at this moment in an open brougham.

I have never heard whether Mr. Burns has alluded to this extraordinary exhibition!

One day two lovely American girls came to see me. Joey called at the same time. I was out. When I returned all three were lying face downwards on the floor. He was explaining the beauty and profit of some Swedish exercises.

I remember a young society lady asking him at my house humbly and politely if she might act a play of his for a charity performance. "No: no one can play my plays who cannot walk a tight-rope!" She replied sweetly, "I can do double splits," and straightway did them. Joey stared in amazement.

Some years later, in his play *Pygmalion,* he succeeded in making me exclaim "bloody"* nightly before a thousand people—he thought to conquer my pre-Raphaelite instinct.

I invented a Cockney accent and created a human "Eliza Doolittle" † for him: and because the last act of the play did not travel across the footlights with as clear dramatic sequence as the preceeding acts—owing entirely to the fault of the author—he declared I might be able to play a tune with one finger, but a full orchestral score was Greek to me.

Some wept at the finish of this play, for no one knew what had happened to the two characters they had grown to love.

After all—Elijah, went to heaven in a chariot—you must end your story somehow.

Later, he wrote the end of the story of "Eliza Doolittle"; when he found I had not read it. He sent me the following letter:

"7th March, 1917

". . . There are four depths of illiteracy, each deeper than the one before:

    I. The illiteracy of H—— I——.

    II. The illiteracy of those illiterate enough not to know that he was illiterate.

    III. The illiteracy of those who have never read my works.

    IV. The illiteracy of 'Eliza Doolittle,' who couldn't even read the end of her own story.

* Sir Herbert Tree implored me to "cut" the word, but, if I must say it, to say it "beautifully."
† The heroine of *Pygmalion*.

"There is only one person alive who is such a Monster of Illiteracy as to combine these four illiteracies in her single brain. And I, the greatest living Master of Letters, made a Perfect Spectacle of myself with her, before all Europe.

"G. B. S."

If an artist has a personality that *will* force its way through, spoiling the effect of Joey's brilliant dialogue—he shudders and laughs murderously. "Tree old chap, must you be treacly?" he said at a rehearsal of *Pygmalion* before the company and "stage hands"; nobody laughed; they knew death should have been Joey's punishment.

And he thought to cheer me when he remarked, "Good God; you are forty years too old for 'Eliza'; sit still, and it is not so noticeable."

To "sit still" with your hands folded in your lap for three-quarters of an hour, a glare of indignation in your eyeballs, while somebody else for the same length of time stands with his back to the fire, and another sits in an armchair—nobody budging except for some practical purpose of turning up a light, or picking up a newspaper, or ringing a bell— is Joey's idea of perfect stage management.

His genius and passion for debate often cut across the rhythmical movement of his drama, harming the natural sequence of emotion, and making the artist feel his own imagination is but an interruption.

Don't think: I have thought for you, is Joey's attitude to us poor players.

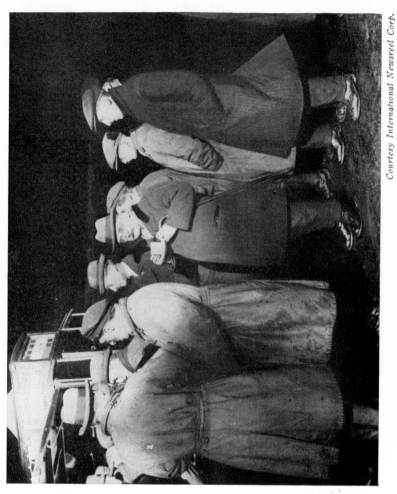

SIR JAMES BARRIE (WITH CUP AND WALKING STICK) AT A COFFEE STALL
IN ENGLAND

CHAPTER XVII.

SIR JAMES BARRIE

I CALLED him "Jim" when I wrote to him, and when I saw him, I said "Hullo!" I never called him "Mr. Barrie," or "Sir James." I do not know why.

I blessed him most at a rehearsal of *The Adored One*.

The producer having put his arm round my waist said, "No, my dear, you go here, and then you turn there, and you say your line like this": I grew silent as doom, cold as the snows on Fuji-Yama.

Out of the stalls on to the stage, with his pipe in his mouth and his hat on the back of his head, came the author, and, with that Scotch accent that leaves you cool and calm, said: "I think perhaps she will do better if you leave her alone."

During the first night of *The Adored One*— what a lovely part Leonora was—he came into my dressing room and told me no one had ever worked for him more beautifully before. Leonora pushed a man out of a railway carriage because her little girl had a cold and he wouldn't shut the window. She says it over and over again during her trial for murder in spite of all the efforts of judge, counsel, jury, and friends to stop her. In the end she is declared "Not guilty."

This little story Barrie made into a play of magical tenderness, fun, and beauty.

Pamela Lytton,* Dolly Gladstone,† Beo, and I went to look for him after the performance. We went to his flat; he was not there. We went to the Savoy; he was not there. Then back again to his rooms; he was not there. We looked at Joey's windows opposite—all was dark; then back again we went to the Savoy and had supper, then once more to Jim's rooms: this time we found him.

With what gentleness and dearness he received us—and how proud we were to talk with him at that time of night!

Whenever I am with him I feel a monstrous being. I want to be a little child and have him tell me about things that only he knows. It is the guilelessness and trust of a child he treasures. I fancy he winks one eye at the wisdom of the grown-ups.

I have a desire to be without a flaw in his presence. This must be because I love and admire him very much.

But it is when life hits you between the eyes that Jim shows the stuff he's made of.

The following is his answer to a letter of mine, asking his permission to publish some letters of his to me.

* Countess of Lytton.
† Viscountess Gladstone.

"3, Adelphi Terrace House,
"November, 1921.

"My dear Stella,

"I am much elated to find that you have preserved for so long those two old letters of mine. Is the faint perfume that I fondly think comes from them really lavender? And if it is (I wish I hadn't thought of this), is it lavender meant for me, or were my little missives merely kept so near the beautiful G. B. S. budget that in time they stole some of the sweetness in which I am sure his lie wrapped?

"This misgiving has come upon me suddenly, and I am rather dashed by it. My two little Benjamins are shrinking before my eyes. All I see clearly now is the sweet Shaw bundle, encircled by a pale blue ribbon. I doubt whether my pair were preserved intentionally. I daresay they got into his lot by mistake, and just fell out one day when the ribbon burst. Or an instinct of self-preservation had made them creep in there. They probably thought that sometime, when you sat in the dusk with the G. B. S. bundle in your lap, you might inadvertently fondle them also.

"All this is a bitter pill for me, who in the first thrill of seeing them again had hoped deliriously that you kept them because you could not part from them. I conceived you (mad fool that I was) carrying them everywhere in a gold bag attached to your wrist, constantly being late for dinner because you must have one more peep at them, climbing ladders for them when the house went on fire. I was proud to feel that (even though you could not read them) they were a solace to you when you were depressed and a big brother if you were almost reckless. A nauseous draught.

"Another thing strikes me—that you preserved them

to ask me to read them to you some day. I tell you flatly that I cannot read them. Even the 'Stella' seems to me (the more I look at it) to have an odd appearance. Hold it sideways and it is more like 'Beatrice.' Were you ever called 'Beatrice'? A horrible sinking comes over me that these letters were never meant for you at all.

"Even if they were, there is no proof nowadays that they were written by me, for the handwriting is entirely different from that of this letter. I am trusting that my new superb penmanship is amazing you, even as you gaze at it through blinding tears. The explanation is that since the days of these two letters my right hand has gone on strike—writer's cramp—and I have had to learn to indite with the left. Perhaps these letters

---

A horrible sinking comes over me that these letters were never meant for you at all. Even if they were, there is no proof nowadays that they were written by me, for the handwriting is entirely different from that of this letter. I am trusting that my new superb penmanship is amazing you, even as you gaze at it though blinding tears. The explanation is that since the days of these two letters, my right hand has gone on strike — writers' cramp — and I have had to learn to indite with the left.

T.

did it; the hand that wrote them then grandly destroyed
its powers, as the true loyalist smashed his glass when
he had drunk a royal health.   At all events, we scarcely
know the right hand nowadays—we pass the time of day
and so on, but nothing more.   At first the left was but
an amanuensis.   I dictated to it, but I had to think down
the right arm.

"But now the left is my staff.   Also I find that the
person who writes with his left is quite another pair of
shoes from the one who employs his right; he has other
standards, sleeps differently, has novel views on the
antology of being, and is a more sinister character.
Anything curious or uncomfortable about the play of
Mary Rose arises from its having been a product of the
left hand.   And now the question inevitably pops up:
What justification has my left to give permission to publish letters written by that other fellow, my right?
They don't agree about you at all (right says you make
people love and writhe).   They don't agree about me,
they even hold contrary opinion as to what the letters
are about.   Left says that unless there is a cypher in
the letters it can't understand why you want to print
them.   (By the way as that is what this letter is about,
you can print them if you like.)   Left has the vaguest
recollections of the doings, apparently referred to in the
letters, when you visited me in order to annoy the
blue-eyed one across the way.   On the other hand, what
memories do these doings recall to right, who is at
present jogging me to let it get hold of a pen again.
The pretty things it wishes to say to you! but left won't
pass them on.

"Ah, me!   You and G. B. S., and the days when I
was a father to you both.

"But enough of this.   I can't pretend any more—not

for long. Left likes you every whit as much as right does, as does the somewhat battered frame to which they are for the moment still attached. And we all send you our love, and wish for you the best kind of happiness and courage for any evil hour, and may the book be worthy of you.

"Yours,
"J. M. B."

"Island of Harris, N. B.
"7th September, 1912

"Dear Stella,

"I thought when I saw your nice little monogram that it meant you no longer adored G. B. S. And that you had crossed the street again to me. You see, I had watched you (a bitter smile on my face) popping in at his door instead of at mine. For the moment I am elated, though well I know that you will soon be off with me again and on with him. He and I live in the weather house with two doors, and you are the figure that smiles on us and turns up its nose at us alternately. However I would rather see you going in at his door than not see you at all, and as you are on elastic I know that the farther you go with him the farther you will have to bound back. I wish I had not thought of this because it suddenly fills me with a scheme for a play called *The Weather House.* Will stop this letter presently to think scheme out, but as I see it just now I feel G. B. S. and I must write alternate acts (according to which door you go in at). When I wrote that, I meant we should each write the acts in which you were nice to him, but on reflection I am not sure that I would not prefer to write of the scenes which took place across the way and leave him to write those of No. 3.

"I have done no work here except a one act play, which

striketh me as being no great shakes, for the Duke of York's, where a triple bill is to be done. I daresay I'll go on with the other, but why, oh, why don't you post, or, better, call on Frohman, as it goes to him if it's done? This place is very remote—nothing alive but salmon, deer, and whales, and I return to London in a fortnight, when I hope this comedy of the doors will begin again.

"Yours,
"J. M. B."

[illegible]

[illegible] House

W.C. 3

7th Sept. 1908

Dear Chester

I thought when I

saw your [illegible] of the [illegible] morning

that it meant [illegible]

paper about G.B.S. [illegible]

[illegible] you had [illegible]

the [illegible] [illegible] to me. [illegible]

[illegible] I had watched you [illegible]

[illegible] [illegible] [illegible] [illegible]

[illegible] [illegible] [illegible] [illegible] [illegible]

[illegible] [illegible] [illegible] for the [illegible]

...... alters tho' .....
I know that you will
..... be if will; was ......
and as with him. He ....
I .... in the ..... house
with his .... and ... on the
..... that smiles on us
and turns up its ... at us
ultimately. However I would rather
... you going on .... his
own than not see you if ...
... and as you are an ......
I know this the further you
go with him the further you
will have to come back.
I wish I had not thought
of this, because it suddenly
gives me such a scheme
for a play called "The mother

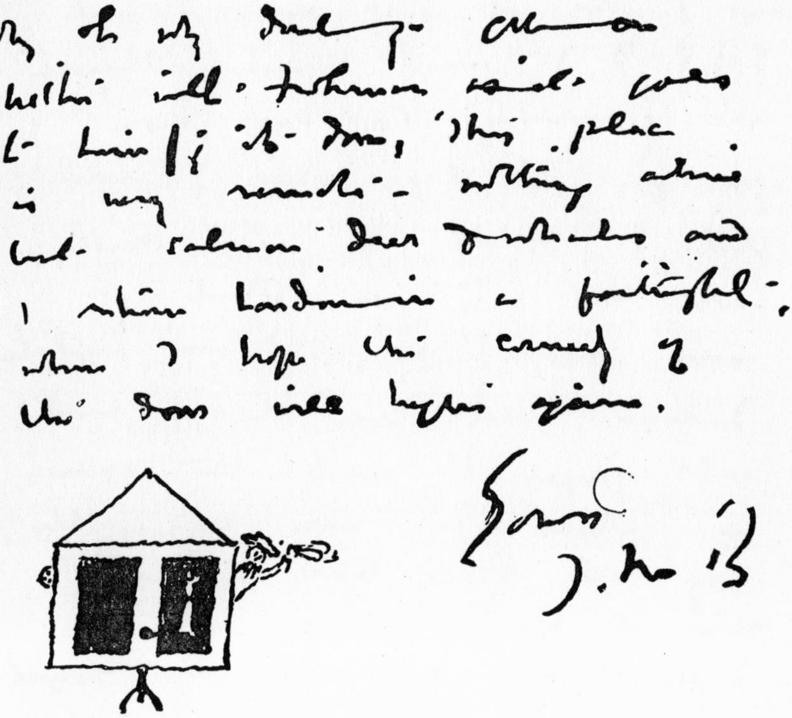

[illegible]

"26th November, 1913.

"My dear Beatrice,

"It is great that you should be recovering so quickly, and I am very glad.   Mr. Frohman arrives in London in a fortnight, so the best plan is to wait until he comes. He knows I want you, and I hope it will all be easily arranged.   I expect that after this long rest your energy will be appalling.

"I have some relations coming to-day to stay with me for a week, else I would have gone down to see you.   I meet the other weather man at times in our street, and ask after you and see him blushing.   I used to find him staring in at the window by the florist's shop, but now he gazes at neckties.   Any day he may blossom out in socks, slips, and spats: 'all for her,' as the dramatists say. I now pause to draw this picture of him on my blotting paper.

"J. M. B."

Someone else must write about my faults.   They will, perhaps, be kinder to me than I could be to myself.

But I can say this,—I shall die wiser than I was born.   I have learned a few things.

"It is mind that makes man, and soul that makes man angel." . . . .

It is far easier for men and women of the world, with keen knowledge of world-values, to see through the glamour of the artist; than it is for the artist— not concerned about world-values, and hampered by imagination—to see through the glamour of the men and women of the world.

———

People we love must be loved as they are. It is a want both of wisdom and courage on our part— a sort of drug—this wilful blindness, to blame them, because they fail our vision of them. . . .

———

I do not like unreal people; but it is dangerous to interfere with their pretence. Slowly a monster may face you, and turn and rend you.

———

I thought once that untruthful people would at least listen to truth—not a bit of it.

———

Want of interest and curiosity in things that are ugly leaves us ignorant of a great deal of useful knowledge.

———

I cannot see the resurrection of cold, callous, and unaffectionate hearts.

———

I feel with Robert Louis Stevenson—I think it was he who said—"The greatest beggar is the man who has no words."

———

Youth is harmed by having wisdom thrust upon it.
Youth must gather wisdom slowly, in laughter and tears.

I remember a little bird beautifully made of wool my mother kept on her window sill. I said, "Darling, that is so dirty and old, why don't you throw it away?"

"No; I cannot, someone took so much trouble to make it."

It is just that effort to make "beautifully," which is to "give" and is the greater part of inspiration.

"To make," "to take," and "to have" is the devil's luck.

This is a good foundation for art criticism.

English dignity and reserve do not impress me—but that they are clever without cunning, and meet injury without treachery—that is what I love.

I have met a reserved and pompous dignity that hid a murky mind.

I like butlers to be official; and those who nurse the sick, cheerful. Superficial amiability I dislike; but an intelligent, straightforward, and frank manner, backed by instinctive breeding, is the best all over the world.

When the animal nature in man is completely dominant, we may be sure that the mind is diseased.

An American doctor told me nobody would be evil if their brain molecules were normal.

I once asked a kind veterinary surgeon why dogs were so much nicer than people. His answer was, "Nearly all bad dogs are drowned, all mad dogs are shot!" And I do believe I heard myself saying, "That is how it should be with us"—but that is God's business.

There is an odd selfishness and egotism about actors and actresses, and most public people. Public life forces this upon them.

We cannot *perform,* unless our trust and faith in ourselves, our power, our taste, our looks, our voice, our movements, and our own thought, are for the moment paramount. If we hesitate or feel humiliated, we are lost; just a few are blessed with the rebound of the brave creative spirit; they are perhaps less selfish and vain, because they are more sure.

There is no doubt artists need much sympathetic and vital companionship, and care of a particular kind.

I remember a story a friend told me of a valuable cob she lent to some gay friends with her dogcart. The creature knew she had to go well that day, and off she flew like the wind, with her burden.

When they returned in the late afternoon the cob fell at the door. The people were ignorant—selfish —they had over-driven her.

I would say to everyone, "Cherish your 'cobs,' your racers, your singing birds and your artists. . . ."

———

I agree with a friend of mine who says, we ought to take off our hats to all human beings who have arrived at the age of forty, acknowledged sane, morally and mentally.

———

It was Abraham Lincoln who said, the one thing he could not pardon was disloyalty in his own house—

It *is* a dreadful thing, but it can be done.

———

The two best things to know I learned last: the meaning of the Lord's Prayer and the word Forgive———

A friend of mine told me a story of a woman she saw praying in a cathedral abroad, kneeling with upturned face before a crucifix.

My friend heard her words: "J'accepte tout! J'accepte tout! J'accepte tout!"

When we can say that, we are indeed "gay, and fit for Paradise."

DD. Lyttelton is among the friends I love who neither spoil nor flatter me.

She never hesitates to tell me my faults: "I wish, Stella darling, people did not call you 'difficult'; but they do, and you are; do be careful."

She was the first to encourage me to write, and

she will be the first to say how amateurish my book
is!

DD. has a wonderful gift of affection, though I
have thought she is sometimes too ready with her
"there are faults on both sides."

She is extraordinarily generous, but not in the
least extravagant.   She would pawn her jewels for a
friend—but wait until someone she loved grumbled,
before buying herself a quite inexpensive hat.

To help a friend in grief and trouble, she will
take endless and exhaustive pains.

My foolish belief that things are what they appear,
and my faith in "instinct"—the only gift given us
for nothing—and my feeling that compromise is a
form of cowardice—she often makes me ashamed of.
And yet, when she says, "Stella, you are so absolutely
ignorant of the world," I am content.

I have heard her criticised; I think this is because
she has no patience with affected charm, and takes
no interest in the "merely smart," and is very critical.

Her joy—when Sir Edwin Lutyens showed her
how her house could be divided in half, so that her
son might marry the girl he loved, and have a home
ready to bring her to—no friend of hers will ever
forget.

DD. loves the theatre more than I do; she will
go in a 'bus, on a wet night, and sit in the pit, happily
watching indifferent actors in an indifferent play.

She has genius for organisation—a passionate love

of literature, and is interested in the whole round world, and—in the echo from the world beyond.

Some day, I fancy she will write a fine play—perhaps, for me.

Margaret and Jack Mackail were blessed in many ways—a pathway made ready for their feet—a light to guide them.

I remember Pamela Wyndham * saying to me at "Clouds": "It would be an honour to black their boots."

Intelligence, goodness, and simple beauty ruled their lives, leaving no room for fools and madmen—and the world is full of fools and madmen.

I think these few letters show the tenderness of their early love for me, and mine for them.

"Rottingdean,
"25th December, 1894

"Dearest,

" . . . Are you really thinking of going to America? I suppose there is something to be said for it, though one can't think of anything except how one would miss you and the queer beautiful radiance that goes about with you.

"I wish you the best Christmas wishes, and my love to Pat and the dear little boy.

"JACK."

"30th September, 1895.

"Dearest Stella,

"I forgot to give you my book last night. How we bullied you, and how well you bore it!

* Now Viscountess Grey of Falloden.

"When one has lost one's first nerve and audacity (a thing that happens to everybody) it is only by 'style' that it can be replaced. That is the second education in art, and a harder one, but in the end more fruitful, than the first.

"My love.
"JACK."

"12th May, 1894.

"Darling,

"We don't come home till Saturday 19th, and the children being at 'The Grange' this house will be empty and glad to receive you and Pat if you should find your-selves houseless a few nights. Please remember that I shall leave my latchkey with mother, who will give it to you if you take shelter here. . . .

"About Duse—it was a great disappointment to find that she did not appeal to us at all; her naturalness, if that is what it is, wore one out, and my cry was, 'More art! More art!' I sat like a stone between two melting spectators whose secret strings vibrated at her every word and gesture; it is so personal, isn't it? I very much want you to see her and to talk about her with you.

"Ellen Terry says she is the biggest of all. I feel left out in the cold, not to grasp her greatness. Duval's father was more comic than anything ever before seen on the stage, but the audience behaved with great self-restraint.

" . . .

"MARGARET."

"20th September, 1896.

"My own Girl,
"I wonder so much how all is going with you, and how

Beo is, and how plans are, and when you will be in London and we can see you.

"Oh I wish I could give you the peace and heavenly happiness Clare makes—I really think it would be happy for you to be with her; like a tender little poultice to your worried heart. She baffles all words. You must come and cuddle her, and see her gay innocent smile, and hear her conversation. . . .

"I am in London, can I do anything for you? . . .

"Now that we are settled, the summer with its long hot days, and you rushing in, and me in your nightgowns seems all a dream. By the way, give me an address to send them to please, and do you like pink or blue ribbon in them? I entreat you not to say, 'Keep them,' in your generosity, for they are no use to me, now, and not as comfy as my own; but they were just salvation at the time, and it was only you in your wonderful realising sympathy who could have thought of such a thing. The teagowns, too, were a blessing: and oh, the turquoises on that yellow one. . . .

"My love and thoughts are all round and about you, and will be with you in that awful country, darling.

"Your loving
"MARGARET."

"31st December, 1894.

"Darling,

"A little line of blessing on you, all next year, and of thankfulness to you for all you have been of illumination and beauty to us both, this year.

"Loving
"MARGARET."

Frances Horner* was another friend who never

* Lady Horner.

flattered me; and often delighted in teasing me. Long ago, I spent happy days with her at "Mells."

I do not fancy she really cared for the theatre, or appreciated the strain and stress of the life. It was simply in the splendid kindness of her heart that she stretched out her arms to me. I admired her tremendously and her lovely home.

I remember her taking me out in a stanhope and pair in a thunderstorm. The horses stood on their hind legs, while she laughed merrily, assuring me her horses always stood on their hind legs, and they loved thunderstorms, especially the lightning.

To swim in the lake at the bottom of the garden, generally at a spot where it was forty feet deep, was the family's great amusement in warm weather. "It is quite easy, Stella. Here's a bathing dress; jump in!" And Sir John said: "I'll help you; don't be frightened!"

I jumped in, and threw my arms tight around his neck; we both nearly drowned. Frances pulled me out amidst peals of laughter from the children. How young we were!

She has a readiness and wit amounting to genius, and a gift for housekeeping that beggars description.

With a smile and a few sweet words she could within a few hours, get her cook to serve a dinner to twelve of the most distinguished people in London, and every dish could be taken as a personal compliment.

She laughs without noise, and weeps with no suggestion of hysterics. She can speak of the dead,
making them live before you, and as she smilingly
tells of their cleverness, their fun, the tears fill her
eyes and roll down her cheeks—dear Frances.

And there were our talks at night, too. She is
a friend who gives confidence for confidence.

I can see her sitting by the fire in my bedroom,
with her hair like fairy gold, her hand pushing
through it, lifting it, an aureole of sunbeams around
her head, as she says: "Stella, life is like that; it's
just a matter of fate whom we love. It may be a
good man, or it may be a bad man; it may be a fool,
or it may the right one."

Mark, her youngest son, as a very small child,
made you love and respect the little world of his
own, where the coachman was "king," and the maid
who used to look after him "queen."

I heard him, as quite a little boy, say to the coachman with inimitable dignity: "And are you a married
man?"

At a certain large luncheon party at Buckingham
Gate the door opened, and Mark came in with a tiny
pistol and some small pink caps. He walked
solemnly round the table, firing a little cap at each
guest. The guests, thinking it polite, no doubt,
took no notice of him, much to Mark's disappointment. Frances smiled indulgently. Mark came
up to me and fired. I quietly slipped off my chair
on to the floor—dead. I remember his mother's

smile of gratitude. From that moment Mark and I were friends. . . .

And the beauty of Edward and Cicely and Katherine—

The happiness of those days in that lovely garden at "Mells" is blurred by what lies between. . . .

On the afternon of the day, when on every placard there was the one word "WAR" I went to see Frances; I remember her bending head on my shoulder and her heart-breaking tears. . . .

Beo was in America. I cabled to him to come and help. He had anticipated me; his answer was: "Have arranged, sailing."

The late Lord Wemyss was nearly eighty years of age, when I first knew him.

His affection and his letters, and his interest in my life, and my children meant a great deal to me.

I remember once taking a famous actress to lunch with him, and how dreadfully upset he was about her fingernails—pointed, reddened an astonishing vermilion—they caught his eye unmercifully. I explained to him afterwards that it was the fashion, but he was distressed. He said: "Nothing should be a fashion that disturbs conversation and attracts the eye from the human countenance."

Courtesy was the breath of his being. I know no one now who makes every woman they address feel a' queen.

At Gosford, I believe my little dog was the only

dog that was ever allowed to sit at the table at meals.

As a child I always felt I was ugly.

When I was about fifteen I remember an old friend of ours saying to me: "Child, your face is silver like the moon; if I were a young man, it would make me weep." I thought he was silly; now I think he must have been a very nice man, with the heart of a poet.

I remember my mother telling me I had red hair when I was born, and how glad she was.

A Canadian lady wrote to me some years ago:—

"I do not feel that photographs can do you justice. You will laugh when I tell you that more than half your facial expression comes from the nervous texture of your skin—your face, or, rather, your skin in moments of excitement is luminous, and gives a curiously beautiful contour to your face. There are little reflected lights about brow and eye that no photo can give. I am so puzzled to know if it is the simple beauty of your character, or the subtle complex personality of your artist self, that attracts me."

My face is not a "mask"—it speaks as I speak, so I have some respect for it.

I look my best when I am very ill, which means the bones of my face are good and my features are placed well. My hands are Italian in shape. "Aunt Madeline" took a plaster cast of one for me and Lord

ELIZA DOOLITTLE IN "PYGMALION"

Wemyss had it done into bronze, and the hand looks lovely.

The following poem to me was written by a well-known London manager. His wife gave me her permission to publish all the poems he wrote to me. Unfortunately, the book they were in has disappeared—she asked me for it and I thought I gave it to her, but she says "no":

To Beatrice.

Come in a dream, beloved, if thy feet
   Are weary, thro' the valley of the night;
Sure are the wings of drowsy thought, and fleet
   To bear thee through the shadows to the light.
Grey is the world between us, let us go
   Far to the land where only lovers are:
All day the hours like laughing waters flow
   And all the night beneath a patient star.

There is a garden where the echoes treasure
   Thy footfall as an old-remembered song.
The ilex and the cypresses will pleasure
   To swathe thee in their shade. O, stay not long!
The oleanders and the roses wait
   Thy coming, and so soon the night is past,
Come, come to-night; wide open stands the gate,
   And Death must close it, with our lives, at last.

Enter, and wander down the winding stair
   Of moon-kissed marble, shadowy with time;
There is thy home, and thou belongest there,

With all the beauty of the southern clime.
The night is warm as kisses to the cheek,
Sweet to the ear as when a song is still,
Or the thrilled hush when thou hast ceased to speak
And all the world is waiting on thy will.

O, blind me with thy kisses, let me swoon
Into the dark, and glide into a sleep,
Till moth-white as the early morning moon
Thy face appear, and I behold the peep
Of wonder-witching dawn within thine eyes
And feel thy breath like soft winds from the South
Stir me to shake off slumber and arise
And kneel and kiss the daybreak of thy mouth.

August, 1910.

These lines were written by Madame Sarah Bern-hardt and Monsieur Maeterlinck in my birthday book:

Je suis très très heureuse d'avoir vu l'intérieure de cet être exquis, dont l'âme est aussi jolie que le visage, et qui porte le nom de Beatrice Stella Campbell.

SARAH BERNHARDT.

1902.

Elle est un de ces êtres qui savent réunir les âmes à leur sourse; et lorsqu'elle se trouve là on ne sent plus rien entre lui et ce qui la vérité,

("Aglavain et Selysette")

M. MAETERLINCK.

In June, 1913, Sir George Alexander revived *The Second Mrs. Tanqueray*.

In the autumn of this year Jenny Cornwallis West divorced George.

On April 6th of the following year we married. The decree absolute had been held up for three months, owing to business reasons.

It looked odd that we married only a few hours after the decree was finally made absolute, but *Pygmalion* was to be produced in five days' time, and then there would be no chance of a few days' quiet together. . . .

Amongst hundreds of telegrams and letters of congratulation, I quote a few which show friends felt the marriage might bring us happiness.

"Wednesday

"Oh, my dear,

"My joy was great, and I feel so interested in life when I think of you, at last brilliantly contented, too.

"Soon I hope to see happy faces.

"How glad I am he talked to me at Alice Keppel's. It makes all the difference to have heard from him what adoration and devotion he has for you.

"His people must love him because of his 'expression,' if nothing else, and if they love him they must be glad to know how happy he is.

"Bless you both. "V. R." *

"16, Lower Berkeley Street, W.

"A thousand loving wishes, darling, and may you have

* The Duchess of Rutland.

much of the happiness you deserve so well. I thought so much of you yesterday, and send you all my love.

"Your loving

"FRANCES." †

"Stella, darling,

"All my love and thoughts to you. Bless you.

RACHEL." *

Beo loved George with much affection. Stella wrote from Africa:—

"East Africa Protectorate,

"April 10th, 1914.

"Darling Mother,

"Your telegram which came on Wednesday, was a great surprise to us, as you can imagine, but I can't tell you how glad it has made us, to be able to think of you as happy, and no longer lonely.

"I am very sorry that I do not know George better, but I hope to some day; and I *do* know, from the little I saw him, how much he loves you.

"I have little news, and can think of nothing but your happiness, so I can't write any more now. . . .

"Do write when you have time. I enclose a few lines to George. . . .

"With very much love and a heart bursting with good wishes for your happiness, and a big hug from little Pat.

"Your loving

"STELLA."

———

We were happy at last—I with my belief in the

love I had struggled against for so long—convinced that George had been a very unhappy man—that his unhappiness had been the fault of others—and that I could help him.

Five days after our marriage *Pygmalion* was produced at His Majesty's Theatre. And surely no first night has ever gone with more success, and with such joyousness. The "bloody" almost ruined the play; people laughed too much.

Before the first night Joey sent me final orders, which show, I had not been obedient at rehearsals:—

". . . I could have planned the part so that nine-tenths of it would have gone mechanically, even if your genius had deserted you, leaving only one-tenth to the gods. Even as it is, I have forced half the battle on you; but winning half the battle will not avert defeat. You believe in courage; I say, 'God save me from having to fall back on that desperate resource,' though if it must come to that it must. I don't like fighting; I like conquering. You think you like fighting and now you will have to succeed sword in hand. You have left yourself poorly provided with ideas and expedients, and you must make up for them by dash and brilliancy and resolution. And so, Avanti!

"G. B. S."

One paper said, "The house rocked to and fro and shook with laughter—they roared, they cried with laughter!" There was a kind, human element in the play, too.

In September I went to America with *Pygmalion,* leaving George in my house at Kensington

Square. The wrench was hard, but he had to remain in England to attend to his financial affairs. As usual I had to make money.

After a few months, George came out to me; and learned to know intimately my life and work.

This close companionship filled me with happiness.

But the rumbling of the war was growing louder— the whole world was on its mettle.

Again he had to return to England to take up his military duties.

Some months later George came out to me a second time, and I felt still more sure of our future together.

This time he insisted on acting with me. I taught him "Doolittle" in *Pygmalion,* and "Orreyd" in *Tanqueray,* and he acted well.

Everywhere in America we were received with great hospitality.

Dear Mrs. Stotesbury lent us her house in Washington, and her servants and motor. We entertained royally in our fine surroundings, and when, at the end of the week, I asked her housekeeper for my bills, she said, "There are no bills!"

I telegraphed to Mrs. Stotesbury, who replied, begging me not to deprive her of a trifling happiness!

In San Francisco I produced *Searchlights,* by H. A. Vachell, and taught George the leading part.

After some weeks he was called back to England again.

MRS. CORNWALLIS-WEST

In New York I managed to get up a matinée for Shelagh's * hospital in France. George had written from England asking me to do this for her. I played *The Second Mrs. Tanqueray,* and sent Shelagh £500.

My mother-in-law wrote to me from England:

"Newlands,

"Stella dearest,

"How truly I wish you were here! Your beloved has just arrived in his uniform, so good to look at. So glad of your dear telegram. Little Shelagh is here too, and so grateful for your grand work for her hospital. Ah, Stella dear, our silver-lined cloud must turn its silver side to us soon.

"As for our beloved—you have made a different man of him, and his men I hear simply *worship* him. What a wonderful success Shelagh's Benefit must have been. *Do* send me a good account of it, and your speech. I am going back with Shelagh to her hospital, and then down to Daisy's villa in the South of France. Have you the least notion what your plans are? Do write to me now and then. But not the sort of writing an intoxicated snipe would make who had dipped his feet in an inkpot and then danced a mad war dance all over the paper!!

"Stella dear, you know you cabled me to spend £30 on George's hut. But it has not come yet. I only tell you because it may be lost in the post.

"God bless you, dearest, in the New Year, and may it bring us peace *together.*

"Loving
"Patsy."

* George's sister, Constance Duchess of Westminster.

"Poor little Daisy * in her flat in Berlin, but she has her boy with her."

George met me at Falmouth on my return from America.

It was the day his bankruptcy was published. We remained away from London a few days—far too happy to worry, and then returned to Kensington Square.

At Rushlin Castle, George's old home in Wales, my father-in-law and I went for some long motor drives together, and he talked to me of his youth and the Italian nurse who had nursed him as a baby; and he seemed to link his great love for Italian art in some way with her. His sensitive appreciation of the beauty of nature, shows in the water-colour paintings of his that I have seen. He was a man of absolute integrity, and treated me with affection.

My mother-in-law lived with me at 33, Kensington Square, during a time of severe trial for her, and for us all: I, with other friends, did my best to help George's mother.

In May there was a revival of *Bella Donna,* at the St. James's.

In October, 1916, at the London Opera House, I produced *The Law of the Sands,* by Robert Hichens.

---

* Princess Pless, George's eldest sister, a beautiful, fragile woman, who was, during the five years of war in Germany, nursing and bearing bravely a difficult position. She and her son stayed with me in England twice after the war, and I grew fond of them.

I encouraged George to write plays, and for some time it was an absorbing pleasure to him.

In February, 1917, I produced his one-act play *Pro Patria,* at the Coliseum, which met with some success. Later I took it to the provinces, and in one town his father and mother stayed with us to see the play.

The following letter pleased us:—

"H. M. S. *Vernon,*
"Portsmouth,
"Tuesday night, late,

"Mrs. Patrick Campbell,
"I feel I must write and tell you of the great pleasure your acting in *Pro Patria* gave me.

"Once in the wilds of Ireland's western side I have often heard my mother speak of you and your splendid acting. I never had the chance of seeing you till to-night. Now I can write home and tell my mother how I have had the good luck of seeing you and hearing you— which was best of all.

"I shall always cherish memories of your wonderful elocution and the power that your voice possesses. I just loved the softness in your voice, and its changes, and its power to thrill.

"Do excuse me writing to you. I shall carry away with me memories and thoughts of a beautiful, good woman gifted with a most wonderful voice. I shall always venerate you.

"I suppose I have no right in writing to you—but I feel sure you won't be angry.

"The pleasure and brief happiness you have given me make me,

"Always gratefully yours,
"GEORGE COLE.

"P. S.—It's awful cheek for a sailor to write to you, but I simply can't help it."

During the next few months the agony and nervous strain that was upon the world had broken up all normal living; and normal thinking. The servant question, and food, had become a tragedy: air raids—the evening's entertainment.

In the home, superhuman courage, and calmness, were needed to cope with nerves, that were on edge.

If there was no cook, and *you* could cook, that was a triumph: I felt more proud of my sudden ability to cook—and that George proclaimed my cooking as good as the "Ritz"—than I have ever been of my success on the stage.

Terrible war news—with the awful awaiting and facing the death roll—seemed more in keeping with the tenseness of the moment, than good news.

Companionship in the home was not expected: that your man was *alive*—your son *safe,* and *sound;* happy on his "ten days' leave": that was enough.

The long grey line of motor ambulances waiting for the wounded, at Charing Cross—what a sight it was to pass, almost every night coming home from the theatre. . . .

At the Savoy one day, a tall handsome officer came down the steps of the restaurant, carrying his friend on his shoulder—an armless, legless, trunk, with a gay, handsome, laughing face. . . .

In October, 1917, *The Thirteenth Chair,* was produced at the Duke of York's—a popular play that met with great success, for four months.

During the run of this play my heart was lacerated:—

> "Admiralty.
> "Deeply regret Acting Lieutenant-Commander Alan U. Campbell killed in action, 30th December. Letter follows."

Beo had been killed in France! I had not realized this could be. . . .

One day's rest to get my heart steady, and then work again! Life was pitiless—the theater, hell.

Friends wrote: "Thank God you have George to love and take care of you"—but George was strangely silent; this made the pain harder to bear. . . .

I was in deep sea, and there was no light anywhere.

CHAPTER XVIII

Lieut.-Commander Alan U. Campbell, M.C.
Age, 32. Howe Battalion.
Naval and Military Service.

H. M. S. *Britannia* (Training Ship), 1898 to 1900—Naval Cadet.

H. M. S. *Endymion,* 1900 to 1904.

H. M. S. *Glory* (Flagship China Station), Cadet to Midshipman. Two years Training Ship, three years on China Station.

Retired from H. M. Navy and proceeded to Oxford University, 1905.

At outbreak of the Great War obtained commission in R. N. V. R. as Sub-Lieut. in December, 1914; would have obtained one earlier, but was compelled to undergo an operation to enable him to pass Medical Board at Admiralty, which kept him two months in hospital.

Served as Sub-Lieutenant in the Anson Battalion at Blandford from January, 1915, until he proceeded with R. N. Division on original Expeditionary Force to Dardanelles; was prevented from taking part in the original landing at Cape Helles by reason of wound (caused by operation) reopening; underwent further operation in hospital at Port Said, and when discharged to Base was unfit for service in the field.

Egypt.—Became Base Quartermaster at Mustapha Barracks, Alexandria, to R. N. Division for one month.

Base Quartermaster to M. E. F. at Base for two weeks.

Appointed A. P. M. to M. E. F. at Base, Alexandria,

and carried out these duties for nearly three months, May till beginning of August, when he was pronounced fit for active service; proceeded to Gallipoli Peninsula.

GALLIPOLI.—Landed beginning of August, joined up with his old battalion, Anson, found himself in command practically two companies (including reinforcements) at the Cape Helles end in the trench, whilst the remainder of the battalion was at Suvla.

Transferred to Howe Battalion, became Trench-Mortar Officer, September, 1915.

In October, 1915, took part in operations carried out by the 52nd Division (Lowland) in taking Vineyard Trenches; employed protecting their left flank, with all available mortars of the division, relieving the French Division on the extreme right of the line. Was put in command of the Divisional Heavy Mortar Battery, 18 guns, afterwards reduced to 12 (Dumezils), firing 130lb. shells, which the French handed over in December, 1915.

He was ordered by the 8th Corps to draw all enemy fire possible from the 52nd Division (on the left), who were taking some trenches near the "Vineyard," which he very effectually did, firing on an average 30 heavy shells from each mortar and having the "Dumezil" gun positions and trenches nearly flattened out.

Prior to the "evacuation," acting under orders of the Divisional General, he invented a means of converting the remainder of the large "Dumezil" torpedoes, into electrical contact land mines, by means of tins of ammonal, lashed to the sides of the aerial torpedoes, and trip wires to contact pieces into electric batteries.

Using the personnel of the Mortar Battery, and with the help of N. C. O.'s from the Divisional Signal Company (R. E.'s), he laid out 13 mine fields in the divisional area, protecting the withdrawal of troops from the line.

The mine fields started from between the firing line and support line and covering the whole front, continued down to the Eski line (or final reserve line). On the night of the evacuation he was placed in command of the last thirty-two men who remained up with Divisional Engineers (who were cutting wires or pulling down obstructions in the trenches), and when all troops had passed through, his party connected up all the trip wires, completely blocking the way, should the Turks attack.

Some of the mine fields had as many as 250 large aerial torpedoes lashed together (about 25,000 lb. of "Melanite"), and from reports of aeroplanes, and news from the Athens papers during the next few days, they appear to have caused great havoc amongst the Turkish patrols (2,000 casualties being admitted by the Turks).

EVACUATION.—Proceeded with the division to Lemnos, given leave to England. Received the "Croix de Guerre" with palm from the French.

Returned and proceeded to Stavros, on the extreme right of the Saloniki line. Back with Anson Battalion, employed digging trenches and sighting machine gun emplacements, etc.

Returned to Lemnos Island with the R. N. Division, and became A. P. M. to R. N. Division for nearly two months until arrival in France.

He was practically in trenches all the time. He put up a "box barrage" with the Stokes Battery in two successful raids in enemy trenches. Took part in the operation north of Ancre on November 13th, 14th, 15th.

Ordered by Brigadier down from bombing post in German strong point to conduct two tanks up; assaulted strong point with tanks at 6:10 a. m. on November

14th, and in one hour took position, and with officers and crews of tanks rounded up nearly 400 prisoners, including seven officers, after which, until relieved on November 15th at 4 P. M., acted as General Brigade liaison officer, keeping touch for Brigadier with all units of brigade.

February, March, 1917, took part in advance on Aisne. April 28th took active part in the operations around Gavrelle.

His division held the Oppy-Gavrelle sector until relieved on September 24th, 1917.

July, August, September, he came home to Senior Officer School, Aldershot, passed out with a most excellent confidential report. Was secretary of school cricket team.

Promoted to Acting Lieutenant-Commander and transferred to Howe Battalion as Second-in-Command. Went through operations in the Ypres Salient, October 26th, throughout the Paschendaele offensive to October 30th, until relieved, November 8th; moved to Cambrai front December 16th, when Boche attacked the position on Welsh Ridge in the La Vacquerie-Marcoing sector.

He and the Commander killed instantaneously by a bursting shell at 7:30 A. M. December 30th. Buried on January 1st, 1918; at Metz en Couture.

Mentioned in despatches after evacuation by General Munro.

Recommended for a promotion by General McGrigor after duties as Base A. P. M., Alexandria, August, 1915.

Recommended for promotion by Major-General Paris, K. C. B., after evacuation, January, 1915.

Recommended for promotion after Stavros.

Recommended for a Battalion Commander by Brigadier-General Prentice, D. S. O., after operations of November 13th, north of Ancre.

Received Military Cross, January 1st, 1917.
Received Bar to Military Cross, January 20th, 1917.
Egypt, Dardanelles, Salonika, 15 months.
France, 17 months.
Gazetted as Captain in the H. L. I.

MY SON

His hand is on my arm, and he says—
"Don't write about me Mother—all the men out
there were such splendid chaps."
He sees my sad face, and adds—
"All right, say what you like, I am going out to
play golf."
Yes, he is happy somewhere—and I may do as
I like.
I wanted to be with him at the Investiture at
Buckingham Palace when he received his Military
Cross * with a bar, but he had left the house early
that morning, and when he came back he handed
me the case, his arm around me, he said with a
smile:
"Where were you?—a poor old woman came up
to me and said, 'Bravo, my son'—everyone thought
she was my mother."
We laughed—we understood one another—pic-

---

* This cutting from a daily paper of 14th February, 1917, describes
the deed that gained this honour:
"He brought his guns into action with good effect. Later, he guided
two 'Tanks' to the enemy first line system and materially assisted in
taking over 400 prisoners.
"The hero of this splendid act of gallantry is Temporary Lt. Alan
Urquhart Campbell, M.C., R.N.V.R., and in recognition of his bravery
the King has awarded him a bar to his Military Cross."

BEO WITH OFFICIALS AT FOURTH SENIOR OFFICERS' SCHOOL

tures in the papers with "Mrs. Patrick Campbell and her brave son" were not to be thought of.

Once he slept in the room next to mine; he laughed at his cough, saying he had been "gassed a bit."

I heard him talking in his sleep—a deep strong voice—I knew he was giving orders to his men——

The thought kept passing through my mind in the night—"Beo risks his life hourly—he gives orders to men who obey him with their lives."

And I remembered how as a baby he wanted a sword—and his first picture was a drawing of a flag—

I saw him, when he was four years old, nodding and smiling at some children he did not know, who were looking at him from a window as we passed.

I asked him who they were; he said in his baby voice, "They are my friends"—*that* was his attitude towards the world: his fellow men were his friends —and they were all worth while—his *enemies* were the enemies of *mankind*.

I, who hate war with a hatred that makes me feel a fiend, learned through war I had brought a *man* into the world—that is enough——

BEO'S LETTERS.

"Somewhere in Gallipoli,
"25th October, 1915.

"Darling Mother,
"I expect all your letters and all mine have been sunk!

I love to get your photos—do send me as many as you can, and of anybody, just to make my dug-out look cheerful and to remind me that there are others things than dead men, shells and smells. I have been in the actual firing line now nearly three months, and am feeling a bit fed up with it all. Flies, sandstorms, shells and smells describes it! There seems no chance of leave until this 'filthy' war is over, and as the Bulgarians and Germans appear to be making their way down here, we shall wake up one morning to the tune of 'Jack Johnson,' and there will be the devil of a scrap. As it is, the shelling is pretty hot, and I can't remember the time when I didn't have a headache.

"Two or three days ago we advanced to within twelve yards of the Turks' line in our sector without a casualty; and as I am now commanding the Brigade Mortar Battery, they seem to think that my beastly heathenish bombs and mortar shells and things helped somewhat. The next night the Turks made an assault with bombs and grenades, etc., but again our fellows bombed them back and my old Battery put the fear of God into them. The mortars are fine, and we fire a shell about the size of St. Paul's, which makes a noise like an earthquake. I direct their fire from the nearest point to the enemy. Our Tommies love them, and the cry is ever—'Give 'em some more "Delight," Sir!' The R. N. D. out here are splendid, that is to say the remains of our original lot (poor fellows, they've been in the thick of it for six months without a rest), and its always one Englishman equal to three Turks at close quarters. Let us hope the new drafts and reinforcements will soon be as good as the old, and then 'Allah help the Turk!' Of course, we get a good few casualties. One young officer under my command had his head blown off by a shell just near me! I've felt squeamish ever since. He was such a cheery soul, and only 18! And the Colonel of the——— was killed by a shell within 50 yards of my dug-out, and also a Major in the——was blown to bits by a Turk bomb quite close to me. (Better not name Regiment on account of the Censor.)

"I have been extraordinarily lucky so far. Have been hit all over my body, but always with spent bullets, or stray spent shrapnel bullets. How long the luck will last rests with the gods, but we all feel here that none of us will get off the Peninsula with a whole skin. . . .

"I am a funny sight in the trenches. My beard's not a success, and I think I'll shave, or my own men will shoot me one night for a Turk. Our average distance from the Turk along the whole line is not more than 75 yards—*i. e.,* from the Aegean Sea across the Peninsula to the Straits—and it is awfully sad to look over our parapet through a periscope, and see all the thousands of dead bodies heaped up between the lines, both Turks and our fellows, killed in the numerous assaults on each side. It is certain death to try and bring them in, even at night, and the stink is awful, and the vultures hop about, and we are not allowed to shoot them—they are USEFUL. And then, when one walks up from the rest camps (rest is only a name, as they are shelled all the time), one passes graveyard after graveyard, and one reads the names of all one's pals and feels sick at heart, but one arrives at the firing line with a firmer determination to beat the enemy to his knees.

"Do excuse this rotten letter, Mother dear, but there are so many things happening every day, and all day and night, that it would take an encyclopædia to record them.

"About 7:30 A. M. the other morning there was a

pretty aerial duel between a German Taube and a French Voisin. The German was armed with a machine gun, but the Frenchman, though only armed with his pistol, manœuvred so well that he managed to drive off the Taube. It happened right above our lines, and you should have heard the cheering.

"I am writing this letter in my little dug-out in the firing line, about 50 yards from the Turks. I am fairly comfortable. Have pinned blankets all around the walls to make it warm, and waterproof sheets on the ground and roof, and have nothing to fear except shells, centipedes, snakes, and—LICE. If you want to send me anything, send me Keating's! Outside my dug-out is a sentry, who is potting away at snipers opposite. I have been keeping my eye in, earlier this evening, but one has to be pretty nippy. This morning about 6.15 I was taking aim through an iron loophole at another loophole in front, when, just as I fired, a bullet from another sniper hit my plate about a quarter inch above the loophole. I just had time to see my quarry throw up his hands and fall back, and then I sat down quietly to recover my nerves. The bullet had hit the plate with such a force as to knock it back on to my head. . . .

"I wonder if you received all my letters from Alexandria. By Jove, I was glad to get out of that place, and it was just touch-and-go. The doctors wanted to invalid me, but I had made great friends in my capacity of A. P. M. with the Surgeon-General, and I practically implored him to get me passed; and I *was,* and here I am; and, except for an occasional breakdown, fever, sunstroke, influenza, etc., for a few days, never felt better. I am afraid the men suffer a good deal from dysentery and jaundice. But their spirits are wonderful, and one is proud to be an Englishman, and amongst them. . . .

"Darling, what wouldn't I give for a long talk with you like we used to have. I wish I was with you and working for you, and helping to make all a success. I get many spare moments to think over my life, and I feel so heartbroken at all the worry I have caused you. . . .

"I'm pretty lucky in this job—that is to say, the Brigadier, and others, seem to think I COUNT, and have made my presence felt. When I first landed I was given command of a company, and then had command of what was left of the 'Anson Batt.' here, the rest being at Suvla Bay. And now I have this command, which is gradually becoming a more and more important factor in the campaign. . . .

"It is very romantic, sometimes; we have a glorious sunrise, and we hear all the Turks chanting the Koran and praying, and then our Tommies play the bagpipes and sing ragtime and pepper them with bombs and maxims to annoy them. How they must hate us! It's like a glimpse of 'Omar Khayyam' suddenly overshadowed by a village fair.

"Remember me to all. Was the new play* a success? Do send lots of photos. You don't know how they cheer one up in this God-forsaken Peninsula. All my love, darling Mother, and do forgive me for all my sins.

"Your loving son,
"BEO."

From "Somewhere in the Mediterranean" he writes to Stella:

"Sunday, March 7th.

"Darling Stella,
    "The Lord only knows when I shall be able to write

* *Searchlights.*

to you again, or even if this one will reach you. We are on the most interesting and history-making expedition, and nobody knows if we shall ever come back, as the forces are of unknown strength. But the fact remains we are going to land and occupy the Dardanelles forts—attacking them from the rear (those that the fleet haven't bashed to pieces), and then we go on to Constantinople and endeavour to take it. We have two battalions on board and the Brigadier-General and staff, and the band plays every night at dinner, and as the weather has been delicious, it has been like a yachting trip so far. Not a sign of a submarine, although, of course, we were strongly convoyed through the zone. Now we are alone and all the transports assemble at Malta, where we arrive to-morrow. Thence we proceed to an island called Lemnos, which is to be our base.

"At what point of the Gallipoli Peninsula we land I don't know, but that we shall have to fight our way all the time is certain, as we have to drive every Turk out. All our men are magnificently equipped, and I myself look like a pirate of Penzance when I am fully armed.

"'It was very exciting from the moment the King inspected us. All was done so secretly. We marched out of camp at dead of night, and all the different battalions entrained at different stations all round the country, and we all embarked at Avonmouth. We marched nine miles fully equipped, with our transport and mules and horses, etc., and didn't get off till about 2 a. m.

"The other battalion with us on board is the *Hood* Battalion, O. C. Asquith, Patrick Shaw Stewart, and Lewis Waller's son are all with it and on board.

"Violet Asquith came to see the ship off all alone.

"We have a new Colonel in George's place, a fine man, Colonel Moorehouse, C.M.G., D.S.O. He was in command in West Africa. There is quite a chance if we finish this job satisfactorily, and there are enough of us left out of the 60,000 who go now, that we shall go and finish off German East Africa. . . .

"How is darling little Pat? . . .

"Good-bye. Love to all.

"Your loving brother,
"BEO."

And some months later he wrote to her from France:—

"Darling Stella,

"Thank you so much for the beautiful photo of yourself and Pat. How lovely he is getting. You are a lucky dog!

"How is the play going? And how do you think darling Mother is looking?

"We have been going through a perfect maze of operations, and the removal of our division from the Salonika front to the French front was a thing of stupendous interest and work for us all.

"I don't think much of the trenches here—very unsanitary and no proper cover from shell fire. We'll have to show these troops what some of our men can do in the way of trench digging, etc.

"We've had a few casualties, but nothing to speak of. They all regard us as veterans out here, which is pleasing, and we have been placed in a regular corps. . . .

"Tell Pat that every time I fire my guns at the Boches I say, 'There's one from Pat!' and it's become quite a common expression—my sergeants use it now!

"My love to all, darling.

"Your loving brother,
"BEO."

"Anson Battalion,
"Royal Naval Division,
"Eastern Mediterranean Squadron.

"Darling, darling Mother,

"Your sweet letter has just arrived. You don't know how it cheers one up to get letters from those one loves.

"I am sending you my 'Cross' * registered. I do hope it doesn't get lost. There is no opportunity of wearing it out here in the field, and I wear the bit of ribbon on my left breast.

"I am anxious to read the despatches on the evacuation at Cape Helles. I do hope I get an English honour, for your sake, Mother, dear. I only want it for you. I was glad to see my 'Croix' had a laurel spray on it, which is the highest grade and differs from the Legion of Honour in that the 'Croix' can only be won in action, whilst the 'Legion' can be won anywhere, and even by civilians. . . .

"Wasn't it rot only getting three weeks' leave after all that time under fire? We are now on the right of General Sarrail's line from Salonika. They must think a lot of the R.N.D., because we have a most important part of the line, practically at the same point where the Greeks beat the Bulgarians in the Balkan War; in fact, we are using some of the old Greek trenches. The Bulgarians are thirty miles off, although we can see their outposts and fire in the mountains. A Greek Army Corps is in between us, like a man holding two dogs apart. . . . But we are prepared, and strengthen our position night and day. The scenery is magnificent, and such a change to that awful Peninsula. My duties are all on the mountain tops, and I come down to our little bivouac to sleep.

* Beo sent me his Croix de Guerre to America.

"I am looking for good concealed gun positions for my battery, and it is interesting and exciting work. . . .

"We have had one man killed by a bear and two torn to bits by jackals, but otherwise we are all very happy and healthy, and the air is wonderful. . . .

"All my love, darling.

"Your loving son,
"Beo."

"1st Trench Mortar Battery,
"R. N. Division.
"July 12th, 1916.

"My own darling,

"Am still in the land of the living, although last night they were 'plastering' us with all kinds of shell and shrapnel. Have just got back to my dug-out, 5 :30 a. m., having been on the 'qui vive' for forty-eight hours, and feel pretty tired and headachy. They have been putting over asphyxiating shells, and one has to be eternally alert not only for one's own safety, but for all one's men. Thank God the prevailing wind or breeze is not favourable to them for gas! Fifteen men were killed about 2 a. m., this morning by one of their beastly big shells. All asleep in a large dug-out. There is nothing now except a large hole as big as our back garden and bits of legs and arms. . . .

"What a morbid letter, but I expect it is because I am dead beat and must get some sleep, but don't seem to be able to. The battery are behaving splendidly, and I am awfully proud of them. It's fine to feel one has trained them all and that each individual man always rises to the occasion, and the worse the shelling, the more dogged they become.

"By Jove I'm glad I'm an Englishman. The Hun is

a beaten man, and it is quite a common occurrence for the Tommies and an officer, to go over the parapet, and frighten the life out of the trench opposite, and come back with twenty or thirty prisoners, at night-time.

"And we never see a Boche aeroplane now. Our men are always ten or twelve up at a time.

"Darling, will you have the photograph films, which I think are in that box of mine, developed and printed? All the stuff is what is called 'Base Kit,' or stuff we cannot be burdened with out here, and I sent it on to you to take charge of.

"The things you sent me are fine, and I don't get wet feet now.

"My dug-out is in a trench called 'Granby Street.'

"Fancy B—— coming to see you! We always think him a little 'off his chump.' He's got a soft job now as a kind of messenger to the Staff Captain, and always lives miles behind the firing line and gets leave occasionally. It always makes us in the firing line angry, to think of all the staffs who get such an easy time of it, and who do nothing but worry us with returns of men and ammunition; and as soon as a shell comes, run deep into a dug-out and stay there. But still, old B—— has seen a bit of fighting and has stuck it out, although he always looks as if he were going 'sick.'

"I must go to bed now; it is 6:30 a. m.

"Good-bye beloved Mother.

"I wish I could see you soon.

"Your own
"Beo."

"63rd R. M. Division,

"My darling Mother,   "18/8/1916.

"How rotten you must think me for not having ans-

MRS. PATRICK CAMPBELL AND HER TWO CHILDREN
JUST BEFORE BEO ENTERED THE NAVY

wered all your sweet, dear letters. You don't know how I love to get them, and how they cheer me up. We have been having rather a hard time of it—nearly fifty days and nights in the firing line now, and I spend all my spare moments in trying to get a little sleep. It was terrible the other day—I lost a Corporal and four of my best men by one shell, which completely buried them in the crater it made.

"It nearly broke my heart; they had all been with me nearly a year, and I was so fond of them. We held a solemn service in the crater less than fifteen yards form the Boche, and, although they were shelling at the time, our poor little band with their steel helmets off, remained untouched.

"The awful part is writing condoling letters to the wives.

"No signs of any leave yet. What do you think? While walking along the trenches, I met 'Polly,' *—a full-blown captain of a Scotch regiment, and in kilts. All his men love him, and he looks quite different and has been through a lot, and he is a real good plucked 'un and very fearless.

"Do write often, Mother darling, and tell me any scraps of news. I don't think they stop illustrated papers; at least, most of the men get them.

"I am writing George a note to-night, and will try and write you a longer letter, darling. I must admit I am getting a little war-worn, and would like to get a cap-taincy or majority in the Scots Guards or Black Watch temporarily—it would give me a little respite.

"All my love, darling,

"Your own,

"BEO."

* Captain Allan Pollock, a brilliant comedian, who played in my

"188th Light Trench Mortar Battery,
"63rd R. N. Division
"France.
"September, 1916.

"My own darling,

"I am so sorry I haven't written for so long, but life has been very full of dangers and excitements, and the only time I have had for writing has to be occupied in sending in reports and despatches.

"You will be glad to hear all the Generals think very highly of my Battery and I had an awfully nice congratulatory message from the General over one operation, in which he said that my comrades were grateful to me and the Battery for their magnificent work and devotion to duty; and that it was entirely due to the Battery that the operation was successful. And *what do you think?* The General sent for me and told me that because I had had such a long, tiring, and strenuous time, and done such good work, he was going to give me '*special leave*' soon, that I was too valuable to him at the present moment, but that I could expect it in the near future.

"Hurrah! ! Hurrah! ! I'll be able to 'pop' at the rabbits yet, and sec 'Beppo' and 'Geeee-n-a' ! ! * . . .

"By Jove, we did get a pounding from the big German guns the other day, and hardly any one of my gun positions are standing now, and most of the guns are out of action—but the men were absolutely, superbly magnificent. Two of them have gone in for D.C.M.'s, and one ought to get the V.C. Mother, you wouldn't believe how absolutely fearless and wonderful these men of mine are. They are just like young gods, all of them —most of them youngsters—but their eyes sparkle and

company in London and made a big success in America; a brave soldier who was severely wounded.

* Our dogs.

their nostrils dilate with excitement when they go into action, and I can rely on them to a man to do exactly what I want. Sometimes they go forty-eight hours without an hour's sleep, working day and night.

" . . . Darling, the coat is wonderful, and everybody is envying me. I sleep in it. It's so awfully cold at nights now. And the pie and all the hairwash arrived safely!

"What's the price of eggs? ? ? You couldn't send two dozen hard boiled could you? They are so frightfully expensive here, and all our money goes on them.

"Tell me about Barnes—he, anyhow, is an honest man!

"I do love your letters so, Mother, so write often, even if only a line, and send more photos. . . .

"Poor Fred. I am writing to him. I've had some of that 'Sand and Flies' in Gallipoli!

"I am sending you a cutting * I found in the *Daily Mail* of the 12th—rather nice of Lady Buxton, and brought back memories of Daddy, and how he would have loved to have been with me here.

"Tell me the name of your playlet, and also Stella's, and has anything happened about George's?

"Is George's Division the 57th or 67th, and what regiments are in it? I hope I get leave before he goes. It will probably only be ten days when I do get it.

"My best love, darling,

"Your own son,
"BEO."

* "During their stay in Boshof their Excellencies decorated with almond blossoms and violets the grave of Captain Cecil Boyle, a brother-in-law of Lord Buxton, who was killed in action in the neighbourhood in the Boer War, and Lady Buxton, noticing that the next grave was that of Sergeant Patrick Campbell, husband of the actress, laid on it some other blooms. Almond blossoms were placed by the Governor-General upon the tomb of the French soldier, Comte de Villebois Mareuil, who fought with distinction on the side of the Boers."

Writing of the Battle of the Ancre he says:

"November 28th, 1916.

"My own darling Mother,

". . . Imagine a huge army lying on the grass in massive waves, with nothing but their greatcoats to cover them; no noise—just a few whispers—a few prayers, and last words to pals before the attack at dawn.

"I felt that we were in the presence of two gigantic figures, who were sitting minutely gazing at us—one was Death, and the other some indescribable being—it wasn't exactly life, or Victory or an Angel, but all I knew was that these two figures were silently summing us up and taking the toll for the morrow. I have never felt near to God in my life before.

"And the men—one cannot describe their magnificence. They were not excited or downhearted—all feeling the same presence of some mighty Being who was labelling them for the morrow, and all filled with the same feeling, that the result to-morrow must be 'V i c t o r y' at all costs!

"I went round to my men and to fellows I knew in other regiments, and one felt proud to be amongst them —and not for all the riches in the world would I have given up my place in that mass of men. One literally felt like one big family. Then about 4 a. m. coats were rolled up and stacked away, and a small tot of rum served out, or hot soup—to keep the cold from one's bones, and then a silent wait at the 'Alert.' Think of it, a whole army—all waiting for the signal.

"Then on that misty morning, just before dawn—one couldn't see ten yards in front of one, but all knew exactly what to do—a lumbering 15-in. shell came on and buried itself away back in the Hun lines, and immediately to the second the Artillery started! ! ! Ten seconds before, you could have heard a pin drop, and ten seconds after, you had to shout in a man's ear to make him hear. Then, as the barrage lifts, over surge the waves of men—I and my men with them, and the rest is chaos—but Victory! !

"What a name our dear old Division made for itself— each man was ten times a hero—and they were up against the German Guards Division that day! Those they didn't kill they captured, until they had accounted for the lot.

"It would take ten volumes to recount the incidents— one gets an impression of blood, bayonets, shells, and blue-grey uniforms!

"My men were glorious, and our adventures many. Seventy of us were holding up seven hundred Huns for a whole day.

"Then all our guns were knocked out, and every man, killed or wounded at his post.

"Then we found the Boche guns, and fired them until all the ammunition was expended. Then we became bombers, machine-gunners, anything that was needed, and we kept fighting for three solid days—with no sleep until we were relieved, when we marched out covered with blood, dust, and smoke, and victory in our eyes.

"We marched past guns and gunners, (what was left of us, alas!).

"You should have heard the cheering. The dear old Naval Division had made history and an undying name in those three days. But what a cost! It's too dreadful—all one's pals gone!

"How I got through I cannot say! My life was saved a hundred times by gallant fellows—one of my best pals pulled me down into a shell hole, saying: 'For

God's sake look out, old man there's a sniper!' And the next minute he had been shot through the head and fell on me, dead!

"And the glorious stretcher-bearers and doctors—you just felt that V.C.'s were not good enough for them—the way they worked under murderous fire! I can tell you the clearing of a battlefield is gruesome work.

"My greatest feat was capturing three hundred and eighty odd prisoners with eight men and a 'tank' ! * You may have read the exploits of that dear old 'tank' in the papers. I saw it in the *Daily News* of the 23rd November, on the second column.

"Well, yer 'umble was the galleant horficer who led the way—'because he knew it so well'—I should jolly well hope I did, considering I had been bombing it with every conceivable kind of bomb for many hours and nearly lost my life a dozen times.

"But fancy getting a notice in the papers! That's more than I have ever done as an actor!

"We are now back resting and refitting and getting reinforcements for the next push.

"I have been very lucky, and billeted with my men in a lovely chateau, rather like Frampton*—there is fishing and duck shooting, and the country is magnificent, and it is wonderful to be away from the noise of the guns.

---

* The *Times,* on the 24th of November, 1916, had said: "One would like to tell at length the tale of the officer of the Trench Mortar Battery, the name of whose father (and still more that of his mother) is known wherever the English language is spoken, who led the 'Tank' into action against the redoubt. It was not strictly his business, but he 'knew the road' (having been putting mortars into the beastly place for half a day) and did most gallantly a service of great danger."

*Frampton Court, Dorchester, the home of Sir Algernon Brinsley Sheridan.

"I expect I shall be able to get leave soon; but, of course, I must first reorganise the Battery.

"Tell George the Ansons did magnificently, and as I am still on their establishment, I will consider myself one. I am now the Senior Officer, except the Colonel, on the books.

"I shall try and manœuvre leave for Christmas if possible.

"I hope you are keeping well, and don't work too hard! "All my love, darling,

"Your own son,
"BEO.

"P. S.—Love to George and Stella.
"We captured a little dog in the Boche third line—he is so glad to be a prisoner."

"My own darling Mother,
"I am so anxious to hear about George's play.   Just a line from the front trenches—it's bitterly cold and I don't think I have ever felt so miserable, frost-bitten, toes, nose, and fingers—and shelling is increasing every day—but we are continually pressing the Hun back, and fighting keeps one warm.   I have had many narrow escapes, but I always carry our little front-door key, * and clutch it, if I feel rather faint.

"A shell burst so close the other day that I was inside the zone of the fragments, which luckily burst upwards, but one jagged bit cut a tree in half, against which I had crouched, just about five feet above my head.

"That was four days ago, and my ears are still singing and my nerves are going slightly.   I think the fellows who get wounded are the luckiest, you can't imagine the

* The key of our home, 33 Kensington Square.

accumulated strain on one's nerves after two years of it. "The gramophone in our little dug-out is a source of great joy. Did you get the cheque for it we all subscribed? . . .

"It is now 11 a. m., and I am lying down on some sandbags resting and shivering after a hellish 'scrap' last night, as the Boche countered, but we drove them all off and didn't lose an inch of ground.

"Our old Division never has.

"Lee, my Irish sub, is trying to fry some bacon on a candle, and is making us all laugh by his language and Irish brogue. Bragg, another of my subs, who is a Warwickshire farmer, is making our mouths water by telling us the tale of a HAM. Wilcox, my second in command, is trying to keep himself warm by writing to a lady in the Argentine. We're more or less a happy crowd; we all know each other's worth in a tight corner, and they all love and respect me, which makes me happy, so life isn't so bad.

"All my love darling, and love to George; my hands are so cold I can't write.

"Your own
"BEO."

"February 6th, 1917.

"Well darling,

"After the most awful journey—bitterly cold—which nearly froze us to death, we arrived into the battle area, and found, as I thought, the old Division in the thick of it again. And now you will be glad to hear that it has kept up its reputation.

"But the cold! ! ! It is indescribable. Some of the poor wounded—both Boche and ours—who have been lying out for days have to have their feet taken off simply because they have become blocks of ice.

"I didn't have a minute to write to George, but have done so to-day. My darling, I never realise how wonderful you are, and what a rock of comfort you are to those around you.

"The whole way over I have been thinking of your goodness, and hoping that I may be spared to really make you happy in regard to me, and my doings, with money and life in general. . . .

"Is George better? I met some of his staff in Boulogne. His Division will be out soon, I think. I am glad he is not coming. He would die of the cold. Even the water in our water-bottles has two inches of ice on it, and our meat, and even bread freezes.

"The Mess are overjoyed with the gramophone. It makes life absolutely different up here in this bleak spot. It took us a long time to get it going, and all the oil had frozen; but now it is playing as I write this, and the guns are booming outside, and we are quite merry and bright, awaiting our turn *again! !*

"My Brigadier is very sympathetic, and he and the Brigade Major have elected me a member of the Caledonian Club in London. I expect my commission in the H.L.I. will be through soon.

"I think I must write to the Paymaster, Blandford, and increase that monthly remittance to you, to £15. It will teach me to be careful with money.

"Did you post the letter for me? It was on your desk.

"Do write and let me know the result of George's play I am so excited about it.

"Your loving,
"Beo."

"188th Trench Mortar Battery,

11. 3. 1917.

"Darling Stella,

"Why don't you write me a line? Here am I, having H—l's own time in a sea of mud—and shells—and not a line from my own sister! ! ! Burghhh! ! ! Boohoo! ! !

"Right! I was going to finish a one-act play for you, but now I'll give it to Sally Brough instead, and eat all Pat's sweets, and dirty Nanny's nursery, and—well—nuff said! ! !

"You will be glad to hear that perhaps I am coming back this month to go to Aldershot, to attend a Battalion Commanders' Course, and that I get from Saturday noon to Monday 9 a. m. off every week.

"Our old Division has been doing marvels, and we are very pleased with ourselves, although I think they have given us a full share of fighting, practically scrapping continuously since I came back and that on the top of the big attack in November we have just about beaten the record out here. So far in our Brigade alone since November 13th we have won ten D.S.O.'s twenty-six Military Crosses, and about forty D.C.M. and Military Medals.

"Do you see much of mother? I do hope so. I realise so much now what a treasure she is, and what a lot we both owe her in life.

"WRITE.

"Your own loving brother,

"BEO."

"Best love to Pat and Nanny, and ask N. to send along any old illustrateds or magazines she doesn't want, as the men love them so."

"188th Trench Mortar Battery.

"Darling, . . . I can only tell you that before the end of the war I *will* make you proud of me.

"With all the love in the world.

"Your own son,
"Beo."

"May 1917.

"My own darling Mother,

"Just a line to tell you I am quite all right. We are back amidst the shelling and noise again; but the weather is warm, and that is the main blessing. . . .

"If you ever send any records out again, try and get one of Caruso singing an English song (it is the only one he has sung, and it is divine).

"Also some needles and some good songs or violin and *Chu Chin Chow* records.

"I am so sorry George is ill. Can't he get a War Office job on "Q" branch somewhere, where he would not have to run about so?

"When I get home you must meet our machine-gun officer, Macgeorge, if we can get home together. He plays the piano divinely. When we were resting in a back area we found quite a good piano belonging to our 'Follies,' and he played for hours, everything from Liszt, Schumann, Strauss, down to Paul Rubens and coon songs. You only have to give him a whisky and soda and a good cigar, and he is a concert in himself—and only twenty-two; but he has studied for ten years all over Europe. He makes a very fine officer, too. He is in the H.L.I.

"Do write often. Stella hasn't written. . . .

"Give my love to George.

"Your own loving son,
"Beo."

"May, 1917.

"My own darling Mother,

"Just a few lines to say we have just come out of the stiffest scrap this Division has ever been in. I cannot describe it, except it was all hand-to-hand, and that we had to fend off at least sixteen counter-attacks of Boches ten times our number—one night seven counter-attacks. But the Division came out more glorious than ever—absolutely magnificent—and my men were almost supernatural—forty-eight hours without leaving the guns—no food or water—and the Germans seething round like tiger-cats; but our men can be super-tigers, and we never gave one inch of ground.

"I am quite well, but dazed and rather weak—the shelling was indescribable. I believe they are going to shower more honours on us, and every man deserves a V.C.; but anyhow, I have one man in for the V.C. and two for the D.C.M., and five for Military Medals. I do hope they will get them.

"Love to all.

"Your own son,
"BEO."

"My own darling Mother,

"I have had no time to write. We have been scrapping and fighting all the time, and I am so tired and weary, and it is only the thought of how unhappy it would make you and others that prevents me praying for a shell.

"I am broken-hearted; one shell came yesterday and knocked out twenty of my men and one officer. It is too awful to think about. It would have killed me, too, if I hadn't just turned back five minutes before to go and telephone from a dug-out to the General. I and the rest of my Battery are so shaken by this horrible loss that we have been relieved from the guns for a day or two, but shall go back soon.

"I expect you will read all about the dear old Division's exploits—we have excelled our last performance.

"How did G.'s play go? I am so anxious to know. I have looked in the only papers I can find and can only find my own name! ! !

"Write soon, please.

"Your own loving son,
"BEO."

"In the Field.

"My own darling Mother,

"I am afraid my coming home has been knocked on the head for some time, as the worrying of the Boche during his retirement requires the services of all the highly trained officers and men in France. We are still more or less in the thick of it and I am afraid will be for some time, and there is no leave to be had for a long time. Things are progressing well here, and there is no doubt the Boche is a beaten man on the Western front, but I cannot see any finish to the war until about June, 1918.

"It is rather hard luck on all of us who have been at it practically from the start to be continually kept at it when there are so many thousands of soldiers at home doing nothing. But still, we are all patriots, and if the services of our highly trained and brave men and officers are necessary for the carrying out of successful operations, well, we give our blood cheerfully and will go on doing so until we are all gone. Do you know our

Division has now in its possession more crosses and medals for Bravery and Valour than any other in France?

"And it makes your eyes dim to see the brave fellows on the march, some with two, some with three gold stripes, and even a few with four or five; and nearly every two or three with the Military Medal or D.C.M., and the officer's with their D.S.O.'s and Military Crosses and a V.C.—our V.C., poor devil, is dead.

"Do write and tell me all news. I am sorry George is not well. Can't he get a staff job in a Brigade or Divisional H.Q.'s, such as Staff-Captain, where the work would not be so strenuous? I know from experience that an A.P.M.'s job, done keenly and well, is as tiring as anything, and in France, during this advancing business, one man is never asleep and has three times the amount of mounted police, and all of them at it day and night, guarding prisoners, traffic, wells, etc., besides the usual routine of a Division. . . .

"The Germans have just started to bombard us rather heavily, so we must get under cover.

"In spite of all discomforts, we are quite a happy crowd, as our Brigadier and staff are perfectly charming and considerate, and such fine soldiers, and so proud of all of us.

"Do go on sending papers and kippers or haddocks. The cigarettes were received with joy by the men, and came at the most opportune moment, when I don't think there was one in the whole Battery.

"Give my love to George and tell him I will write him a yarning letter soon.

"All my love, darling.

"Your own son,
"BEO."

"My own darling Mother,

"Thank you again and again for the Map Case. It was a lovely one, and it never left me in the last attack, in which I continually had to be referring to my maps. . . .

"The old Division is praised on all sides, and really it is a marvel what we do; for forty-eight hours we held off what seemed to me to be the whole German army, but, as a matter of fact, it was two German Army Corps, of ten times our number, and we never gave an inch. There was no souvenir hunting, and the prisoners taken were under 1,000, but all the time it was: kill, kill! ! ! We out here see the Boche as he is—with the veneer of civilisation off, and there is only one thing to do—*kill him!* as quickly as possible.

"So you see, darling Mother, letters from home are the only things that keep us fighting troops from becoming ferocious beasts ourselves. So write every day if you can. . . .

"One cannot talk of 'after the war.' None of us really expects to come out alive—least of all a Trench Mortar man. It's simply by watching the Boche manœuvres and shelling, that I have managed to keep any of my men alive, also myself; but it is weary work. The gassing I got last November is beginning to tell on me—the slightest bad smell makes me sick, and cigarettes and cigars are no enjoyment. My left hand was badly lacerated by German barbed wire in the last attack. . . .

"I wonder if you could send out my old cricket bag with all my cricket things and a ball or two, and a few old golf balls and iron clubs, for when we do come out of the line we shall probably go back a good way to rest, and the men would love to play cricket.

"When we get out I am going to finish and send you two little one-act plays.

"How is Stella? . . .

"Well, darling Mother, I have talked a lot about myself and my doings. I want to know all about you and yours. Is the tour a success? How wonderfully plucky George acting like that—with you, too! I bet he was nervous. Tell him to keep it up till I come back. I'm dying to see him and will write him a play called 'Beppo * and the Brigand.' Give him my love; I wish he were here. He would have been a Brigadier by now! . . .

"The Anson Battalion won the two football cups to-day and yesterday! Fancy, every match of the season has been played under shell-fire and in sight of the enemy!

"My French has become quite good; that is to say, I have been telling stories to the French staff officers to wile away a weary hour or two in the trenches. . . .

"All my love, darling.

"Your loving son,
"BEO."

In the summer of 1917 he wrote from the Senior Officers' School:—

"Lille Barracks,
"Aldershot.

"Darling Mother,

"I feel so anxious about you in these raids. I do hope you are not suffering from shock or anything. *Do* be careful.

* My husband's dog, a dear, black retriever.

"I will see you on Saturday.   We are having a most strenuous week.

"All my love, darling.

"Your own son,
"BEO."

In a letter to George he says:

". . . The more I see of them (women), the more keenly I appreciate what a wonderful person my own Mother is—so far, far above all the rest!"

I find a letter from a girl friend of his in America, written to him at the Front, about her marriage:

"Irvington-on-Hudson.

"Dear Alan,

"My memory of you is precious and beautiful.   No one in the world knows the fine, brave Beo better than I do.   Your letter makes me know that all the things I have believed about you are absolutely true. . . .

"I am happier than I ever thought I would be. . . .

"We were married when we had known each other six weeks! . . .

"You are a good man, and a brave one. . . .

"Esther."

"My darling Mother,

"Just a line to let you know I am quite fit.   We had a few days' rest and I went some motor rides with a pal. It was funny.   I ran up against Phil Carr, a Captain in the Intelligence Corps at St. Pol.   He gave me dinner and tea, and we had a long talk about things.

"We are now off into the thick of it again, and the rest is in God's hands. I know you are praying for me, and that, and the excitement, and my wonderful men keep me going.

"Write often.

"Your loving son,
"BEO."

"France.

"Darling,

"I am all right—awful noise, and we've lost a few men, but have the Boche under our thumb.

"Will write when I get a moment, to all.

"All my love.

"BEO."

"188th, Light Trench Mortar Battery,
"France.

"My darling Mother,

"No news from you for ages. I haven't written for some time because I am in the thick of the fight, and one's nerves are so keyed up that one cannot relax for a moment, knowing that one mistake means not only the loss of one's men, but one's own life as well.

"My men are working splendidly, and I am very proud of them; of course, I have had casualties, but mostly wounded, and they are very cheerful when I manage to get down to an advanced dressing station or hospital.

"There seems no chance of leave for ages.

"You will be glad to know I was mentioned in despatches—Sir G—— H——'s belated Gallipoli despatch, vide *Daily Telegraph*, July 14th, page 12, 4th

AS AMERICA REMEMBERS HER

col., under Howe Battalion, next to Colonel Collins.

"I was attached to Howe Battalion during latter part of operations.

"So, darling Mother, with a lot of luck I may have an English honour to give you to keep with the Croix de Guerre.

"Do write and let me know how you are, and do take care of yourself, Mother darling, and don't do too much.

"My Battery was lent the other day to one of the finest old regular Divisions, and to my surprise I was placed in command of five Batteries, and went to all the Conferences of the Generals. It was most interesting, and they all treated me well and took my views and advice on several matters, which was quite an honour, wasn't it?

"I am feeling rather sore about the head and stomach to-day, as I had a very narrow escape yesterday—one of their beastly shells fell about ten yards away. I heard it coming just in time to fling myself down a mine shaft, but I was very sick afterwards; all my stomach seemed to be turned upside down and my head aches. I'd give a lot to be able to have forty-eight hours' sleep in dear old thirty-three.

"By the way, do send me some weekly illustrated papers, because, of course, we have no mess now and get no papers except the *Daily Mail*.

"My best love, darling, and do write soon.

"Your loving son,
"BEO.

"Gladys Cooper's photo hasn't arrived yet, but the others brighten up things greatly."

"France,
"November 30th, 1917.

"My own darling Mother,

". . . George tells me you are not well and are suffering a great deal. Do please take care of yourself—it makes me more nervous than all the shells and bombs in the world.

"You must give up all those extra matinées and parties for charity; you will kill yourself. . . .

"I wonder if any of us will have any nerves by peace time, if we are alive!

"It's wonderful about the cards*—the padre and I think that we will give one to each man, and if he wants another, or any more, he will pay twenty-five centimes for it and the officers fifty centimes each, the proceeds to go to the Battalion Band Fund!

"We are progressing favourably with our Band, and have a real professional Orchestra leader as Bandmaster.

"But do tell me what the cards cost, because I feel it must have been such an expense for you.

"Gladys Cooper sent me such a lovely new photo of herself, which now adorns my tent and sometimes the mess when we can get one. . . .

"Your loving son,
"BEO."

"Howe Battalion,
"17th December, 1917.

"My own darling,

"The cards are wonderful and a huge success. I have given everybody one.

---

* He made a sketch for a Christmas card. I was able to get 1,000 printed for him in time.

"We have fifteen instruments now, and although they have only been going four weeks, they have already given a concert.

"I am so afraid we shall be in the trenches for Christmas, and I expect the Boche will attack again, but we are ready for him. He has never driven the old R.N.D. back a foot, and never will while any of us old 'uns are alive. The *esprit de corps* is fine, and I flatter myself the Battalion is in as good fighting trim as it has ever been; but it has been hard work training the new men and lecturing and putting new morale into them—eight solid hours a day, and the weather abominable. . . .

"Your loving son,
"BEO."

Beo and his Commander, were killed instantaneously by a shell near La Vacquerie, at about half-past seven in the morning of December 30th, and were buried on January 1st, at Metz-en-Couture.

"Headquarters, 13th Corps,
"B. E. F.
6/1/1918.

"Dear Mrs. Campbell,

"I was indeed grieved to read of the death of your son, and my old comrade, Alan Campbell. We served together in the same Brigade, of which I was Brigade Major from the beginning of Gallipoli till our arrival in France, and in the same Division until the beginning of last year.

"You will doubtless know with what gallantry he fought in Gallipoli. Certain arrangements for our final retirement were entirely in his hands, and the

Turk knows best how efficient those arrangements were.

"In France he quickly became known as a daring and expert Trench Mortar Officer. I have no hesitation in saying that he was out and away the best I have known, the next best being an officer he had trained, and who later became the officer in my new Brigade.

"How he led a Tank into action at the Ancre on November 14th, 1916 is probably known to you. It was a particularly gallant act, and cleared up a very awkward situation.

"As to his later work, you will doubtless hear from his present Commander, but I feel that I cannot let slip this opportunity of expressing my admiration for the gallantry and leadership shown by my old comrade, and also of expressing my sincerest sympathy with you in your loss.

"Yours sincerely,
"C. F. JERRAM
"(Major)."

"11th January, 1918.

"Dear Mrs. Campbell,

". . . During the short time we served together in the Dardanelles and in France he stood out as one of the very best officers, a splendid character and full of grit. He did fine work all through, more especially in connection with the evacuation, which meant for him a week of danger without rest.

"He soon got known in France, where opportunities were, perhaps, greater, and I had hoped to hear of his rapid advancement. His death is a grievous blow to the Division and to the Service. His proud record and example remain—and this must be some little solace in your present great trouble.

"Yours sincerely,
"A. PARIS
(Late G.O.C. Naval Division)."

"6th January, 1918.
"Dear Mrs. Patrick Campbell,

". . . I knew him so well, and realise so much what a loss he is to his country, and his regiment.

"I was more pleased than I can tell you when I read that he had been gazetted as Captain in the H.L.I., and I had been counting on him at the end of the war as being one of our most tried and trusted officers—and one who, I knew, would be warmly welcomed by all of us who are left.

"As his late Brigadier I cannot speak too highly of him. The most gallant fellow I have ever met—always reliable and very capable.

"He would very soon have had command of a Battalion—and was doing such good work with the Howe Battalion, while his Commander was on leave.

"He was beloved by us all—officers and men alike—and he leaves a real blank, and though he never joined our regiment, I can assure you the Highland Light Infantry will always be proud to have borne his name on their roll.

"For myself I feel a better man for having had him as a friend. . . .

"Yours most sincerely,
"R. E. PRENTICE (Lt.-Col.),
"(High. Lt. Inf.)."

"6th January, 1918

"My dear Stella,

". . . Beo has shown himself to be an absolute hero, not once, but many times during the war. Surely he surpassed even your good opinion of him. Certainly he was one of the great soldiers of this war. If we win, it will be due to men of his courage and example.

"I know how much you loved him. For such love there is no consolation except, perhaps, the knowledge that all men who know what he has done are moved to the deepest of their feelings with reverence and admiration.

"NEVILLE LYTTON." *

"7th January, 1918.

"My dear Beatrice,

"I am so sad that you should have this ordeal to go through, and I wish I knew any way to comfort you. How much rather would you have this sorrow than never had a son who would go to the war and die fighting gallantly for his country. How good that you have had a son who stood the supreme test of manhood. And in those three years he lived thirty of such lives as mine; he had in them the work he was so fitted to do superlatively well, all the joys—that come to most lives that are spread over many years. He died in great honour. Surely you are a proud woman as well as a sad one.

"I shall, of course, come to see you any time you want me.

"Yours affectionately,

"J. M. BARRIE."

* Major the Honourable Neville Lytton.

"Stanway.

"Dearest Stella,

"How can I write? You are never out of my mind for a second. I heard the sad, sad news yesterday, and knew that the cruel blow which had fallen on so many hearts—the cruellest blow—has fallen upon your poor heart, and I think you will believe that there is no one who feels for you more than I do, for every reason. I know how you adored Beo, and Beo is associated with our happy past. He and Ego*, what happy days they had together here; what fun they had at the stump cricket—their test matches in the barn.

"If you have one of the Christmas Cards left, I'd love to have it. Dearest, I can't write more now. I wish I could save you from the suffering—the anguish; but, alas! one can't, except by just deep, loving sympathy, which does strengthen just a little. You have joined the band of those who mourn for heroes—and Beo was a glorious soldier. Bless him! and God comfort you.

"Your loving friend,
"MARY WEMYSS."

"Taplow Court,
"February 6th, 1918.

"Dearest Stella,

"This is only a tiny line to thank you for sending me the card. I think Beo's spirit and his generous braveness are shining through you and helping you!! I know, alas! that nothing can save you from all the agony of longing and *missing;* disappointment and the long, weary way one has to trudge through! But I see by the strength and bravery of your beautiful letter that you

---

* Lord Elcho, the eldest son of the present Earl of Wemyss, killed in the late action against the Turks at the battle of Katia.

are, indeed, a worthy mother of your glorious soldier son. I remember a story you used to tell me of Beo, when you were scolding him, falling asleep hugging his cricket bat! * What boys they were! Their eagerness at games; their self-training and courage. Seriousness and fun helped them to be the soldiers they were.

"I have a lovely letter to show you some day, that Beo wrote, with pictures of himself and Ego at cricket in the pouring rain, and at golf on Cleeve Hill playing up and down precipices. You must come quickly to see us at Stanway some day when you can leave your work.

"Your words are a help to me; each one helps the other, for your courage comes when one feels inclined to flag and fail, and it helps one on again.

"God bless you.

"MARY WEMYSS."

A brother officer wrote:

"In the trenches,
"4th January, 1918.
"My dear Mrs. Cornwallis West,

". . . His indomitable cheerfulness, his faithfulness to his comrades and his own Division, his staunch patriotism and lofty ideals, all endeared him to his fellow officers and the men who served with him.

"I hope you may see with his own clear vision the Great Cause for which his sacrifice was made, so that the pain of your own sacrifice may be lessened somewhat by the knowledge of how he died—and for whom.

"RICHARD DONALDSON,
"(Lieut., R. N. V. R.)."

* I remember his words, too—"Your voice is so lovely it sends me to sleep!"

"11, Charles Street,
"S. W.

"Dear Mrs. Cornwallis West,

"I was Brigade Major to the Brigade in which your son was, and saw a great deal of him during the last year. May I tell you how deeply I sympathise with you in your sorrow? Alan was one of the most popular people in the Naval Division, and certainly one of the most plucky people I know. He had done so well, and he is a great loss to the Division. General Prentice and I were very glad when he got his commission in the Highland Light Infantry, and it would have been so nice to have had him in the regiment.

"He often used to talk to me of you, and I felt I would like to tell you how very much I feel for you. . . .

"   . . .

"ALEXANDER TELFER-SMOLLETT."

'3rd Bn. Machine Gun Corps,

"Clipstone Camp.
"5th January, 1918.

"Dear Mrs. Campbell,

"   . . . He was a great friend of mine, and a finer soldier was never born. I crossed to France with him last October, and he saw me off to my Base. My wife, too, asks me to convey her sorrow; she knew him almost as well as I.

"The tributes I have heard of his work in Gallipoli and France from his brother officers were magnificent. . . .

"   . . .

"WM. GOODALL, LIEUT."

"10, Adephia Terrace, W. C. 2.
"7th January, 1918.

"Never saw it or heard about it until your letter came. It is no use: I can't be sympathetic; these things simply make me furious. I want to swear. I *do* swear. Killed just because people are blasted fools. A chaplain, too, to say nice things about it. It is not his business to say nice things about it, but to shout that the 'voice of thy son's blood crieth unto God from the ground.'

"No, don't show me the letter. But I should very much like to have a nice talk with that dear Chaplain, that sweet sky-pilot, that . . .

"No use going on like this, Stella. Wait for a week, and then I shall be very clever and broadminded again and have forgotten all about him. I shall be quite as nice as the Chaplain.

"Oh, damn, damn, damn, damn, damn, damn, damn, damn, DAMN.

"And oh, dear, dear, dear, dear, dear, dearest!

"G.B.S."

I found the following quotation amongst Beo's papers, that came back from France:

"To be glad of life because it gives you the chance to love and to work and, to play and to look up at the stars: to be contented with your possessions, but not satisfied with yourself until you have made the best of them; to despise nothing in the world except falsehood and meanness, and to fear nothing except cowardice."

CHAPTER XIX.

ABOUT six months after my sorrow, life began to teach me its hardest lesson; which must be learned if we are to comprehend in any measure the grace of God:—That there can be a fundamental gulf of gracelessness in a human heart which neither our love nor our courage can bridge.

*   *   *   *   *

My mother-in-law was brought back very ill from the South of France. For a short time she was in a nursing home in London. Daisy Pless asked me to go and see her. I watched Patsy as she lay in bed; her expression of mysterious defiance touched me: leaning over her, I said: "Is there anything in the world I can do for you?" After some moments, in a voice that seemed to come from some other being, she said slowly: "God bless you."

I asked her maid whether there was anything I could do.

"Tell Major West to come to her."

I had not seen George for a long time—I wrote to him begging that he would go to his mother.

*   *   *   *   *   *

On February 10th, 1920, there was a revival of Mr. Bernard Shaw's *Pygmalion,* at the Aldwych

Theatre, and again this play went with all the old merriment.

On the 3rd of June, the production of *Madame Sand,* by Phillip Möeller at the Duke of York's Theatre.

Dear Madame Sand—she thought it was *love* that made life worth living.

She loved men of genius, and they loved her—and inspired her work—

Some people liked the play, some praised me, some laughed at my trousers; some would not believe the cigars I smoked were real.

One man came to the stage door and asked how we managed to get the smoke into the "trick" cigar.

And these are some of the letters that were written to me:—

> "Plumpton,
> "Sussex.

"My dear Mrs. Campbell,

"I am so sorry if I was rude about your trousers, but quite sincerely they wounded me. If only they had been pretty trousers—but they were not. They may be historically correct. But in a play which outrages history in so many vital points, to outrage it further in the stuff and cut of 'George Sand's' trousers, would have offended nobody, and pleased one person at least. C—— glared so formidably at me when you complained of my criticism, that I did not dare to ask her how she'd like to wear trousers like that. I don't think she would look very nice, do you? . . . .

> "Affectionately yours,
> "RUDOLF BESIER.

"P. S.—I hadn't really time to tell you that your performance was pure genius—like everything you do."

"62, Cadogan Square, S. W.

"Dear Stella, they all told me untruthfully that the play was bad and unnecessary, and that you were no good.

"I may have failed to disentangle the respective merits, but it seemed to me the play was almost worthy of your acting—more one cannot say.

"Many thanks. I enjoyed it enormously.

"Yours,
"WEMYSS." *

"2 Robert Street,
"Adelphi.

"Barrie took me to your play the other night, and we both thought you *marvellously* good and looking too beatiful, especially in the last act in your pink dress.

"You are a wonder!

"I do hope it's going to run.

"Bless you.

"Loving,
"CYNTHIA." *

"10, Adelphi Terrace,
"June.

"I went on Thursday night. I thought the British public absurdly illiterate and stupid. After the second act I felt inclined to come before the curtain and explain to them that the Coliseum was across the road, and that they had come into the wrong house. If they think that Alfred de Musset's part must be sacred music,

* The present Earl of Wemyss.
* Lady Cynthia Asquith.

at least Grock will make it clear that they are meant to laugh at him. Pigs!

"What induced you to imitate Oscar Wilde? It was an inspiration, and amazingly like the original. . . . Your lovely performance is too good to be thrown away; it is a repertory part. Why can you not act as intelligently as that for me, devil that you are?

"G. B. S."

"Leytonstone.

"Dear Madam,

"Thank you so much for the very clever and artistic play that I have just seen for a second time in a week, and only wish I had the opportunity of a third visit. In spite of critics and letters, a good many people have enjoyed *Madame Sand,* and personally I think the play has gone to show a far more pleasing side of her character than one gets from reading her life.

"There are, unfortunately, so very many ordinary plays produced nowadays, plays that one sees one day and forgets the next. But *Madame Sand* is the only one of the great many I have seen this year, that remains with me as a very real enjoyment.

"Hoping it will not be a great while before the public have the pleasure of seeing you act again, and with apologies for writing you.

"Yours truly,
"M. G."

On October 11th, 1920—at the invitation of the British Rhine Army of Occupation—I played *Pygmalion,* with the members of their Dramatic Company in Cologne. They played extraordinarily well, and it was an interesting fortnight. I was overpraised, over-entertained, and over-photographed.

On November 2nd there was Mr. J. K. Hackett's fine production of *Macbeth,* at the Aldwych Theatre. No doubt I deserved some of the bad reviews I received. I lacked spirit and physical strength at that time.

> "The Empress Club,
> "35 Dover Street, W.1.
> "November 26th, 1920.

"Dear Mrs. West,

". . . Now to the sublime! I feel sure that we shall never witness such a great performance of *Macbeth* in this country in the future unless you give it again together. It is too rare a combination—two geniuses— which makes the whole so powerful.

"I think Mr. J. K. H. tremendously strong in his part, and I hope he is as grateful to his Maker, as his audiences are, for that beautiful voice! But it is his lovely, wicked wife who sends the thrills all over the house.

"You are a wonderfully gifted woman, and it is great art for so gentle a being, to be able to impersonate a fiend of fiends.

"The public are intelligent and loyal, and they appreciate and love you and expect great things for many, many years to come. Don't let selfish, unkind, and stupid people rob us of a vestige of your vitality. You are too richly endowed by Heaven with such gifts to let the common herd affect or depress you.

> "Yours very sincerely,
> "E. H."

Then my doctor advised me to make no more effort, but to stay quietly in bed—and there he kept me for three months—I am sure it was only my anxiety about money that made me get up. I had acted so seldom during the last few years—and then only short engagements—that I was hard pressed.

A good offer was made to me, to recite a Prologue and Epilogue for a film called "The Dawn of the World"—*three performances a day*—I got out of bed to go and see this film. D. D. Lyttelton came with me, and we both thought it was not so bad: thankfully I accepted the engagement.

When this engagement was over, my doctor was very severe with me.

He said I must go away into the country alone, and speak to no one—for six or eight weeks. I obeyed him.

I had waited in London nearly two years, for a miracle to happen. . . .

* * * * * *

Publishers asked me to write my "Life"— a hundred thousand words! I laughed, and said I could not write a letter that anyone could read, and I knew only about thirty words—and some of those were "swear words." How could I write the same words over and over again?

But this did not seem to frighten them, and so, after some hesitation, and a few pangs, I agreed.

I found a cottage in Lancashire, sold my London house, and settled down to my job.

On the 10th of September I acted at the Play-house, Liverpool, in a very effective little one act play by clever Miss Clemence Dane, called *The Terror,* for a fortnight—I could not spare more time from my writing: it was a success, and had six and seven calls every night.

The country and I have never lived together until now—a week or so, visiting at country houses, that was all, some happy weeks in Dorsetshire, six weeks in Wiltshire, a month in Surrey, and a few months in Wales.

Breakfast once in the woods at Long Island—Before me, lay the silver sand—beyond the Atlantic—behind me, the undergrowth, the American white dog-roses, the tall trees: my companions, my American girl friends with their intoxicating wild spirits.

Nature gives me happiness and beauty every moment—the wild birds in the hedges—the robin in my hall—his hide-and-seek way of greeting me in the garden. And my fifteen Irish ducks, the silly hens, the fresh eggs. The Japanese garden, the Japanese teal—the Irises that will be up in the Spring—the thousand daffodils in the wood—the fritillaries and other lovelinesses that I am awaiting, and that are ready with their many blessings.

And the wind blows from the sea, fourteen miles away, into my garden.

There is a sunken rose garden in front of my sitting-room window, where the roses were blooming late into November.

On my cottage is a yellow jasmine, and a white jasmine, and two pear trees, that were heavy with fruit when I came here in the autumn. And then there are the privet hedges and the birds' nests—what singing there will be in the Spring!

Beautiful hills can be seen far away on the left; on the right, many fields and plowmen with their horses and dogs—their homes and farms in the distance—and crows and seagulls feeding as the earth is turned over.

And rooks talk like mad in the morning—and at nine o'clock little feet and children's voices hurrying to school—a small part of my garden and a hedge separating me from the road where they pass.

At the back of my cottage, the country road, and a smithy and duck pond—and in front at the end of my wood, an old Manor, empty now, where I saw the picture * of Mrs. Wilbraham Bootle, which makes you say, Mr. Romney was the greatest of portrait painters.

So long as that picture exists, you can meet and know intimately Mrs. Wilbraham Bootle, and the best work of a great master.

It is not too quiet here: near by is the beautiful home of the young Lord Lathom: he and his sister come up sometimes from London, and have wonderfully gay parties.

* Now at Blythe Hall, the Earl of Lathom's new home.

GEORGE SAND IN "MADAME SAND"

And these are a few more things that I have learned:—

Religion and love inspire the spirit of martyrdom—Why?—a profoundly troubling question.

It is this spirit of martyrdom against which the world to-day rebels.

The limitless martyrdom is martyrdom to self.

———

A man built a temple, high towards the heavens—built it of all the wisdom, knowledge, beauty, art, true speaking, honour, glory, patience, virtue, and goodness that he had gathered together.

But the four winds of heaven blew upon the temple and it fell to the ground.

"I have made the best I could; with the best that I have found; and all is destroyed," he cried.

A voice whispered, "You built in vanity—lay your treasures one before the other on the ground, upon your knees, making a pathway through dark places."

He did as he was told, laying his poor wisdom, patience, goodness, and all the virtues he had gathered together, humbly upon the ground—one before the other.

And behold the pathway led to a great Light that filled his heart with song, and great peace was about him: and he smiled at the memory of the temple that had been destroyed by the four winds of heaven.

———

Moral education, not experience, should teach us, instantly to recognise what the Americans call—a "spook."

It is never an "instinct"—an artificial fly can catch the finest fish.

We only believe the fallacy that love can triumph over the character of another when our own love has failed in the attempt.

Callousness never takes the place of love—only of what people are apt to call love.

The instinct of self-preservation is an animal instinct.

The instinct of the preservation of the community is the highest instinct man is capable of—it must in the end lead to the preservation of the individual.

There is a strange desire in the world to-day, to speak the truth.

It is the wailing that follows war—it comes in the wake of grief.

A child speaks the truth from want of guile. Men and women speak it in despair.

Our best loved friend is always in some way our peer.

I have lain my cheek upon the earth and felt it my mother's bosom.

———

I knew a shy man who told me his timidity was born of his dread lest people should guess how foolish he knew them to be.

———

Refinement and breeding in a man or woman will take care of itself.

It is the lack of vital energy that so often goes with these qualities that must be looked to continually.

———

We are sensitive to the human eye—

I have known a cunning eye in a most intelligent man that made me set little value upon his words, and the principles he laid claim to.

———

A lovely gentle feminine eye in woman has stolen manhood and honour since the beginning of time.

———

The look of trust in the eye of a child and the clasp of its little hand can send the Devil to sleep.

———

To see through a kind but crafty nature we need a super-intelligent knowledge of human character; or else a similar cunning.

———

I have known a lie, built upon a truth, that broke a heart.

———

I have known a truth, built around a lie, that saved a soul.

Actors and actresses possess a very wonderful honesty in their endeavor to please the author.

They would rather brave the censure of critics, the disappointment of dearest friends, than feel the author was dissatisfied with their work.

There is a story of an author who at rehearsal, when the actor fell, said: "No, no, that's not the fall I want at all, I want you to fall—inert." The actor said: "Would you mind showing me?"

The brave author got up, and threw himself down —hurting himself very much—and the actor said: "That's splendid; would you mind doing it again?"

The loveliest performance I ever saw was Ellen Terry as "Imogen."

When she entered I felt she had come from the moon: when she left the stage I was sure the stars were greeting her.

No one has ever had her magical step—that extraordinary happy haste, that made you feel she must presently arrive at the gates of Paradise.

The evening I saw her in "Imogen," she forgot her words, and—giving a delicious look at the audience and then towards heaven—spoke three times in a voice that melted your bosom, this word: "Beyond—beyond—beyond——"

There was no "Beyond" in the text, but it was the loveliest word I ever heard, and described her "Imogen."

I have seen the great Eleanoröa Duse only in modern plays *Magda, Hedda Gabler,* and *The Second Mrs. Tanqueray.*

To me she was too sad, and too slow. But in her work there is a great dignity, sincerity, and a fine introspection—and a tremendous appreciation of the nobility of suffering.

I wish I had seen her in a poetical play—or in a purely romantic, decorative rôle.

Her personality is not new to me, for she resembles strangely an Italian aunt of mine.

Sympatica morbidezza is her great charm, and she commands almost slavish attention and admiration from her audience. The atmosphere of a Madonna was about her work. The Madonna-like atmosphere of her personality eclipses sometimes the charm of her sincerity in modern neurotic rôles. This atmosphere often renders criticism of her technique a small affair. Her beauty pulsates, and never for a moment is there a feeling of "tricks."

Though perhaps not aiming at quite such a classic standard, I think there are just as many clever actresses to-day as there were yesterday.

The "school" to-day is lighter—the personalities

have somehow adapted themselves to a more girl-ish, or what is termed a "flapper," style.

We were neurotic, weary ladies in teagowns, when Ibsen gripped us.

To-day is the day of the girls the soldier boys left behind them, and rightly so.

That will pass, and to-morrow the woman who "comes through with a smile" may be asked for—

Anyway, surely the enthusiasm for the theatre is greater than ever.

*   *   *   *   *

I have never known the "art of *acting*" really cared for in this country. It is first the player, then the play—and always, "Who is your favorite actor or actress?"

I do not find people discussing exquisite gesture—variety of tone—and above all, that most difficult of technical difficulties, the subtle tones, tempo and manner, which indicate the difference of feeling to-wards each character in the play—or broad human effects—atmosphere breeding and style.

Now and then, a critic points out these things, but an English audience does not look for them—or rec-ognise them.

When authors produce plays, it seems to me, the absorbing idea is that their words are heard by the audience.

I have known it carried to such a point that the

actors talked *at* the audience the whole evening, making one feel not only a fool, but a deaf fool.

It is a fault to drop the voice now and again, but it is a worse fault to bawl for two and a half hours unceasingly.

When actor-managers produce plays—it is that the play should "go"; the thrilling scenes thrill; the comedy lines call forth laughter; and the tender scenes tears—and they themselves make a personal success.

But the real "art of acting" is not considered.

This art has nothing to do with impersonation—beyond the *means* by which the artist impersonates. If a personality suits a rôle a fine impersonation may be given with little or no knowledge of the "art of acting."

It has nothing to do with youth or of age unless the feeling of youth is to be suggested.

It has nothing to do with any *real thing*—only with the technical means, apart from inspiration—by which the *real things* is given to the imagination of the audience.

There is a certain artistic hysteria on the stage, that is exasperating—a stare in the artist's eye as he waits at the wings, a stiffening of his muscles, and a throatiness ready in his voice. Oh, that he would trip, or sneeze, and suddenly become natural, and begin over again—the right way!

I made the remark to a brilliant writer, before I had heard of the Clarendon Handbook, that I found punctuation very difficult—where to put a semicolon, and where to put a colon.

He replied: "That is not what troubles me, it is what to put between the semicolon and the colon!

The gods laugh when man would make his genius confederate with his clay.

Art is a form of worship and thanksgiving—the rest is invention, ingenuity, a business, a compromise, an imitation, or a bag of gathered, or stolen articles unpacked.

It is a common form of self-indulgence to burden one's friends with confidences; to tell them those things which we would consider a breach of trust on their part if they repeated.

How eagerly such confidences are sought—and given.

When we lose trust in people—in time we lose interest in them.

To be tolerant towards sluggish natures and unresponsive minds, is very difficult, and needs Christlike patience.

A fine heated discussion is a sort of mental tennis. There are rules to the game, and the more intelligent keep to them.

I have hurt a loving friend who wanted to see me off by train, by remarking to her: "I like porters, not sentiment at railway stations."

The silly last words as the train starts—the other passengers, dreading the fate of their toes, as you retire backwards from the window to your seat.

Or if you shout your familiar farewell, without moving from your corner, you have the impression that you have forced an intimacy upon the rest of the people in the compartment, which they resent, and that secretly they despise your want of self-control.

Some time after the train has started you have an odd sensation of nakedness; you cannot clothe yourself quite in the garb of a stranger again.

I heard a lady say, in a mysterious voice: "You won't forget, will you my dear, to tell Nora that I left the brown——" Her friend interrupted her hastily, blushing furiously, and said, "No, no, I won't."

I wasted the better part of an hour wondering whether Nora was her sister, daughter, or maid— and what *was* the brown——I did not ask, so I shall never know.

*   *   *   *   *

There is my beloved grandchild, "Pat"—Stella's

boy—he calls me "Mother Beatrice." He has the radiance that goes with a great kindliness of disposition; and a very quick intelligence—an elasticity—without which life is a dreary battle, and possessing which—a battle fit for the gods.

And my beloved daughter Stella, a courageous, beautiful woman, full of gentle talent. She has a delicacy and distinction of inestimable value in plays of a certain calibre. Her "Roxane" in *Cyrano de Bergerac* is remembered.

* * * * *

It is not want of gratitude or grace, on my part, that names of some loved friends are omitted from these pages.

I have no diary to help me, and so the daily sequence of events is lost; and with this loss has gone the names of friends; kindly deeds, fun and happy hours.

They will come to my mind by and bye, and I know the omission will fill me with regret.

* * * * *

And here is the book I have written and dedicated to you, little girl, because you walked all that long way to see me act, and all the long way home again—I hope you arrived home safely.

FINIS

INDEX

443

INDEX